I0461739

A ROAD THROUGH HELL

A TRUE STORY ABOUT ALCOHOLISM, DRUG ADDICTION, CHRONIC RELAPSE, AND RECOVERY

RAY VANCE

A ROAD THROUGH HELL

A true story about Alcoholism, Drug Addiction,
Chronic Relapse, and Recovery

© 2022, Ray Vance

The moral rights of the author have been asserted.

All rights reserved. No part of this publication may be reproduced, stored in a retrieval system, or transmitted, in any form or by any means – electronic, mechanical, photocopy, recording, scanning, or other, except for brief quotations in critical reviews or articles, without the prior written permission of the author.

Published in USA

ISBN 979-8-9855321-1-1 (*paperback*)
ISBN 979-8-9855321-2-8 (*ebook*)
ISBN 979-8-9855321-3-5 (*hardcover*)
ISBN 979-8-9855321-4-2 (*dust jacket*)
ISBN 979-8-9855321-5-9 (*audio cover*)

Book cover design Marko Markovic, 5mediadesign
Book cover photo www.stock.adobe.com

Thank you, God, for making me who and what I am.
Thank you for allowing me the knowledge of the truth.

In remembrance of my dad, you always said
if you were to write a book it would change the world.
We miss you every day.

To Franklin Schaffer, meeting you has absolutely
changed my life. Thank you for extending the hand of AA,
your patience, tolerance, and love have been instrumental
in teaching me how to live life on life's terms.

To my Home Group, every time we are together, I learn
more. With your help I have found myself. With you I have
found an existence beyond imagining. Your faces, your
words, and your love are with me always.

To the rest of my family and friends, what a ride it has
been. Thank you for being part of my life.

CONTENTS

Chapter One: Tongue Tied..9
Chapter Two: Gettin' High..29
Chapter Three: The Campus 47
Chapter Four: Hugs Not Drugs 53
Chapter Five: A Proposal 61
Chapter Six: Back into Addiction.............................. 73
Chapter Seven: 21 At Last...83
Chapter Eight: Becoming a Father............................ 87
Chapter Nine: Unemployable and Rehabbed 101
Chapter Ten: Insanity..111
Chapter Eleven: Another Rehab 125
Chapter Twelve: Hopeless..129
Chapter Thirteen: New Horizons...............................145
Chapter Fourteen: The Workhouse............................155
Chapter Fifteen: Lycanthropy 163
Chapter Sixteen: The Big House................................175
Chapter Seventeen: Lumberjack................................183
Chapter Eighteen: Geographical Cure.....................203
Chapter Nineteen: Bradford 221
Chapter Twenty: Dumbass..233
Chapter Twenty-One: The Bitter End 245
Chapter Twenty-Two: On We Go................................249
Chapter Twenty-Three: Life on Life's Terms..............261
Chapter Twenty-Four: Rescue......................................269
Chapter Twenty-Five: Are You Shitting Me?.............. 279
Chapter Twenty-Six: No Middle of the Road Solution .. 287
Chapter Twenty-Seven: The Dream............................293
Chapter Twenty-Eight: Eminent Disaster 299
Chapter Twenty-Nine: A Visit from An Angel............305

PREFACE

As I begin this project, I am quickly approaching four years sober. I've thought for some years about writing a book on addiction and recovery, a topic that I have ample experience in. I am discovering that changing thought into words may take some practice.

I have been through at least seven inpatient treatment facilities and a two-year stint in prison as a direct result of my alcoholism. Today I have a choice of whether I will drink or use again and that my friends, is nothing short of a miracle! I have lived a great deal of my life without that choice; I'm sure we will explore this phenomenon more later. So how do you tell a story full of embarrassment, shame, self-pity, suicidal thoughts, homicidal behavior, and all-around demoralized self-will? I guess you start at the beginning, but there are a few things I need to address before I start. I belong to a 12-step fellowship that believes that anonymity is the spiritual foundation of all our traditions. So, in a nutshell even though this is my story, I don't want to harm anyone in writing this. So as an act of anonymity, I will write under the name Ray Vance and I will change the names of friends and family, as this isn't meant as a platform to embarrass or shame anyone.

So, with that in mind here we go. How do we start? Well haven't we already decided, at the beginning.

1

TONGUE TIED

I was born June 8, 1971, in Zanesville, Ohio. I was the third of what would eventually be four siblings. I have an older brother Jordan five years my senior and a sister Terry seven years older.

I don't feel like I'm doing a very good job introducing my family, let's remember I'm an alcoholic not a writer. So, I'm just going to muddle on through, it gets to be a habit when you are using.

Our father Roland and our mother Paula are the parental units of this story. They were loving, and hardworking parents and I'll say right up front I never saw my parents drink, smoke, or use drugs, ever. Apparently, I just caught a lucky break and got the alcoholism and addiction gene. A little footnote about my loving little family - about a year before I was born my father uprooted the family from a rather fancy living in California with a family business, large pool in the backyard, and an airplane to go where you want. Now I will add, my memories from childhood are I believed that dad actually owned an airplane, however mom has corrected me and said he would rent or charter planes and fly himself to Ohio. Dad had a dream to be a farmer, so he literally moved the family from California to the middle of Podunk, Ohio. Remember, it's June 8, 1971, I've just been born so what the fuck do I know, I'm just a baby. Everything is new and bright. Everyone is smiling and so happy to meet me; as far as I know, I've just landed in paradise. However, the rest of my family excluding my adventure-seeking father, just might have been pissed.

Eight days less than a year after I was born, my little brother Mick was born. He was born with spina bifida, and he was paralyzed from the waist down. So here we are, the Vance's. I'll say again that this is really about my life, but at the beginning they are some of the main characters.

Of course, I don't recall very much about being a baby, but I will share some stories that have been passed down to me from others. I'm told my first word was *bitch*; this is attributed to Grandma O'Malley who watched me after Mick was born. Apparently, bitch was one of the grandma's favorite words. When I was three years old, my father was building a new section of our farmhouse and he was building it from a kit he had ordered. Apparently, I ate one of the bits for the drill that fit the screws. They had to halt building and wait for the bit to come back. Sounds like a shitty job! When I was four years old, I would stand in front of the TV with my arms out and wag my butt back and forth so no one could see what was on. It's quite possible that I had an attention problem. Like if I wasn't the center of it, I had a problem! My real memories start in kindergarten. I remember taking naps on my own rug and watching *The Letter People* on PBS. By this time, we lived just outside of Somerset, Ohio, most noted for being the hometown of Civil War General Philip Sheridan. My father by that time was living his dream of being a farmer during the day and earning a living working the coal mines at night. I should say that I was always very close to my dad. He was probably the best friend I ever had. To me he was like a superhero, there was nothing he couldn't do, and he taught me everything good that I know.

I was a small kid and had asthma. I was allergic to every known animal, grass, mold, pollen, and buckwheat, so I was perfectly suited for the country life of a farmer. I was on a strict regimen of allergy medication and probably miserable most of my young life. After an attention deficit disorder diagnosis, I was put on Ritalin, which I'm told I liked to take. I do remember that I always felt different, not quite good enough. I always wanted to be somebody else. We lived outside of town, and until I was old enough to ride my bike into town, I didn't really have friends of any kind or a social life outside of family. If I really think about it, I wet the bed until I was twelve, so I was afraid to stay at friends' houses on the weekends.

My first real friend was Charlie Brown, a calf whose mother died. I bottle fed Charlie Brown from birth, so he wasn't treated like the other cows. He wasn't confined to the pasture, and he was free to roam lose in the yard. I would come home from school, and he would meet me on the lane like a dog. I could yell or whistle, and he would come running and we played together. He was a good-sized steer when dad sold him to another farmer. Dad would take me to the farm that Charlie Brown moved to, and I would call from the fence, and he would still come running. We visited several times. One day on the school bus that farmer's kids told me Charlie Brown sure tasted good!

There are a lot of lessons you learn growing up on a farm. One of the most powerful that I learned was that things you love can and will die and sometimes they get ate! My first memory of physically being hurt was on the farm. I was riding with dad while he was brush hogging around the edge of the field, we were on a Ford 3000 when he drove under a low branch, the muffler broke off and stuck right in the top of my head. A quick trip to the old town doctor a few stitches and I was good as new. There was an old farmer that I would see around town that had two hooks for hands, he had lost them in a hay bailer. Another good lesson from farmers that I learned very young was to be careful around the hay bailer and the P.T.O. shafts on the tractors because they could literally rip your arms off! I will state here that growing up on a farm is very educational. I learned how to drive equipment and how to repair everything. As farmers we built houses, grain bins, we repaired barns and tended and fed livestock. We birthed calves, raised chickens and pigs. We butchered and ate what we raised. We learned soil conservation, and we learned about breeding livestock. My father was an electrician in the coal mines, my grandfather was a high-powered lineman in California, so I also learned how to wire houses and barns and find electrical problems on equipment. If there is a more well-rounded way to be educated, then I don't know what it is. The education is really fantastic, I'm quite sure I hated every second of it. We will get into that a little more later.

Well, back to early adolescence. I should mention that after the birth of my younger brother Mick, my mother spent a good deal of the rest of his life in the hospital with him. And from one year old, I spent most of my time being raised by other family members. My father worked the coal mines from 3 p.m. to midnight then he was up with or before the sun working the farm. I want to say that I had incredible parents. They lived with the hand they were dealt, and they did the best they could. And again, I was a baby, so what the hell did I know?

I suffered abandonment issues from not being with my parents. As you will see later, one of my greatest fears is being alone. It has been a haunt and a torment for most of my life. So, let's see, I'm a Vance, I'm being raised a farmer and I'm learning the things that will make me a competent employee in any field and I hate every minute of it. Yep, that sounds about right. At this point I'd like to make a brief disclaimer - this is my story and I've changed my name to protect the privacy of my family and friends...that's if I ever get any, so far, they ate the only real friend I've had, other than my dad. Being this is my story, I am willing to share my shame and embarrassment but in no way do I wish to shame or embarrass anyone else. This book is a direct result of my recovery, and I don't want to hurt anyone. I want to tell my story the best way I can and in good faith I am attempting to spare any animosity or blame to anyone other than myself. My perception of my life then, is greatly different now. In an attempt to relive the past, I want to show first what my perception was then. If that didn't make since, shut up, I'm an alcoholic not an author.

I will say here that I was insanely jealous of my little brother Mick, he got everyone's attention. As crazy as this is to say, I remember wishing I were paralyzed so that I would be loved too. Wow, that's pretty fucked up isn't it? Mick never complained about not being able to walk or run or play like other kids.

Subconsciously, I learned a great deal from him, though I wouldn't know it for many years to come. Our little family of Vance's did our best to be normal, we sometimes went to church. Early in life we were active with extended family, we went to reunions and I have many memories of uncles, aunts, and grandparents on both sides. We also went on vacations, we had family in California, so I remember several cross-country trips. It was a lot like the Chevy Chase movie *Vacation*; we had to see all the sights.

We saw Big Musky I don't know how many times, but it was a lot. We went through the painted desert numerous times, we went to the Grand Canyon, the Redwood Forest, and we stopped on bridges that were exceptionally high or long. I'm sure we spit off the sides, and I'm ninety percent sure I hated every minute of it.

On my eighth year of what I'm pretty sure I perceived as one of servitude and misery, we were on a family vacation in California. My grandparents had a nice house in a neighborhood where everyone had a pool in the backyard and on this particular trip my life would be changed forever! Even though I'm in my forties, still today this takes some contemplation to write about, as this was a pivotal point in my life, and it's difficult to write it in the manner I felt then – but with guidance from God and a reassuring thought that I am no more or less important than a single grain of sand on the beach, I will do my best. Sorry, that was some recovery slipping in a little early, it really is an amazing thing so have patience, I promise we will get there.

So, we are in California, I'm a whopping eight years old, we go to lots of neighbor's houses and swim. This summer my brothers are there and a few older cousins. I don't think my sister made the trip, she stepped on a nail a week before we left and had to get a tetanus shot, so she stayed with family in Ohio. Anyway, on one particularly hot day we were swimming at a neighbor's pool and their teenage son took me inside and violently molested me. Even today the memories are indistinguishable. I don't remember if it happened more than once, I do know that it was so traumatic that I suppressed it until I was twelve. I do remember being threatened with a knife at my throat and made to perform oral until he came. As if that isn't bad enough, afterwards when we came out of the house my older brother and my cousins teased me and called me a fag. The latter might have been worse than the molesting, it forever changed my and my older brother's relationship. I think I was more hurt by the betrayal of family not protecting me than I was by the actual molesting. Side note: I've caught myself in the last few years jokingly saying "But did you ever have to suck a dick?" Now, this situation for anyone to be forced is totally without humor, but I never really thought about what I was saying when I was joking around. It never really occurred to me that I actually did! We have to note here that the off-color humor of an alcoholic and drug addict probably stems from living a life of such misery and depression that our funny bones get twisted a little. Okay, maybe a lot. So, let's look at a few things from the perspective of an eight-year-old. I didn't understand what happened or why I felt shame and embarrassment that I was teased by family members. "In all honesty, my memories focus this feeling on my older brother even though my cousins were there too."

I'm no psychiatrist, but evidently the trauma was so severe that my eight-year-old mind couldn't handle it, so it was filed away for a later date. Some of the direct results, however, was that at eight years old I became sexually aware. I'd say that would be about five years sooner than normal. I also experienced dreams of male genitalia, which I'll say, didn't boost my confidence much. I was very confused as to why I would have dreams about male parts and of all curses I was and still am a very vivid dreamer. I often remember my dreams, I am happy to report that I don't still dream of dicks. We can now take a look at my first ad-dick-tion, no pun intended but my first addiction was sex. It felt good and I couldn't really control the desire to learn more, feel more, and do more. Again, this is my story, it's about me, so there will be no names, fake or otherwise, on this subject. There was, however, some pre-teen experimentation with anyone willing to participate. Somehow, I knew there was more. I had yet to experience an orgasm, and I was already addicted so it's safe to say it was only going to get worse.

My second addiction was candy - let's remember I'm eight - but I took candy to a whole new level. Over several years, I stole off my older brother's coin collection to buy penny candies at the town store. To this day, I'm still as thrilled as a pig in a poke to shop in a candy store. All the colors, smells, the different tastes, oh my God sensory overload! If I knew then what I know now it was a sure sign of trouble to come. I'm just a little kid, what kid didn't like candy. So here we are, little Ray Vance, I have severe asthma, I'm scrawny as a bean pole, and I'm secretly skimming off my brother's coin collection for candy. I live on a farm; the animals are fucking more than me, and I dream of dicks. Holy shit! No wonder I got made fun of!

I forgot to mention that I was held back in first grade. I had a bit of a speech impediment, so I had trouble pronouncing my Rs. Just thought I'd throw that in there, as it sort of adds to my charm!

You may recall that I wrote my first real addiction was sex and I lived on a farm. I am generally alone when I'm doing my chores, one fine spring day I was in the milk barn bottle feeding some calves... So there I am, in the milk barn watching this calf suck the bottle with quite a vigorous intensity and the idea strikes me like I just came up with the formula for rocket fuel. "If the calf sucks a bottle, it will probably suck a dick." Now, being a little unsure, I thought to test my theory, I pulled the bottle out of the calf's mouth and put my pointer and middle fingers out in front of it to see what would happen. Eureka! The calf took my fingers just like the bottle. Let's again note that I am very young and there is a huge difference between two callused fingers and the barely used soft skin of my unprotected manhood, but I just figured out the formula for rocket fuel so here I go. I opened my pants, pulled down my underwear and exposed myself. The calf immediately sees it and takes to it like a bass to a night crawler. It took me all of a millisecond to realize that I just stuck my dick into a belt sander and there was a very real possibility that I wasn't going to get it back. Another valuable lesson learned on the farm is if you are looking for sexual gratification it's probably best if you just touch it yourself - a lesson that has served me well for a great many years.

So, let's look at some behaviors, actions, and feelings from my adolescence, and I might as well break it to you now, these are some things that will be looked at on the road to recovery. We can start with some behaviors. I was already stealing money, such as my brother's coin collection. I was sneaking into the pantry and eating cake icing, I would leave the icing in the pantry and continue to go back to it to get more. I would eat bowls of powdered sugar. I fought with my siblings like I was fighting for my life. I was insanely jealous of my younger brother for being paralyzed and getting everyone's attention. I could already lie like a used car salesman and was a pretty fair hand at manipulating people to get what I wanted. Here are some general feelings that I felt at this time - I spent a great deal of time fantasizing about being someone else, anyone else besides me. I felt less than everyone else. I felt humiliated, ashamed and embarrassed. I don't suppose sticking my dick in a belt sander helped that much, and I lived in constant fear that someone might find out how I really felt. So, in a nutshell, I was a full-fledge addict, and I hadn't even used drugs yet, other than Ritalin. But by that time, I had stopped taking it, so my own thoughts in my head ran by like they were on fast forward. My internal dialogue was just as fast, and I could barely understand myself. I think sometimes I didn't.

The summer between fourth and fifth grade, I remember going to the county fair. We went every year. Dad would mingle with the farmers, look at livestock and tractors, just a regular ho down. We were there the day before the fair opened while everything was being set up. As we walked in, I looked down and there was a $50 bill folded in half laying in the gravel. I picked it up and showed dad and I remember being excited. I just hit the jackpot! I could throw darts at balloons, shoot ducks with pellet guns, I was in hog heaven. I'm already spending the money in my head when my dad informs me that we have to turn it in. "Fifty dollars is a lot of money and someone worked hard for it," he said. Are you shitting me! I was going to have the best year at the fair and now I had to turn my money in. Dad saw the disappointment in my face. Clearly, I didn't do well enough at hiding my feelings, so he further lectured me on how hard he worked for his money. I was well aware of how hard he worked for his money. Anyway, the $50 was collected, and I was given a $5 reward for returning it. Now, I don't know this for a fact, but there is a very strong possibility that my father put up the $5 himself.

The next day at the fair, that $5 was gone in the blink of an eye, so I'm running around the fair with my little brother, and that rocket fuel formula sensation hits me. I've got a doozy of an idea; it takes a little time to explain it to my little brother and my idea went something like this: if he asked someone for some money, they would probably give it to him because hell, he's a cripple for gods sakes.

Mick asked why we don't ask mom or dad for money?"

"Because we won't get enough."

He wasn't too sure about the idea but after some fast talking I convince him to at least try once to see what happens. Of course, it works, apparently all of my ideas aren't completely stupid. I don't know how much we got, because it bought candy and games until my dad came and found us and threatened extermination if we didn't quit. I'm quite sure I didn't make it back to the fair that year.

I should say growing up in a farm community was quite an experience. People helped each other on a regular basis; if a neighbor called for help, you went and you were insured that if you called him, he would show up. Everyone knew who you were - which made things a little difficult when I got older, but we're not there yet. There were cookouts and ice cream socials where the ice cream was cranked by hand; there was always something going on, and oh yeah there was sweet corn and maple syrup made from the trees in the yard. Little did I realize then the incredible childhood that I was being given. I spent most of my time in my head, I thought, as a slave being forced to do chores that were never done. Feed the steers twice a day (grain feed and hay from the top of the barn), mow the yard, which was around five acres, brush hog the pasture, another thirty acres, and by the end of the fifth grade I was a regular farmhand; I was being primed for some time.

At the end of fifth grade, I went on the school camping trip terrified because I still wet the bed. I did have a few friends by this time, I was sometimes sleeping overnights during the weekends at their homes. I would try not to sleep much; I had a great fear of my friends finding out that I wet the bed. No wonder I'd rather be Indiana Jones; God damn I thought I was pathetic. So anyhow I went on the school camping trip, and the only thing I really remember is while we were at the zip line a teacher went ahead of us to show us how it worked. She was going to go down the zipline backwards and unfortunately, she by mistake put on a kid's harness instead of an adult harness because when she stepped off the platform, her harness let go, and she fell about three stories to the ground below. She broke both legs maybe an arm and who knows about her back.

I remember a lot of kids crying and a lot of really upset kids. I don't remember crying or even being scared. Let's remember my best friend was eaten and my little brother was born paralyzed, so bad shit happens.

Around the same age, I was riding in the grain truck with dad going to Columbus to the granary. We were in a traffic jam, and as we were approaching a semi-truck on the side of the road my dad told me not to look. Of course, as we got closer, I did, and apparently a driver had stepped out from in front of his truck and was hit by another semi. What I saw was not much different than what you see when a deer is hit at high speeds and everyone from the country has seen that. Another lesson, bad shit happens.

There were deaths from farming accidents with people we knew, it was around this time that I learned that dad had owned an appliance repair business in California with a brother; evidently the risk of electrocution while working on appliances wasn't enough excitement for him, so he upped his game to dangerous equipment, angry bulls, and wiring equipment three miles underground in the mines. No wonder I'm crazy, it's in my blood.

So, let's go on to the sixth grade, I'm pretty sure that here is where I had my first real drink, on an overnight with several friends in town while camping in their yard. Their parents left, and we raided the bar. I'm sure we all got sick, we definitely all got drunk, and I have to say that on the whole it was a rather enjoyable experience.

I got in quite a lot of trouble that year in school. I was always against everybody - teachers and students alike. I'll say by this time I had already been attempting relationships with probably all the girls I met during the previous several years of elementary school. We will round it out and say from the third grade on I was interested in the girls in school and probably looked at a few teachers! I had an insatiable appetite for sex, and anything had to be better than the belt sander experience that was forever lurking in the back of my mind. So, I always was willing to hold hands, steal a kiss or two, and grab an ass if I could get away with it. I'd play get married or house with any of the girls who wanted to, but it was the wedding night or doctor that was always on my mind.

I will say that I would already feel attached and better if I was trying to be in a relationship. It was for the most part all innocent and normal except in my mind, in there it was already an orgy of lust and an unwholesome desire for more. Let's get back to the sixth grade; that was a rough year by the end. I had thirteen demerits, several suspensions, and I was just starting to feel comfortable. Two big things happened at the end of that year, on one of my overnights with friends. In the middle of throwing tomatoes or rocks at cars, one of my friends pulled out a joint, and we smoked it. Instantly, my whole life changed. Oh my God, I was going to be all right, it was easily the best thing that had ever happened to me! From the very first hit, I was changed. The racing thoughts slowed to a manageable speed, my almost overwhelming feelings of inadequacy faded to the back of my mind, and the unreasonable fear settled to a little worry. After the next hit, fear left me altogether. It was wholly a new me. I wasn't ashamed, oh help me baby Jesus, this shit show is about to get real.

I honestly can say that I wasn't immediately consumed with getting more, but it was really close. Most of my friends were drinking beer when they could. We were in the country, so everyone drank. There had to be under a thousand people in the community and there were like five bars. We were farmers in the country, everyone drank, oh except my parents. Dad didn't like it, and mom's sister died while driving drunk with kids in the car, so she didn't drink either. I didn't learn about this until much later. I didn't like beer; I couldn't figure out why anyone would want to drink it. I hadn't experienced whiskey yet, but back to where we were in my life - weed was fucking great! Like I said, the daily search for more wasn't instantaneous, but it was close.

The second big thing that happened in the end of the sixth grade revolves around the trouble I was getting into. As I think about it, let's set the stage for what happened at the end of the sixth grade because there was a definite build up to what all happened, and if I look at it a little harder and ask for some Devine guidance, maybe we can sift through it a little and have it all make a little more sense. So, we will go back to the end of the fifth grade about the time of the school camping trip. I was informed by my parents that I would be flying to California for the summer between fifth and sixth grade. At first, the thought of the trip was exciting to me; I was going to spend time with several different family members, and there were a lot of activities that would keep any young boy thoroughly interested. I was to spend time in the mountains with Grandpa O'Malley on his job site; he was a lead electrician on a huge hydroelectric dam. I was to go to Disneyland with cousins and swimming in the ocean, the list went on and on. So naturally I was excited at first. Of course, the whole trip was planned because there wasn't going to be anyone at home to watch me, and I was less than trustworthy to stay home alone. Dad would be busy with the coal mine at night and mom would be at the hospital with Mick all summer having surgery after surgery. I was still jealous of Mick; lucky bastard gets all the attention and so. The family plan was to ship me off for the summer break from school. This wasn't really a new plan; by this time it was really the old faithful fall back, something I started to recognize when I was a few years younger. My perception was, "I had a terrible life, no one really wanted me, and my opinion of myself was so low why would they."

As we approached summer break, however, I felt some apprehension about going. There was a recurring dream cropping up; I was waking up from dreams of dicks again. I was really confused about this; I had put the dreams out of my mind, and I was clearly interested in girls not boys, so why was I having this dream over and over? I continued to become more and more agitated, as we got closer to summer break. I finally told my parents that I wouldn't be going to California, which I don't suppose they took so well. They kept asking me why, and I didn't really know I just wasn't going. So, we argued back and forth for a while like any well-bred family would. Actually, I argued, they just said I was going, and I said, "No I'm not."

In the hope of a truce, we ended up at a Pizza Hut just mom, dad and me to hash out this California debacle, and as we talked, I just got more and more agitated. I literally felt like I would die if I went to California, I was on the verge of exploding in Pizza Hut. I couldn't hold back the tears and finally the dam broke, memories came rushing in and I understood why I was having dick dreams and I told my parents everything. When I told them what happened when I was eight, they were in worse shock than me. I'm sure some other families heard some shit that night. I didn't care, I couldn't stop it. It just all spilled out. I was crying the whole time shaking it felt like I was reliving the whole experience, and trust me, it wasn't any better the second time. Again, they just looked at me like I was an alien; they were dumbfounded. I guess it really is a lot to throw on someone, I was about to be twelve and this had been bottled up since eight. There was some relief telling my parents I was still completely embarrassed and ashamed, humiliated, and probably a few dozen other feelings that I couldn't identify.

I still was sent to California that summer. Overall, the trip was really nice. I didn't swim at any neighbors, I can tell you that. I had a few drinks that summer, but I don't think I got drunk though I'm sure I wanted to. But there was an allusive magic to even a little drink, an excitement that took away the racing thoughts, a thrill that I couldn't quite get ahold of, as it took me away from myself. It was akin to the same feelings I got when I stole a cigarette and smoked, or when I snuck into the pantry and ate icing, or when I fantasized about being someone else, or when I masturbated. All of these things took me away from myself, and being that I truly hated myself, away was always so nice.

Let's recap my summer in California, I spent a lot of time in the mountains with grandpa. Grandpa and his work buddies took me Snipe hunting. For anyone who doesn't know, there's no such thing as a Snipe. They put me on a rock and told me to wait for the Snipe. I suppose the jest of the gag is to find out how long a dumbass will wait. I went to a family reunion/fish fry where it was rumored that one piece of fish might have been left out in the sun too long. Guess who got that piece of fish. I was as sick with food poisoning as I've ever been. To this day, I remember puking out the window the entire way home.

I spent my twelfth birthday at my cousins, and they had a cake that I remember as being half the size of a table we had cake for breakfast for two weeks solid. I remember the shower at my cousins being big enough to play a football game in. On the whole, I found my family in California to be quite cosmopolitan. My summer was more than any kid could ask for. I remember a few weeks with another cousin and his very pretty Mexican wife, and she would make homemade burritos for breakfast and spread jelly on them. They would feed the baby things that were so hot I couldn't even smell them without my eyes watering. They were all wonderful to me; they all watched me and filled my every waking moment with activities. Even with all that, I'm pretty sure I was miserable. You know that old adage, "Wherever you go, there you are." I remember the trip was cut a little short, I wanted to go home so Grandma O'Malley bought us tickets and away we went, she took me home and stayed with me! I guess it's better to be miserable around your own shit.

I'll say here that I have very vague memories of seeing psychiatrist, but they don't really stand out. I think my parents knew I was miserable and wanted to see me get help, but I wouldn't be honest with any of the doctors, so it was all for not.

Let's get back to the sixth grade; oh my God I was hell on wheels - and the wheels were on the best blue and gold Huffy a kid could get." I got in an excessive amount of trouble that year. By the end of the year, I earned my thirteenth demerit chewing gum in the Memorial Day parade. I was in the school band and played the snare drum. I'll quickly add that Memorial Day was a big deal in our community. I guess it's easiest to say we were an incredibly old community, and the veterans were held in very high regard, as there were military tombstones dating back to the 1800s, and every year all the veterans in the graveyards were honored.

I probably picked up on this more than I realized, as my family had a military background, my father had served, and my grandpa Vance was the last World War I living veteran for all the surrounding counties. The year before, my fifth-grade teacher, the same one that fell during the camping trip, asked our fifth-grade class for volunteers to write an essay about Memorial Day and the American flag. There was to be a contest, and the winner would read their essay in front of the town at the Memorial Day parade. It's probably not a good idea to ask fifth graders to volunteer to write an essay, as no one did it. Well, as it turned out our teacher didn't take the whole thing very well actually, she was quite pissed, so as a class punishment we were all forced to write the essay. She suspended regular lessons, and we spent a day writing. I opened my mind to what I thought America was, and I wrote some shit down; we were really none too happy about the whole thing. As it turns out. my essay was chosen as the winner. So, on Memorial Day that year I had to read my essay in front of the whole town. My teacher, however, wasn't present she was in the hospital recuperating. I do remember that I was terrified to read in front of the whole town; my fears were unfounded, but they were still real to me - what if everyone knows what I really think about myself; oh dear God, what if they find out I stuck my dick in a belt sander? Of course, no one found out, and with a shaky voice I read my essay, and everyone seemed pleased, I think my parents were especially proud, my mother put the essay in a photo album and has it to this day:

What the American flag means to me!

The American flag stands by me as a sign of peace and Freedom. It makes me feel at home wherever I am. The American flag, all those stars and stripes, just floating In the air, waiting to be admired! I can think of all the fun and happiness I've had in America, like Kings Island, Disney World and the oceans, but there's more than fun. I'm proud to be an American. I love America and I always will! I hope every American loves their flag. The American flag is a statue of liberty, justice, and freedom. That's the American flag.

Paul Ray Fullmer

All right all right, let's get back to the infamous thirteenth demerit (I think thirteen really was a school record). They spent a lot of time beating my ass that year. So, I was chewing gum while marching and playing the snare drum. The music teacher was marching with us, and I was caught red-handed if you will. I was asked to spit my gum out and I refused. I'm sure in my mind if I spit the gum out while marching someone would step in it. Ok, that might not be true; I just really hated being told what to do. An argument ensued and "cunt" might have slipped out a little louder than I would have liked, and there you have it, the demerit was incurred. The next school day I was called to the office; as the year is over, I'm expecting one more ass whopping on the way out the door. What happened next was something else entirely, so earlier in the year our principal had become ill and took a leave of absence and my sixth-grade teacher was made acting principal. We didn't get along very well when he was the head of the classroom and now, he is the head of the school, so I was fairly sure I was about to be in the shit.

Let's recap just a little. I was in a lot of trouble that year; I was living like James Dean in *A Rebel Without A Cause*. The phrase wasn't coined yet, but I was just like the honey badger - I didn't give a shit! So, the acting principal can't really be blamed for being at his wit's end with me. I stroll into his office as smug as always and I stand in front of his desk and stare him down, fully expecting an ass whooping before I leave his office. He gets up from behind his desk and walks over and shuts the door; I'm thinking "Here we go." He sits on the corner of his desk and asks me to take a seat. "Now this is different," I think. He informs me that I am an undeniable piece of shit, and he can't wait for me to get into junior high where I'm surely to have my ass kicked on a daily basis. As I'm watching this man tell me this, his veins are sticking out of his neck, and he is close to slobbering with the dislike he feels for me. I'm sitting there slack-jawed staring at this man thinking to myself "This guy is fucking crazy." He insults, brow beats and berates me for about ten good minutes then tells me I'm free to go.

I go home after school and repeat everything he said to me to my mom, and oh boy, she hits the roof. She tells me she will be taking me to school in the morning.

We get to school on time the next day, and mom drags me upstairs to the office and tells me to stand outside the door. What ensued next I'll never forget. There was quite a bit of yelling, enough that teachers and students were looking out doorways trying to see what in hell was going on. I have to say I wasn't concerned nearly like my mother was. I pretty much felt the same about myself as the principal did. My mom informed the school, pretty much like she was on the PA system, that I would be leaving and not coming back for the last few days of school. She stormed out of the office and dragged me to my classroom where she emptied my desk so I wouldn't have to come back. My friends were all in shock at how pissed my mom was. I was a little in awe myself; I had plenty of opportunities to see my mom pissed, as I was generally an even-keeled ass all the time - it wasn't just reserved for school. But I ain't never seen pissed like this. Out of an uncommon act of good, I just kept my mouth shut and road the storm out.

2

GETTIN' HIGH

In junior high, I got to meet more people and step my using up a notch. Let's look at my award-winning attitude and do a quick check on some feelings. I lived in a state of perpetual fear and envy. I was quite sure that everybody's life was better than mine, even my little brother who by this time I had visited in the hospital more than once. I was dragged to the I.C.U. to say goodbye because the doctors said he wasn't going to make it. That taught me another little lesson: "The doctors don't get to decide when we are going to die." Mick kept pulling through. My world was 90 percent fantasy that I lived inside my own head, and my attitude that everyone saw was make believe. I couldn't let anyone know how scared I really was, so I acted fearless, my fear even existed in my sleep. I was not only afraid I would wet the bed, but I had very vivid nightmares. One that was particularly frightening had me in the house looking out, and all I could see were giant spider legs. The spider is so big that it is above the house, and in the dream, I know it's going to eventually get me! To this day, I have a fear of spiders.

So, the summer before junior high I was given my older brother's motorcycle, a Kawasaki KM100 street/dirt bike. It topped out between 75 and 80 miles an hour, and that's how I went, about as fast as I could. Going fast produced a feeling that seemed to ground me, a kind of peace. Maybe it stilled the shit show in my head a little. In no time, I could map out twenty square miles in my head of every road or path around. Of course, I wasn't allowed to ride on the road, but we had a half-mile driveway, and I could disappear down it for hours. The road and top speed is where I liked to be. Let me say here that all of my time wasn't just spent in fantasy and fear; I was raised in the country on a farm. I learned to hunt and fish, I searched for arrowheads in the fields, I was learning how to operate equipment when we baled hay, I drove the tractor, I could already back up the baler with a wagon attached (for those of you that don't know that is basically impossible, but I could do it). I learned how to operate a bulldozer, how to read a tape measure, how to use a table saw without losing fingers, how to use about any kind of hand tool, power or otherwise that you can imagine.

How could I learn all these things while being completely and totally consumed with fear, you ask? I learned to separate my mind; I could do more than one thing at a time. My dad had a horrible habit of listing the day's chores, which usually were more than twelve different things to do, and he wasn't very thrilled about having to repeat the list. So even though I didn't know it, my mind was expanding and my ability at retention was also expanding. I fought education every step of the way, I hated going to school, but I was learning even though I didn't know it.

My older brother left the farm to join the Navy the summer before junior high. My pot smoking was slowly increasing I had friends that were smoking, and we did any chance we got. As school got started, I met new friends that were doing the things I was. The more my social networks grew the higher I was getting. I was being paid while working the farm it wasn't much, but it soon was spent entirely on weed and when it wasn't enough, I'd steal money out of dad's wallet or mom's purse. I could always ask for more money and nine times out of ten my dad would give it to me. I didn't find out until years later that Grandma and Grandpa Vance didn't tell my dad that they loved him; I guess it was implied. They were good people, and we knew they loved us all, but they weren't going to tell you so. I reckon due to this my father was uncomfortable saying "I love you," so instead he would give me money. Oh boy, when I figured this one out, I beat it like a dead horse' it was almost like he couldn't say no when I asked for money. It was like always having a winning scratch off.

I joined a couple sports in junior high - cross country and track. My brother ran, and I guess I was following in his footsteps. We trained after school with the high schoolers, and I quickly found the guys that got high after practice. My world was slowly being consumed with the next high.

My older brother came home after basic training before he was shipped out on the *Nimitz*, and we were talking in his room. He was showing me how he packed his duffle bag, and he pulled out a bottle of Jack Daniels. At that point, I hadn't had whiskey, but I knew what it was. Being raised on the farm and the fact that dad wasn't a sports fanatic, when we had a day off or when it rained, we watched a lot of old John Wayne movies - and John Wayne knew how to drink his whiskey. So, I asked my brother if I could have a drink. He said "I shouldn't, you're too young to drink," but being a good older brother, he opened the bottle and took a swallow then handed me the bottle.

I held it in contemplation. I don't know how I knew, but I knew that what was inside of this bottle could change the way I feel. I put the bottle to my lips, and I set to drinking it like it was a glass of water.

After about three or four good swallows, my brother snatched the bottle away from me and asked, "What is wrong with you?"

If I only thought he would listen, I could have answered his question at some great length, but I was pretty sure it was a rhetorical question. I was right, of course, the whiskey definitely changed how I felt, and I didn't feel nearly as prejudiced toward it as I did beer!

When he left to return to the Navy, in the bathroom at the airport, he grabbed me and told me he better not find out I'm using drugs. For all intents and purposes, I believe he wanted to be a good big brother, and really it wasn't his fault that I hated his guts. There was a deep anger in me I didn't understand. I had never really forgotten about being teased after I was molested. One good thing, though, after I had told my parents about being molested, I never had a dick dream again; we can chock that one up to a small blessing.

My seventh-grade year was filled with new friends and activities at school and of course girls. My relationship game was stepped up severely; I was always in one and I was usually looking for the next one at the same time. There was a standing family joke that I was likely to be the first sibling with children.

I remember that dad had a huge cookout that year, and a lot of families and coworkers from the coal mines came. It was a real shindig. The party was going nicely, and people brought beer. There was a bonfire, people were roasting marshmallows and hot dogs on sticks. I had found more interesting things to do; dad's boss had brought his daughter, and she was quite lovely. Things were progressing quite nicely when we were caught in the hay barn! My dad was pissed, his boss was pissed, and really, I was a little pissed myself, things were really starting to get interesting.

Dad was in fear for his job for months afterwards. When I was with a girl and it could be just holding hands - it didn't necessarily need to be rolling in the hay if you will - there was a curious phenomenon: I felt better. I didn't feel the overwhelming self-loathing that I normally did. And I liked to feel better...hell, who doesn't? A closer look will reveal that girls gave me a feeling akin to using drugs, as it changed how I felt, and it was added to my arsenal. I was quite fine to use any girl I could to feel better. Now, I should say here that I experienced love with them all; I was very quick to attach, and I very rarely initiated a breakup because I always felt better being with someone. And to be perfectly truthful, it lessened my deepest and darkest fear of being alone!

I was quite sure that we could be in multiple successful relationships if everyone would stop being so priggish about the whole thing! But what did I know I was only in the seventh grade? I will say that I started to learn this and experienced the phenomenon from my first real kiss and the memory of it is with me to this day. It was the summer between fifth and sixth grade, I was in town with friends, and we were hanging out in someone's house. I was sitting on the washing machine, and we were laughing and joking around, and one of the girls had called me out on the way I acted, she said I probably hadn't even kissed a girl, and really, I hadn't other than a quick lip smack. She was in the seventh grade and was quite sure of herself. I informed her that of course I had, and she said prove it. Well, what's a kid supposed to do, so I did, and it was born with passion and lit a flame inside of me like I had never known. Afterwards, I was sure that we should further explore this flame and passion, but it wasn't in the cards, however, some years later I was afforded the opportunity to continue that conversation with my first kiss, and I can assure you it was worth the wait!

So back to the seventh grade. it was no wonder by my behavior that I got a bit of a reputation as a womanizer, but I lived with so many hidden fears and anxieties that I basically just shrugged it off. My feelings kept me essentially on sensory overload I could be watching TV with family and something embarrassing happen on the show and I would have to walk away. I couldn't handle watching it I could feel their embarrassment like it was my own. I was like a feeling amplifier; I would cry and feel pain and loss, as my mind didn't distinguish the difference between real and make believe - just another thing I used to wonder what the fuck was wrong with me why was I like this.

So, the seventh-grade sort of passed by with me chasing weed and skirts with about equal vigor, my duties on the farm were becoming pretty extensive by this time we owned 500 acres and leased at any given time another 300 to 500 acres.

Dad and I had a fairly sizable operation; we mostly grew corn and soybeans and cross-cropped with winter wheat. We were staying with the times and learning new farming techniques. No-till was becoming more popular, and we were moving away from granular fertilizer to liquid. I spent many hours working on the farm plowing, disking, spraying fertilizer and weed killers. You wouldn't believe how great it felt to get high while disking a field, and it certainly didn't hurt my mind-splitting activities of fantasizing while I was working. Most of my fantasies revolved around getting rich so I didn't have to drive that fucking tractor anymore; they often consisted of finding buried gold in a field and striking out to my own tropical island where weed grew aplenty and the native women were always naked! They were my fantasies, so I tried to cover my bases.

By the time I reached the eighth grade, I was getting high multiple times a day. My friends had shrunk to a smaller group, as I only hung out with others that got high. I had a best friend; we'll call him Mortimer Pennfield. Mort and I hung out every weekend at one or the other's house. We started to dabble in minor league distribution, as it helped to keep the supply steady. The eighth grade was a very eventful year; I was high, though, so much of the time it was kind of a blur. I was growing less and less careful about hiding my using; I would try to hide my using when my parents would ask but it was really becoming rather tiring. I should say that one of my favorite places to get high was in the hay barn. I would sit in the haymow and get as high as I could; my body would feel like it was on a conveyor line if I sat forward, I would continue going forward even after I stopped, and when I would sit back it was the same. I would sit high for hours and just rock back and forth on the conveyor line thinking about how it felt. I was in heaven all my fears left me; I was all right with who I was. I had found peace. When I would leave the hay barn and walk from inside to outside, it was like I was being reborn into a new world every time.

I started spending a lot of time in the workshop on the farm making bowls and bongs. More and more of my time was being consumed with not only the act of getting high but also the preparation to get high. All my friends had a bowl or bong that I made, and I spent a fair amount of time smoking out of a pop can, and I became a pretty good hand at rolling a joint.

As I was perpetually high almost the whole time, so I thought I was having the time of my life! Mort and I spent almost every weekend partying at either his place or mine. His mother was a night nurse at a hospital, so his place was usually the safest bet when we were at my place. We had to come up with a reason to disappear. Being from the country hunting and fishing always was a good excuse to be away from the rest of my family though my parents did express on more than one occasion that they didn't think Mort and I were up to anything good. I'm sure in my mind I was being very clever and could find new and amazing excuses for why I always looked like I was on the verge of pink eye. I had asthma, and that was always a sure fallback. I remember one time Mort and I and a few others were camping out in his woods; we were of course getting high. We were on the verge of starting the stoner zombie apocalypse when Mort reached behind him, grabbed a box of 22 ammunition, and throws the whole box into the fire. We all scattered like roaches when you flip the light on in a seedy motel. Ammo starts going off like its World War III, and we are all running and laughing and ducking and dodging behind trees. "We're having fun now isn't this great!" I thought. I don't know how any of us survived. That is the kind of stupid shit we came up with on a regular basis.

On another occasion, Mort was staying at my house, and everyone else was already asleep, so we snuck out and headed for the barn to get high. I'm sure we were in the middle of quite a fascinating conversation when we realized that I had run out of weed. Now, I have to say I'm sure that we were high as a kite, but I immediately experienced that feeling of dread and an overwhelming feeling of loss. Whatever are we to do with no weed? The whole world might as well come to an end. In my mind, I'm experiencing the second coming of Christ and I'm sure to get left behind because there isn't a good bone in my body, when Mort says he has some weed at his house; well hell, speak up man, that solves everything. Except Mort lived a little over twelve miles away. Now we could both drive - not legally of course - but we knew if we stole a truck or car from the farm, it would likely wake up my parents because the dogs were sure to bark as soon as the engine turned over and we weren't so high as to think that shit would turn out very good at all. So, after putting or heads together we came up with an acceptable solution. We pushed my KM 100 street dirt bike out to the end of our half a mile driveway where we fired up the bike for an Enduro run to the outskirts of Thornville to get his weed. The moon was waxing almost full, and we had pretty good visibility for a quick dash to his house and back the trip to his house was for the most part uneventful if you can call two kids in the eighth-grade ridding at plus 75 miles an hour on back country roads without head lights or taillights uneventful. Praise the maker we made it to Mort's house. Now if we had just grabbed the weed and headed back, we would have been far better off, but it wasn't in the works we had to celebrate a little we just had a fantastic ride in the dark we've got more weed so let's get higher and we did. As I said before as we were getting high, I'm sure we were on our way to solving many of the world's great injustices and if we could get any one to decipher the mad ravings of a couple stoners world peace was sure to quickly follow! So, by now we have left the realm of high as a kite and we are somewhere north of stoned begonzys, we decide it's time for the Enduro trip back to the farm. All was going almost as well as the trip to Mort's when the road decides to not be under us anymore and we are shooting across a field at 75 miles an hour, we dump the bike and go a tumbling for a while laughing historically all the way. We finally get up and brush ourselves off and fire up the bike to finish this quest only this time I suggest that I'll drive the motorcycle. We get back on the road and get this little bike cranked back up to speed and damn if the road doesn't leave us again shot across a ditch bouncing across another field motorcycle going one way me another and Mort yet another again it's the funniest thing in the world, we are laughing the whole-time flipping end over end cartwheeling across this field when we finally come to a stop it takes sufficiently more time to get back up. I believe we were both contemplating just sleeping right here in this field maybe by morning the road would stop being so uncharacteristically unfriendly. After some heavy discussion we decide that if we are going to survive this without certain punishments we needed to get back to the farm before the sun decided to make an appearance. Needless to say, we got the motorcycle back to the road and drove the rest of the way back like a ninety-six-year-old woman on the way to church! Hallelujah we finally made it back to my driveway. We pushed the bike back to the shop and feeling a little less than ok we decided to call it a night. The next morning there were several stares and shaken heads at the fact that we went to bed heathy and woke up scratched scabbed and bruised over a good portion of our visible bodies a phenomenon to be sure that I was in no mood to explain "hell we are in the country maybe we were abducted by aliens and they beat the hell out of us for several hours" that would have about explained the whole situation.

Here might be a good time to talk about the elephant in the room. As an alcoholic and drug addict, I can always come up with an excuse or a lie to justify almost anything, but typically the questions don't ever get asked. This is due to the elephant in the room; though there can be a problem so glaring and obvious, but our loved ones don't want to address it or even give acknowledgement that the problems exist at all hence we don't talk about the elephant in the room even though it keeps shitting on the rug.

On another excursion that I had I was with friends in Thornport on the canals of Buckeye Lake, and we ran out of weed. Then my buddies tell me they think they know where we can buy some more. Now we're talking, this is always a solvable problem. My dear old pals tell me of a high schooler they have heard of that they are sure sells weed! Eureka, problem solved. Not so fast, my friends tell me this high schooler has quite a reputation for being on the mean side, but if I were willing to find out they would show me where he lived. I was told that his name was Ray, too, well hell I'm sure we will be fast friends we have the same name and all. So, we pull our money together and my friends are all standing on the canal pointing to a yellow house saying that's it there, are you sure you want to do this. Hell yeah, we're out of weed, and that just won't do. While they are telling me about Ray, they happen to mention that he has a really hot little sister, and in my head I'm thinking "this just keeps getting better," so off I go. I stroll up to this yellow house with absolutely no idea what's going on inside and I ring the doorbell, a guy answers the door and asks,

"What you want?"

"Well, I'm looking for Ray."

"Oh," he says, "come on in!"

"Ok, seems ok so far so I walk into a living room and there are half a dozen guys sitting around talking all of whom are a lot older than me, and the guy says, "Ray, this kid is looking for you!"

Ray gets up, and the first thing I'm aware of is it would take ten of me even to push this guy over; he is literally as big as a house. He says, "What do you want kid?"

As I'm looking around, I don't notice any parental units lurking around, so I figure it should be fairly safe to talk. I decide to hit him with my personality first just to warm things up.

"My name's Ray too."

He looks at me like I just said the dumbest thing he has ever heard and says "So?"

"Well a few of my buddies told me they thought that if I came by and asked, I could buy some weed here."

When I said "buy some weed here," all other conversation stopped, and I became very aware of the pressing silence. Then the room exploded into an up roaring laughter. By now I'm feeling a little past nervous and, in my head, I'm half expecting a scene from *The Lord of the Flies* to be carried out at any minute. While everyone was laughing, Ray's little sister came out of her room to see what's going on, and I'm lost immediately, for she is beautiful.

As the laughing dies down, which I barely noticed, Ray asked me how much I want. I'm lost starring at the future mother of my children and am totally at a loss for words.

"Hey kid, how much do you want?"

Drawn back to reality by the fear of Ray's size and the fact that he looked like he could tear my arms off and beat me with them, I say "A $25 sack."

Ray disappears for a minute, and his little sister goes back to her room Thankfully, I can concentrate on what I'm doing. Ray comes back, hands me a sack, takes my money, and out the door I went.

When I get back to the canal, my friends want to know what happened. I pulled out the weed, and they look in shock and inform me that they never thought for a second I had a chance of getting a sack from Ray. So, we get high and laugh the whole thing off. It helped give me a reputation of being fearless, and I liked that a lot.

Another one of my great debacles that year was one of the most uncomfortable situations I was ever in. On a sleepover - I should really say on a getting-high-over, I stayed with one of my buddies and through an unfortunate chain of events (even though that's not how I viewed it then), I slept with his single mother! Now I'm sure in my mind this whole debacle was caused because I was the great Don Juan in reincarnation "it just wasn't possible for women to resist my unearthly ability to charm," as all of my 90 some pounds of asthmatic self were just too much to handle! Now might be a good time to point out a character flaw that a great many addicts and alcoholics share we simply believe that the whole world revolves around us and it takes a great many disappointments and disasters before there's much hope of changing our minds. So, this great debacle plays out with me being rather ashamed of myself, but I would never admit it, as I did value my buddy's friendship and I was very tightlipped about the whole thing. Though it is entirely possible that I was so tightlipped because my buddy was somewhat larger than me (Who wasn't?), and I was quite sure that there would be an ass whooping involved if he ever found out.

His older sister did, however! I was in class and was called out over the intercom to report to the office by the principal. I was slowly making my way to the office playing out the last few days trying to figure out not what I did but what I was caught doing. There's a great difference, you know. I couldn't come up with anything, so when I entered the principal's office, he looked at me and asked, "What the hell did you do now?" At that point, I'm wondering if this is some kind of set up; I'm pretty sure I'm committing several felonies a day. He proceeds to tell me that there is a high school girl in the next room that says she has to talk to me and she is in hysterics. He goes and gets her and brings her in, and I'm pretty sure I know what's up. The principal asks us if we would like to use his office. I reply no. I'm almost certain I don't want anyone to hear this, so we go out into the hallway where it's empty, as everyone else is in

A Road Through Hell

class. My buddy's sister asks me how could I and if it were really true. All I could think was, Thank God I wasn't caught red-handed; it could surely have been worse." After some fast talking and a fair amount of groveling and an explicit promise to stay away from her mom, we parted ways, and she had at least stopped crying. I was nervous that she would tell her brother, but it never came up again.

Around that time, I was out riding motorcycles with another buddy whose mother leased land to my father for farming, and as we were out riding, we happened across a couple lovelies that we went to school with, so I informed the two young women that we were on our way to roll a joint under the bridge and would they be interested in coming along. They both seemed agreeable to the offer, so they went with us. After we had rolled and smoked the joint, I was feeling quite a lot better about the day's happenings and I asked one of the lovely ladies if she would be interested in a kiss. To my great disappointment, she informed me that she was not interested in a kiss. That's not really much of a story, but that beautiful young woman is my second wife standing in front of me and had she given me that kiss, it could have altered the course of events that made up my life. And as a good recovering alcoholic, I would like to say that everything that happened was for a reason, and unbeknownst to me I had to go through everything to get to where I am.

On a short side note, my wife informed me last night that it was her sixth-grade teacher that fell during the school camping trip and I was in the fifth grade the year we went. I informed her that it was pretty much a miracle that I could spell my own name, and this was my story, so I'd tell it and remember it how I wanted, even if she was right. I lived a good great deal of my time in a fantasy inside my own head, so to have only missed the truth by a year is pretty fucking close. Now as a disclaimer we were both at the camping trip at the same time and I was standing beside the teacher when she fell, so I was only off a little on my memories.

So back to my story of addiction and recovery ... we are quickly approaching my first introduction to recovery! Now, in my head I'm fairly sure I'm doing a good enough job covering my using. Toward the end of the eighth grade, my parents approached me and informed me that they thought I had a problem. "Now where is this coming from?" I thought. They told me that they had been talking to a juvenile treatment facility and they really thought I should go. Now I should say that this conversation was happening in the shop on the farm, and I was in the middle of making a great Ray Vance bowl to get high out of, and I had the gall to ask why-ever they thought such a thing. As I wasn't hiding what I was doing, they informed me that my actions and behavior led them to believe I was on a crash course to prison and that a week later I would be checking into "The Campus" rehabilitation center. I gave a great thought to flight immediately.

I begged and pleaded that they change their minds, I promised that I would quit, and I could be better, a promise that was surly to be made a million times. My parents, however, already under the influence of this treatment center from hell, weren't having it.

So, as it came to be on May 13, 1986 with a bag packed and a carton of cigarettes - which my mother really didn't approve of but apparently the treatment center told her that if I smoked, send me with cigarettes for God's sakes - I was driven off the farm to the big city of Columbus, Ohio, to the suburb of Westerville. I was high as a kite when we left the farm, and when we reached the Campus we were set in a room with a counselor and informed that there would be a seven-day evaluation period where we would have no contact with each other, and in a shocker to me my parents said ok and left. Now in all fairness, they gave me hugs and wished me well and probably told me not to be a dumbass. Then I was introduced to Vladimir another patient who was also just admitted that day, and we would be sharing a room together.

My first seven days of treatment were consumed with taking tests, blood tests, which early one morning when they took mine, I swear it came out green which earned me the nickname green blood for a short while. We had psychiatric evaluations and test after test. I probably even looked at ink blots and was asked what I saw. We were fed almost no sugar or caffeine. At breakfast, when we were able to get it, Captain Crunch was quite a treat, and we would eat it until our mouths hurt.

At the end of the seven days, my parents were coming to visit, and I thought, "Here's my chance to get out. I'll make another apology and proclaim that maybe things got a little out of hand, but I was better." So, my parents showed up. and I was called to the lobby for a visit. I was seven days off drugs and still hadn't told anyone how terrified I was that without the drugs there was no way I could live with myself; I was fully caught up in a scheme in my head to get my parents to let me come home so I could do a better job of hiding my using. When I saw my parents, my mother gave me a hug, and I could tell that my dad wasn't very happy. They said I looked better and asked me if I was being treated ok, I told them that I was. The whole meeting was rather uncomfortable, and as our time together was about over, I was just about to make my play for freedom and plead my case, but before I could start in on why they should let me come home my dad says, "Ray I'm sorry I let your mom talk me into bringing you here." He started to cry and said, "Go get your stuff, and I'll take you home!"

Now I have to say that I had never seen my father shed a tear, and as I looked into his eyes, I could remember being much younger and seeing his headlights on my bedroom wall at ten till one in the morning, as he was getting home from work and I would climb out of bed and be at the door waiting for him, when he would come in he would be head to toe covered in the black dust of the coal mines. He would smile at me and go get a shower and then we would sit up together and talk, I loved my dad so much and missed him enough to wake up in the middle of the night just to have a chance to spend a few minutes together. I saw my dad as Superman; there was nothing he couldn't do, and I loved him with every fiber of my being. Now all of these thoughts passed before me in the blink of an eye. My father had just said that he would take me home and that's all I wanted, yet I couldn't help but feel the pain I was causing him and my mother who sat quietly at his side and I thought about the pain I was putting them both through. This possibly was a "white light moment." I was made aware that my actions and behaviors were affecting others besides myself, and I realized that the pain they felt was mine. I had caused it, so I looked at my dad and the decision was made inside of me, and I don't believe I can really take credit for it. I told him, "You know what, Dad - I'm going to stay. I love you, and I'm sorry." And for the first time I think I really meant it. We all hugged, and I turned around and went to treatment.

3

THE CAMPUS

Now, you would think that by going to treatment I would minimize my drug use, so I didn't look like such an addict, but remember I am an addict and I seldom do what is expected. Anyways, I was quite sure that if everyone found out that I was in treatment for basically smoking pot, I was afraid I would be laughed right out the door. So being an adept addict, I fell back on old faithful, and I lied my ass off. I embellished my drug use to the point of complete ridiculousness. In earnest my recovery started, we were introduced to Alcoholics Anonymous and Narcotics Anonymous, we were given a book for both and encouraged to read them. We were being introduced to a twelve-step form of recovery that had been changing lives of people worldwide for a very long time. We were told that we would be working the first four steps as part of our treatment before we would be released for an aftercare program that would last for at least three months. The twelve steps of recovery were:

1. We admitted we were powerless over drugs and or alcohol, and our lives had become unmanageable.
2. We came to believe that a power greater than ourselves could restore us to sanity.
3. We made a decision to turn our will and our life over to the care of God, as we understood him.

4. We made a searching and fearless moral inventory of ourselves.
5. We admitted to God, ourselves, and another human being the exact nature of our wrongs.
6. We were entirely ready to have God remove all these defects of character.
7. We humbly asked Him to remove our shortcomings.
8. We made a list of all people we had harmed and became willing to make amends to them all.
9. We made direct amends to such people wherever possible except when to do so would injure them or others.
10. We continued to take personal inventory and when we were wrong, we promptly admitted it.
11. We sought through prayer and meditation to improve our conscious contact with God as we understood him. Praying only for knowledge of His will for us and the power to carry it out.
12. Having had a spiritual awakening as a result of these steps, we tried to carry this message to alcoholics and addicts and to practice these principles in all our affairs.

These are the steps as were paraphrased by the Campus; they encompassed the ideals of both twelve-step programs, AA and NA. One of our first and greatest lessons was that alcohol was a drug. Now it behooves me to say that I had a great misunderstanding of just how important these twelve steps really were, but my road to recovery was gaining a foundation that would span a lifetime!

There were about twenty-eight men and women in the Campus, we were all under eighteen, so really there were twenty-eight boys and girls. We grew together, and we got to know each other, as we worked our first four steps on our way to being released. I still have the books I was given at the Campus and inside are all the signatures of the people I got to know and messages from them wishing a happy future.

There was a retirement home behind the Campus and the yards of the two complexes were together. Every day we had free time and would sit out back on picnic tables and smoke and talk and generally flirt with the opposite sex. We started to notice every day when we were outside there was a very old gentleman that sat inside of a trellised walkway that was strewn with flowers; we would wave hello, but he never waved back. Eventually we would shout a hello, and still we got no reply. One day the nursing home had an attendant outside, as we were shouting our hello's; most of us had by then decided that the old man was most obviously a codgety old bastard because he wouldn't reply. The nursing home attendant came over to us and told us that the man we were waving to and shouting hello to was blind and deaf. She asked us if we would like to meet him. "How the hell do you meet a blind and deaf person?" I wondered, so me and a few others went with the attendant just to see how this was going to work.

The attendant put her hand in the palm of the elderly man and using sign language in his palm told him that he had some guests that would like to say hi, we were shown how to sign hi in his palm, and we all took a turn. You could see in his face the recognition of each different hello and his appreciation was shown with tears standing in his eyes. We were given printouts of sign language and the alphabet and when we could while we were there, we would visit this old man and feel the welcoming sense our attempt to communicate gave him. He would light up when you reached out and turned his hand over so you could sign into it. Now I have to say that we had no great conversations, but the little selfless act of generosity was growth for us by leaps and bounds. One of the founding fundamentals of a twelve-step program is getting out of yourself by helping others, and we started to learn this lesson in treatment talking to an old, blind, deaf man.

I spent my 15th birthday in treatment at the Campus. Now we had a lot of fun together, really, I suppose just trying to be regular kids, but all kids inherently want to be adults, "a fault that unfortunately isn't realized until it's too late" so as it was, I genuinely got along better with older kids. Again, I point out that I always wanted to be different than I was even if it was as little a thing as being older! During my stay in treatment, I began to work on the first four steps in earnest, the First step wasn't a huge leap of my imagination to see how I had become powerless over using and that my life had become unmanageable. I was spending everything I earned on weed, I was dabbling in trafficking to help meet my needs, I was also stealing money from both my parents. Looking at the legal aspects, I was committing several "albeit minor" felonies a day. That my friends, is an example of good old justification, a felony is a felony. Like we say on the farm, if it looks like a ground hog, if it acts like a ground hog, it's probably a ground hog. Justification is our enemy as an addict and alcoholic when I am in active addiction I can and will justify all of my actions. I always can find an excuse for the reason why I'm doing things, and whether or not it's the truth, really has very little relevance.

So, I believed that I admitted I was an addict and that my life was unmanageable. Now if we look at that last statement, I've left out alcoholic, in my mind I had very rarely drank and even though one of our first lessons was that alcohol was a drug I didn't believe that I could be an alcoholic. This was the set up for future disasters, and it left enough of a crack in the door of reasoning that there harbored a thought that maybe one day I would be able to handle this thing like everyone else! It was only a sliver of a thought and it was hidden behind a door of reasoning and It was allowed to grow in hiding and would resurface some years later. This disease of addiction and alcoholism is like no other; even when treated, it's still there, and our only defense is a daily reprieve based on the spiritual principles of a twelve-step program. Now, don't get too worked up about that last sentence. I assure you I had no fucking idea what that meant, as I was preparing to leave treatment at fifteen. So, I moved on to step two and again I didn't really see a great leap of faith was needed. I had been raised going to church and had been to vacation Bible school many times, so I believed in God and Jesus. But here again I had my own perception of what the step meant. The step simply says, "Came to believe that a power greater than myself could restore me to sanity." And being a good addict, I twisted this step in my head to be, "found a religion to learn to pray the right way, to contact God" and this step clearly says nothing of the sort. This is a failing of mine that is a direct result of my belief that the world revolves around me, so my ideas and perceptions must be correct.

I moved on to step three, "made a decision to turn my will and my life over to the care of God as I understood him." Again, not really an overwhelming thing in my mind. It was, however, contingent upon finding the right religion to be able to correctly contact God, but I thought that was just a minor technicality.

Step four posed a little more of a problem. I was to write down everything that I had done and that was done to me, now that clearly was to encompass the fact that I was molested when I was eight, and I still harbored great shame and embarrassment about this. Taking a leap of faith and encouraged that the fourth step was the beginning of the freedom step, I added it, however I did not add that I was teased by my older brother and cousins after. I'll say here that it's a true blessing that the programs are set up where we grow with progress and not perfection, a start had been made, and a foundation was laid that could and would be built upon.

Treatment at the Campus was coming to an end. I was approaching a discharge date. Vladimir and I were to be discharged on the same day. We had started and were to finish treatment together. Vlad was a few years older than me, so he was already driving, and he had his own car, a little red Fiat convertible. On the day we were released my parents came to sign me out of treatment, and I was allowed to go with Vlad for a few days; we were going to go to some meetings in Columbus, and he would bring me home and stay on the farm with us for a little while. Vlad and I had started what would be a very long friendship, one that has lasted to this day. Now I can't speak for Vlad, but I was scared to leave; I was sure that once I left the Campus the feelings of worthlessness, self-pity, and despair were sure to return. The day came however, and we said our goodbyes to our treatment friends, and we left.

4

HUGS NOT DRUGS

Our plan, as we sold it to our parents, was that we were going to go to meetings for a few days in Columbus, and that's what we did. The day we left treatment we went to an NA meeting that evening. Now I will say here that we were introduced to both AA and NA through treatment, and Vlad and I both leaned more toward NA. As for myself, because AA introductions were in the form of a handshake and NA introductions were in the form of a hug and the fact that NA was chock full of beautiful women had nothing to do whatsoever with my choice. Ok, that might not be entirely accurate; it was an overwhelming experience to be welcomed with a hug by people that didn't know me, and it was an unexpected bonus that you could hug every woman in the room if you were willing to introduce yourself and somehow, I found the willingness.

Our very first meeting the day we left treatment we met Ian F. He came riding in on a Harley Davidson Cafe Racer wearing leathers and no helmet. Being young and impressionable, I thought it was quite possibly the coolest thing I had ever seen. Ian worked in a juvenile treatment facility in Athens, Ohio, had a striking resemblance to Frank Zappa, and had about four years of clean time. He invited me and Vlad to visit Athens and to come to meetings there. Ian was to be a great influence in my recovery; he wasn't my sponsor, but he nonetheless taught me a great deal about recovery. Ian was also instrumental in helping me to learn to have fun in recovery and there is more on this to come later.

Now I have to say that being a farm boy I had very little experience with the city, it mostly consisted of trips to Eastland Mall, a few restaurants where my family liked to eat and Children's Hospital where coincidentally, my younger brother Mick was having a biopsy the day I was released from treatment. Columbus was a little overwhelming, it had a population somewhere around 900,000 people so needless to say there were meetings going on at almost any given time. Vlad and I spent several days going to meetings before he took me home to the farm.

When I came home to the farm, I felt different, I didn't seem to be so self-consumed with dread and fear. I was showing Vlad around the farm, the tractors and the barns, the grain bins, and the pastures, when I noticed a cow down in the pasture, so I told Vlad let's go see what's wrong. We hopped the fence and set off across the pasture, as we were getting closer my suspicions that the cow was about to give birth to a calf proved to be accurate. Now I thought my new city friend was going to get to see something that everyone doesn't get to witness. As we approached the cow, however, I saw that she was in trouble - the calf's rear hooves were coming out first. Knowing there was no time to get help, I sprang into action, I had been involved in deliveries before, and I had even witnessed a calf being turned around inside of the cow, however we were well past that option here, so I sat down behind the cow put my boots on her rump, grabbed the hooves, and pulled for dear life. After a few minutes of struggling, I was rewarded with a slick and slimy calf in my lap, and I'm pleased to say the cow and calf were both all right! Now Vlad was looking at me like I was a little cracked ,and the show I hoped he was going to get to see turned out to be a little more "hands-on" than I thought. Soon mother and calf were both on their feet, and the calf was nuzzling around us, and I thought with no small amount of pride that maybe Vlad could see just how country I really am. On a side note, I think that most of my apprehension of being in the city revolved around finding a bathroom, for at home when you had to go you just went!

While Vlad was visiting the farm, we got a call from Children's Hospital the biopsy on Mick came back positive he was diagnosed with Hodgkin's lymphoma he was to undergo radiation and chemotherapy right away. We all cried and were scared for Mick and Vlad was there like part of the family.

Vlad and I saw each other and a few of the others we had met in treatment every other week at aftercare for the next three months. My responsibilities on the farm were growing as I was. I went to meetings in Columbus, Newark, Lancaster, and Zanesville. My mother started going to Al Anon, and she learned a great deal about recovery and addiction "later in life what she learned would help her in dealing with my addiction."

When school started back, I was going into my freshman year of high school. I had learned in treatment that I was going to have to change the people, places and things in my life if I was to stay in recovery. I thought this wouldn't be so hard, then I became aware that almost everyone I knew used in one form or another, so I hung out more in the rooms of recovery than with my old friends from home.

I did still work on a few relationships with girls that I went to school with. I was in recovery not dead! I even had a short fling with Abigale Ray's little sister. It didn't go very well, though, as she informed me that she thought I was a bit of an ass and more than a little stuck on myself. I thought "The force is strong in this one," and she was going to take a little more work.

I started spending more time in Athens, and every now and then Ian would ask me to come and speak at the treatment center where he worked. It was kind of scary talking in front of people, but if I prayed before I talked it usually turned out all right.

I met a friend of Ian's in Athens and asked him to be my sponsor; his name was Tony. I later learned that Ian and Tony both had roots in New York City. How they ever ended up in podunk Athens, Ohio, I'll never know, but I was sure glad they were there. Between the two, my education in recovery was tripled. With Tony, I worked through step five. I learned a new level of how to have fun, there were regular dances and functions going on in all the cities around me. I'll state here, though, that there are twelve steps for a reason, and the fact that I didn't work past the fifth could have direct impact on what was coming in the future.

Deer season of my freshman year, I shot the one and only deer I've ever gotten. I had been hunting for a good part of my life because when living in the country that's what everyone does. That year, I decided to give deer hunting a real go and hunted every day. The weather was cold and snowy most of the days, so the hunting wasn't particularly fun. I scared up a few deer in a waterway but nothing I wanted to shoot at. I should say I wasn't really hunting for meat. We raised beef cattle, so we had all the meat we could want. I was after a trophy deer. On the last day of deer season, I had pretty much given up hope. I was still in bed when dad came and got me up telling me several family members were on the way to drive the property and he asked me if I wanted to be involved. I said, "Sure why not?" We had posted up in several different places around the fields, and my dad and an uncle went to the back of the property and started working toward us when the deer broke out running. I remember feeling an overwhelming excitement, I watched as about twelve does broke out in different directions, and there he was a buck so big he could hardly hold his head up. I had other hunters in line of site, so I tracked on the buck waiting to take my shot. The buck was close to one hundred yards away when I was clear to shoot, I emptied my twelve gauge of all five shots, and down he went. It turned out to be a spinal cord hit; it really was a lucky shot but in the end I had a fourteen-point buck with a twenty-three-inch spread on the rack. He was a real beauty, and he hangs on my wall to this day. This was virtually the end of my deer hunting career, as there wasn't much hope of ever getting a better deer, and I wasn't an avid enough hunter to try!

Toward the end of my freshman year, Gloria moved back from California. Gloria was an elementary school sweetheart, and we started dating. It wasn't really dating yet because I didn't have my license, so I couldn't legally drive. I should say here that after I came home from treatment, Mort and I sort of struck up an enmity; apparently, he felt betrayed when I came home, and we didn't hang out and get high anymore. Whenever we passed in the halls of school, Mort would call me a snitch, so I did my best to avoid him. Actually, I was rather hurt over the whole deal, as I considered Mort more of a brother than my own.

At one of the last school dances of our freshman year, Gloria and I were at the dance together and here comes Mort! Mort accused me of being a snitch and threatened me in front of Gloria. I pretty much ignored him, so he takes a swing and punches me in the face. I turn and look at him, and he asks me if I'm going to fight, and I reply, "No,

I'm not mad at you, and I consider you my friend." So, he swings again, and I get another punch in the face. Still, I don't anger, and I tell Mort I'm not interested in fighting him because I'm not mad at him.

Years later, Mortimer told me that he thought that was one of the manliest things he had ever seen. Well, it certainly didn't feel manly at the time, and I beat myself up for a long time worrying about what everyone else thought. Some few years later, Gloria and Mort were married. Apparently, she didn't think it was very manly either. So, my freshman year ended with my pride hurt and my girl lost. Man, this life business is really tough.

That summer, I went to several conventions and campouts that were program organized. I spent most of the summer with Vlad, Ian and Tony; we regularly referred to ourselves as the sicker-than-most group. On a side note, there were a lot of war stories being told, and being an impressionable youth, I listened. I learned an entirely new level of drug using and war stories being usually of the best of times, a lot of it sounded good. By that time, I was over a year clean and my life was certainly changing.

We all went to a convention at Kent State University, and I met a girl there that wasn't with the convention. Stacie was a student at Kent State and still there even though classes were out. The convention was only a few days, but in that time Stacie and I got to know each other. On the second night, I decided to make my move. We were alone in a dorm room making out when she broke down and started crying. *Well,* I thought, *this isn't good,* so I ask what's wrong. Stacie proceeds to confide to me that she had been raped when she was much younger and that she had never gotten over it. In my head, I'm thinking what do I do with that, what am I supposed to say. So, thinking of someone else's pain and hurt, I told Stacie about how I was violently molested when I was eight. I told her that I was sorry for what had happened to her and that it wasn't her fault that she shouldn't be blaming herself. We spent several hours holding each other and talking. To my disappointment, there wasn't any more kissing and I didn't want to make her feel uncomfortable. Later, we said goodnight, and I headed back to the dorm room that I was staying in with Vlad and another guy we had just met.

The next morning, while I was sleeping, Stacie came to my room and threw my two roommates out and climbed into bed with me and we made love! It was the one and only time I was ever intimate with a girl while she cried. Afterwards, we went and had breakfast and spent the day holding hands and talking. Stacie and I wrote back and forth for a long time after Kent State, but I never saw her again. I like to think that in some way I helped her start to get over what had happened to her. As I saw it, if you could help someone and get laid at the same time, my friends, that's a win-win!

Vlad just shook his head at me and asked how is it that I was always meeting girls and that they seemed to be falling for me. What do I know, I was the horniest sixteen-year-old on the planet, and I really liked to meet girls. We had a great summer in recovery, and it was going to get better yet "little did I know that my disease was building steam locked away hidden in the far reaches of my mind" I stayed clean on meetings and fun and an endless supply of girls.

5

A PROPOSAL

The beginning of my sophomore year started, and I decided to join drama class. I was also in home economics - there were girls there - and when a few of my school friends found out what I was up to, they took the class too. I liked drama class; I had spent most of my life pretending to be someone else, so acting came very naturally. In the first few days of school, I stood at the door of drama class and asked every girl that came in if she would marry me and who walks through the door but Abigale, so I drop to my knee and with my best most charming smile, I ask Abigale, "Will you marry me?" She glares at me and walks on by. Yep she still thinks I'm an ass, I thought, looks like it's going to take a little more work.

School that year was fairly smooth. I was in several plays and asked by Ian to speak at several different functions, as well as the treatment center. I worked the farm, went to meetings, and toward the end of the year started dating a very pretty senior who had her own car, which made dating a whole lot easier. We would sneak off together every chance we got. I didn't think life could get much better. I had forgotten all about that boy that was always scared and that hated himself and thought his little brother, who was living a pure hell always with a smile on his face, had it better. Those old feelings were so far away that I just didn't remember them anymore. And still my disease waited in the corner doing push-ups. Ian, Vlad, Tony and I made plans for a camp out that was being held in Kentucky coming up in the summer and I was really looking forward to going! So, my sophomore year came to an end, I was still dating my lovely senior who had just graduated, and we were getting along very well together.

The time came to go on the camp out to Kentucky, and Vlad came to the farm to pick me up. We packed his Fiat full, I kissed my beautiful girlfriend goodbye and told her I would be home in a week. We had been dating for about four months and to my memories we never had a fight.

Vlad and I were off for adventure. The campout we were going to was called The Weenie Jamb, and it was at Big Bone Lick State Park just down the road from Beaverlick All-Girl's Academy. I swear you can't even make shit like that up! What could possibly go wrong? The campout proved to be worthy of its name and I had the time of my life. We went to meetings, we swam in a pond, and we jumped of a bridge down the road into the river until the sheriff showed up and told us to quit.

Ian met a girl that he would later marry, and I met Cindy. On the second day, Cindy and I spent the whole day together. We talked, we laughed, we went to meetings together, so we got to know each other. Cindy lived in Reynoldsburg, Ohio, a suburb of Columbus. Later that night, Vlad was less than pleased when he found out that I was commandeering our tent to spend the night with Cindy, leaving him to fend for himself to find a place to sleep. That wasn't much my concern, as I had bigger and better things to worry about - starting my relationship with Cindy. Now I still had my beautiful senior at home, but that was a problem to worry about later. I might point out here that by moral standards I knew that what I was doing was wrong, however, it was very much like when I was using, I didn't really have much control. A closer look will reveal the truth that I was very much using relationships and sex as a replacement for the relief that I was getting from the drugs, so it was a substitution, one for the other. Infidelity is also a glaring character defect that had I considered working past step five might have been addressed. So, Cindy and I spent the rest of the camp out together with Vlad, who was a little sour about the whole thing.

When I returned home from the Weenie Jamb, I had to call my lovely senior and explain that I had met someone! I was easily able to justify my actions to myself because my senior had graduated and would surely need to move on to bigger and better things. Breaking up with her was one of the hardest things that I had ever done - I didn't want to hurt her, we had a really good relationship - but I was going to do what I wanted so I pushed through. I will say that it was one of the only times that I left a relationship usually they always left, I'm sure on account of my behavior. I still was very aware that I was terrified of being alone and again I was convinced that it should be ok to be in multiple intimate relationships if everyone would just stop being so priggish about the whole thing.

Cindy was the one and only relationship I've had with someone else in recovery, and there were a lot of problems that came from the whole experience. We had a tendency to want to control each other's recovery, and we argued to no end. We were both addicts, both consumed with self-will, and both sure we were always right. Still, Cindy and I spent as much time together as possible. We would take her car and go to meetings in Athens and Columbus. On one occasion, we were headed to Athens, and I was driving. Even though I was seventeen, I had not gotten my driver's license; I didn't need one to drive farm equipment and that included the truck, another one of those little technicalities. On the way to Athens, I was pulled over and given a driving without a license ticket. I pulled a rush job and got my license before I went to court, hence, I lost my license a few days after I got them. My suspension was for ninety days, but I was given driving privileges to meetings and my tutor. Cindy's mom suddenly became "my tutor." You might notice a little pattern of manipulation to get what I want!

My junior year of high school started as normal, except I started getting calls through the school and invited to other schools to talk about drug and alcohol abuse. The whole thing started when Ian had asked me to come with him to speak in a school the year before, and somehow the thing just started to spread like a fire in a field. I would get called out of class and sent to the principal's office; when I walked into the office, the principal would say I had a phone call and hand me his phone. The calls were usually principals from other schools around the state, and they would ask me if I would come and speak at their school. We would schedule an agreeable date, and I would go. By the end of my senior year, I had more than 200 hours of speaking in other schools, and it earned me several credits toward graduating.

Going to other schools and speaking was really a different experience. I was an unknown in that environment and seemed treated with the respect and notoriety akin to a rock star! Now, I should just say here that once I left treatment, I started letting my hair grow, and it was getting rather long. My hair hadn't been cut in over three years, and not that this big-headed alcoholic is vain or anything, but I didn't look much like a farmer. When I would go into another school, I would go straight to the teachers' lounge, light up a cigarette, and drink a cup of coffee! I was the same age as the kids in every school I went to, yet I was treated completely different. No one ever acted like anything was out of the ordinary with a kid sitting in the teachers' lounge smoking and drinking coffee. We will touch on this topic a little later, because it definitely caused a few problems even though I was performing a service that was obviously doing at least some good.

By my junior year, I was practically running the family farm. Dad still made all of the "decisions" while working full-time at the post office delivering mail, as some years earlier the coal mines were shut down. I was doing 75 percent of the work, and so I would miss some school. We lived in a farm community, and missing school to work on the farm was considered reasonable. My time during my junior year was pretty well used up. I was farming, going to meetings, speaking in other schools on drug and alcohol abuse, going to school, still participating in plays in drama, and maintaining a relationship with Cindy. Wow, that seems like a lot. I guess I was busy enough not to have time to use. I was, however, rebuilding friendships with classmates that were still drinking, and there were a few occasions that I was elected to be a designated driver. I was no longer uncomfortable around others who were drinking; I would stop by parties and cookouts, and I was maintaining my own "clean time," as I didn't use or drink. Around this time one of my buddy's dad had a heart attack and I helped out on his family's pig farm while he was recuperating. Needless to say, I was rather busy, but I did notice that I wasn't seeing Abigale around school anymore, I found out that she had went and got her GED. I was in a committed relationship with Cindy but committed to me left a lot of wiggle room.

While I was speaking at other schools, I often got invitations for a little fooling around, and I used these opportunities when they presented themselves. There was quite a lot going on. Again, had I continued working the steps of the program, I might had seen that I was starting to rely more and more on my will than my higher powers and my disease was really working out hard in the hidden recesses of my mind.

There was a convention in Jekyll Island, Georgia, coming up toward the end of my junior year. Cindy and I had been dating for about eight months, and we decided we would go to Jekyll Island together. When the time came to go, we decided to take Cindy's car. The convention was one of the largest I had ever been to; there were thousands of recovering addicts on the island. The convention was so large that there were multiple hotels completely booked full of people in recovery. Ian, Tony and a lot of other people that I knew were there. We spent the days going to meetings and talking about recovery and the nights, we went to dances and out to dinner and we had a wonderful time. One of the nights, I came back to the room I was sharing with Cindy and there were half a dozen people sitting around on the floor listening to a guy sing and play the guitar. I didn't really think much about it, so I came in, introduced myself to Cindy's friends, and joined in. I noticed that Cindy was acting kind of strange, and she seemed to want to pick a fight about just about everything.

The next day, she informed me that we were splitting up and she was leaving with the guitar player and heading to Atlanta! I was floored - not only was she leaving me, but she was also quite literally leaving me stranded in Jekyll Island. I was devastated, I was heartbroken, and I was stuck in Georgia. I was pretty sure that I was going to die over the pain I felt. I was consumed with the old feeling of not being good enough and was overwhelmed with self-pity. Not sure what to do, I found Ian and Tony and poured my heart out about how I just might die over the whole thing. They reassured me, like the good friends they were, that the pain I was experiencing wasn't fatal and that with time I would get over it. I didn't really believe them, but I was most grateful for a ride back to Ohio, which they assured me we could work out. The return trip to Ohio wasn't very pleasant; to be quite honest, I cried a good part of the way. The carful of people that I was stuffed into were all for the most part very supportive, though I'm sure that after a few hundred miles of my crying they would have rather just pushed me out the door on the side of the road. However, I did make it back to Ohio, and I swore that I was done with dating, as I didn't ever want to feel this way again.

There were a few more weeks of school before summer break, and I was really not handling the breakup well. Cindy called and apologized and asked if we could try again, but I told her to get bent. I was going around school like I was a kicked dog when one of Abigale's friends told me that Abigale wanted me to call her! Now I thought that's just what I need someone that thinks I'm an ass to pick me up. I called Abigale, and she invited me over; she told me she heard about my breakup and was sorry. We talked for a while, and I informed her that I would like to be friends with her, but I was quite done with the whole getting hurt thing. Abigale laughed and said she would like to be friends too. I don't remember how it happened, but about a month later we were so in love with each other that we were sure death was imminent if we weren't able to see each other.

As the school year was coming to an end and me being back to myself, Abigale was invited to go to Alabama to spend some time with her grandpa. Abigale's grandpa was going to send her a bus ticket for the trip, I informed her that no girlfriend of mine was going to ride the bus to Alabama and that I would take her. Well, she thought the idea was perfect "being we both knew we would surely die if we were apart for that long," so off to Alabama we went. Alabama was so nice that Abigale and I decided that we were going to move there. Who cares that I still have a senior year of school to complete? We were sure that we would be together forever, and we were ready to start our life on our own. Abigale and I drove back to Ohio, got some of our things, put them in the back of my truck, which belonged to the farm, and headed back to Alabama. I have to say, my parents were really good sports about the whole thing. I had a little bit of money from a car accident that I was involved in, and I was sure that I was making a sound decision. Might be a good place to point out that I was doing what I wanted with absolutely no consideration for anyone else - that is, basic addictive behavior. I was living on my will alone. My dad needed me on the farm, and I had school to finish. In the end, it worked out that we came back just before school started my senior year. We had lived together for the whole summer, so my next great idea was that we were going to move in together, and we did. We rented a small apartment in Newark, and I was driving twenty-five miles to go to school and to work on the farm. I only went to school half a day my senior year; it was a lot to handle, but we were together, and that's all that mattered to us. My dad saw that we were going to stay together so, he found us a trailer in town to rent where I would only be a few miles from the farm and only six miles from school.

One night shortly after we moved into the trailer, Abigale was in bed, and I was laying on the couch watching *The Shining*, and I experienced the feeling that I was being watched. I felt like someone was looking at me from outside. I was watching a scary movie, and I thought that had to explain it, but again I get the all-over willies that someone is watching me. After gaining my nerve I get up off of the couch and I head for the door. As I am slowly reaching my hand out toward the door handle, *bang*, someone kicks the door in and standing before me on the porch is the biggest man I've ever seen! I'm frozen in shock, he looks at me, I look at him, and I can see confusion in his eyes. He takes two steps back and is gone in the fog. Yep had to be foggy. Needless to say, I've not watched scary movies since. It turned out that old boy was looking for the guy that rented the trailer before me; it had something to do with a wife and an ass whooping. Thank God I wasn't involved because I'm very sure big dude could whoop some ass.

I should say that every now and then Abigale would have a drink or even smoke a little weed, but I was still clean. I was still going to meetings but not very often. I was still speaking in other schools, and my senior year I was invited to speak before prom at a school on the Ohio River. The date was set up a week before prom, and I was to address the whole school at one time. Around 1500 people sat in the assembly room while I spoke; it lasted for about an hour and a half. When I spoke, I didn't usually remember what I said after it was over, and that particular day, I must have been on fire, I just told my story, and it really seemed rather common to me. When I finished speaking the school principal came on stage with tears in his eyes and thanked me, even hugged me. After I was done with any presentation, there were a lot of students that would want to talk to me, so I would just hang out and visit. Sometimes people would open up to me about things that had happened to them and sometimes they just wanted to meet me and say thank you. On that day, however, I was approached by a very good-looking girl that informed me that she didn't have a date for prom and that she would very much like to go with me! Now I was totally in love with Abigale, and I even told this young lady that I was very much in a committed relationship, and she assured me it would only be as friends. I thought, "What could be the harm in that?" so I agreed. Abigale took the whole thing much better than I had expected with my assurances that it was only as friends. So, I went to the prom at another school with a beautiful girl and stayed completely faithful to Abigale not for the lack of my date trying after prom. She invited me to stay at her house, so I didn't have to drive the long way home so late, and I fled with my honor barely intact.

While this was all going on, I was working on a serious issue, Abigale was pregnant, and we were trying to decide what to do! Eventually after a lot of very serious talking, we decided that we were just too young to be parents. She had an abortion, and it was not an easy thing to decide. In the end, I was more concerned with myself than with raising a child. Again, had I completed the steps in the program there is a great chance that things might have turned out differently, but I relied on myself for guidance rather than my higher power. So, we made our decision and lived with it.

I was doing as well as I could in school, which wasn't all that well, as I really hated going to school. I had a fight with my American history teacher and was kicked out of his class. I should not have called him a dick in front of the class, but I did. When it came time to graduate, I was lacking an American history credit, so I had to take a correspondence course in it.

A few months before my senior year was coming to end, I was headed out the door to go to work on the farm. Abigale was on the porch, and as I was about to get into the car, I said how 'bout we get married, and she smiled and said she would like that, and so we were engaged. After some planning, a date was set for August. It was still May, and I was only days away from a four-year anniversary of being clean and sober.

I was disking a field at the farm getting ready for planting I remember the day being like any other. I was working, I was happy that Abigale and I were in love, and I knew that we would spend our life together. Some friends from school stopped by the field to say hi, and we were just talking when one of them pulls out a hard pack of cigarettes and opens it up and it was full of joints. I thought, "I'll surprise Abigale and get her a joint," so I bought three. I spent the day disking, and the three joints rode all day in my cigarette pack; I really had got them for Abigale. That night at the trailer after I had showered, I told Abigale that I had a surprise for her. I took a joint out of my pack of cigarettes, put it in my mouth, and lit it. I can honestly say that I wasn't thinking about what I was doing. I never for even one second thought that something was wrong with smoking a joint with Abigale. I told her I had a surprise. How about "Fifteen years of misery and debauchery - surprise! Your about to marry a drug addict!" When I look back, honestly, there were signs that trouble was coming; I wasn't going to very many meetings; I wasn't praying; I was living on my own will; and I was making my decisions without any guidance from a sponsor or a higher power. I had forgotten what I was like, I was feeling happy and in love. I was secure in my job, and I was on the way. So as a good addict, what's my best solution? Let's fuck it up a little or, hell, a lot. I can say I don't ever remember being so high, as Abigale was in a little bit of shock that I had just lit a joint and was smoking it, but she loosened up after I gave it to her. We laughed so hard, and we had a serious case of the munchies. It's really hard to remember how we laughed because the bedlam that was to become of my life really isn't funny at all. Fifteen years later, addiction and alcoholism would ruin our marriage. However, we aren't there yet, and now I believe I need to take a little time to think before I proceed, the absolute mess that is ahead isn't very easy to think about let alone to put into words!

6

BACK INTO ADDICTION

The year was 1990. I was about to be married, and I was within a few days of having four years clean. A close look and a little honesty will reveal that I was not working and had not worked a complete program. I worked the first five steps, and my life started to improve and I didn't finish working the steps. Leading up to my relapse, "I shouldn't really call it a relapse it would be ten years before I'd draw a sober breath and that would be court ordered" anyhow, leading up to my relapse I was going to fewer and fewer meetings, I was running on more and more self-will, but the real kicker and the real warning was that I had stopped praying! Now relapse is really a misleading term because I went straight into using like it wasn't any big deal. Abigale and I made plans for our wedding, and it was in quick order that there was always weed in the house.

After graduation, which I missed, I had to complete an American History correspondence course so I could get my diploma, I never once looked at the course, Abigale took it for me. We were married in August of that summer; I was working full time on the farm and Abigale stayed home. Our first year of marriage was relatively peaceful and quiet, other than I had started using with no more apparent thought than drinking a glass of water. I really didn't even think that "I might just be making the worst mistake in my life" but that would get to be a habit, no pun intended. We were happily married - that's not to say that we didn't fight because we did - I was young and was pretty sure I was always right "not to mention that I was back in active addiction and I was quite sure the world was revolving around me." Our first little sign that what I was doing wasn't all too smart came within our first year of marriage. As I said, I was working the farm full-time, and Abigale stayed home. I would come home from work, and she would be thrilled to see me; we would hug and kiss and hold hands and talk. Thirty minutes later, she would be chasing me around the trailer with a knife trying to stick me. I was quick and thin and always able to avoid the knife. I started to think that maybe something was wrong. She was so glad to see me then so violently angry, so I finally called her mother for help. We saw a few doctors and they ran a bunch of tests; the end result was that Abigale was having a reaction to the THC in the weed, and the estrogen in her birth control, it was causing violent mood swings. What I heard was Abigale was allergic to estrogen, the doctors put her on a low estrogen dose birth control and life was good again. Stopping smoking weed never crossed my mind; of course, it wasn't really an option.

Toward the end of our first year of marriage, Abigale's parents rented a large farmhouse on the outskirts of Thornville and asked us if we would like to move in and split the rent. The house rented for $250 a month, so $125 a month from us seemed like a good idea. However, as good as the rent sounded, the farmhouse was right down the road from Mortimer's house and whenever we passed each other on the road, he still swerved at me like he was trying to run me over! Well, we thought long and hard and money won out; it was only logical that less money on rent equals more money on drugs. By this time, I was smoking weed every day, and I was also eating pain medication -

Valium and Xanax - whenever it was available. I wasn't really biased; I was willing to use anything that gave me a buzz. Remember, I had heard all kinds of wonderful war stories, and I wanted to find out for myself if they were true!

So, as it was, money won out and we moved in with Abigale's parents. About the second night in the farmhouse, Abigale's parents, who owned a gas station, sat at the kitchen table counting money. There were stacks of cash all over the table when there came a knock at the door. I opened the door to the farmhouse to see who was there and who is standing outside but Mort. Mort takes one look at me and says, "Hell no, not Ray Vance!" So, I invited him in. After introductions, Abigale and I invited Mort to our room where we rolled a joint. Mort's and my friendship was rekindled instantly. Mort invited us over Friday night to play cards with him and his fiancée Gloria; we accepted the invitation and showed up Friday at the appointed time. We were all under 21, and Mort informed us that he knew someone that would buy us liquor if we wanted, seemed like a good idea, so we were off we came back with a fifth of vodka and a fifth of Jack Danial's. We played euchre, and the girls drank the vodka while Mort and I drank the Jack.

This became a weekend routine for the next several years. Every Friday and Saturday night, we got together to play cards and drank. It also started my love of alcohol and Is partly why I identify as an alcoholic now. In short order we were buying a half gallon of vodka and Jack Danial's every weekend night and we drank, and we played cards together until the liquor was gone. I learned an important lesson during this time - I could drink or get high, but I couldn't do both without becoming violently sick, it would make me spin so hard that I had to put a foot on the floor when laying down to try to stop spinning. You would think that being armed with the knowledge of what it would do to me would be enough not to drink and try to get high at the same time, but you would be wrong. I spent a great amount of time sick trying to figure out why everyone else seemed to smoke weed and drink together so I figured it was the combination of the two or the timing that made all the difference, no matter what I tried, and I gave no small attempt at every conceivable angle that I could come up with to make it work. However, every attempt ended with the same helicopter ride and vomiting. Years later I would beat this phenomenon by adding cocaine to the mix, but we aren't there yet. We stayed in the farmhouse in Thornville for almost two years my in-laws, however, only stayed for a short time, I believe we may have run them out with all the parties and using.

That two years became a huge party that didn't end. I expanded my drug use to include acid and every known prescription drug available. There may have been some horse tranquilizers like ketamine, there was an endless party at my house and people stopped by and sometimes stayed for a month or more while we partied. We went to the Grateful Dead concert at Legend Valley several summers in a row. We would go to the concert and hangout at the campgrounds and get totally and completely fucked up for an entire weekend. We would eat acid, drink, smoke weed, do balloons filled with medical nitrous, and I loved every minute of it. There was absolutely no concern about anything I did, that it could possibly be unhealthy or that I could be endangering others by the level of my using. I was always impaired in one way or another and usually several ways at the same time.

One incident I clearly remember was over a Fourth of July weekend. We had stocked up on liquor and had spent a night drinking and playing cards when we decided that some acid would make the party even better. Mort, Gloria, Abigale, and I took a trip into Newark to buy some acid; we bought and took the acid and headed to Blockbuster to rent some movies, you know classics like Pink Floyd's "The Wall" and a few others, movies that would enhance the enjoyment of the trip. We spent a good deal of the night driving around the backcountry rounds listening to Black Sabbath, and we watched a thunderstorm laying on the hood of the '79 Camaro that we were tooling around in. We saw the corn in the field grow more than a foot and tassel before our very eyes. The whole night seemed like such an inspirationally religious experience, I felt one with God and what I was doing had to be all right.

The next morning, after being on a trip for around twelve hours, Mort breaks out a bag of mushrooms that he had hidden away after the last Dead concert. That was something I could never do, for if I had drugs in any form, I used them until they were gone; it was never an option to "save them for later." So anyway, Mort produced a quarter bag of mushrooms and handed it to me and asked, "What do you think?" I reached into the bag and grabbed about half the contents and stuffed it into my mouth and started to chew. "I think I'm about to get even more fucked up," I said. Mort and the girls were more than a little put out that there wasn't going to be an even split of the mushrooms. Mort shared what was left between himself, Gloria and Abigale. Oops party foul, my bad. The truth I was only concerned with getting enough for myself and I was always first and foremost important, and so it was that we left on an epic trip, just coming down off acid and eating a bunch of mushrooms on top of it! We sat around for a little while just recouping from the night before. Mort and Gloria were in their bedroom and Abigale and I were on the couch in the living room. Mort asked, "Are you feeling anything yet?" and I replied, "No." I got up and walked into his bedroom and told him they must have been bunk. I was standing in his doorway, and I looked toward his waterbed. It expanded like a balloon I looked down at the hardwood floor that had drink stains and bong water stains all over them, and it was like I was standing in the middle of a constellation of stars, as all of the stains had risen off of the floor to hang at different levels all around me. Mort, seeing my expression, asked, "What?" I told him to get up, and before he made it to the door, he said "Oh." We were literally in outer space. I had achieved "higher than a kite," something of which I felt immense pride in. I looked out Mort's second floor window and saw piglets running all around. Mort didn't have pigs he did have a dog that had just recently had pups, but I saw pigs.

It was Sunday morning, and Mort's grandpa showed up to take his mom out for breakfast. When they returned, Mort was supposed to help his grandpa do some farm work. As soon as they left, we all fled to my house just down the road. When we came outside, the sky from horizon to horizon was purple. I finally understood what Jimmy Hendrix meant when he wrote *Purple Haze*. I let Gloria drive my truck down to my house; I was so bent I didn't trust myself to drive. It was a five-speed, and I remember she put it in first gear and drove all the way to the house without shifting. Mort and I walked down the road. It was like we were in a new world - everything was new, everything was different. Abigale's parents stopped by for a visit, and we were all worried that we were caught, but after a while they said goodbye and left. We then had an hour-long discussion trying to decide if they were tripping too! We continued to party all day, and we were all quite hungover Monday morning, we all skipped work and subsequently we were all fired from our jobs for not coming in. Abigale and Gloria worked at the Cracker Barrel; Mort was working at a service station. We thought it was hilarious that we were all fired, and we laughed about it for months! I was still working on my father's farm, and he was rather pissed off that I didn't show up for work all weekend and then called off Monday, too; I eventually talked him into letting me come back to work for him with a solemn oath that it wouldn't happen again. Of course, it did.

I was paid $200 a week from the farm and buying a quarter pound of weed about every week. I would sell three ounces to pay for the quarter pound and keep an ounce for myself. My auto insurance was paid by the farm, and I had credit cards to every known gas station all on farm accounts. I also had farm accounts at every auto parts store in the area. So, I was very dependent on my job at the farm. I could and would ask dad for more money whenever I needed it, always with an excuse of a bill to be paid or something I needed, and he almost always gave me what I asked for. I always needed more money because I always needed more drugs. Sometimes dad would say no when I asked for more money, so while he was at work at the post office, I would load up a grain truck full of corn and run it in to Zanesville to the granary and have them make a check out in my name for the load that would be anywhere from $1200 to $1800. I never thought twice about stealing money from the farm; I needed more money, and I did whatever I had to get it. I thought I was entitled to more, and I wanted more, so I took more. It's a great character defect that runs in all alcoholics and addicts, and I shared it greatly. Eventually the money wasn't enough, and I started working other jobs as well as the farm as a way to make more. Abigale got a job at the Kmart portrait studio, and that was good because someone was going to have to pay the bills, as almost all my money went to drugs and alcohol!

There was one more great debacle at the farmhouse in Thornville that surely helped play a part in us moving to Newark even though I'm sure I used the excuse that we moved to get Abigale closer to work. Abigale's older brother Ray and I had become fairly good friends; we both liked using, so we got on quite well. One night Ray showed up at the farmhouse, and he was already pretty buzzed. We were sitting around getting high and talking when he asked me if I could run him down the road that we lived on a few miles so he could see a buddy? I thought for a half a second that this was kind of odd being he had a car in the driveway, but I was high, and I said sure. We headed down the road about two miles, and he pointed to a driveway and said, "Here it is." We pulled in and he jumped out of my truck and headed straight for the house. Ray walked up to the door and instead of knocking he kicked it in and marched into the house. I could hear screaming, and I thought this isn't going to end well, but I sat outside in my truck and waited. A few minutes later, Ray came out and got back into my truck and said, "He isn't home; well, his wife and son were." Ray told them that when the man of the house gets home, he can find him down the road at my house. We went home and back to partying, and a few hours later that fellow and a few of his friends showed up. They were posted up out in the field and they were shooting at the house, so I grabbed my shotgun, loaded it, and was headed for the door. When I opened the door, Ray grabbed the shotgun out of my hands, rolled out the door across the yard behind some shrubs, popped up, and started firing rounds into the field, we exchanged gunfire like the Hatfields and McCoys for about thirty minutes. Thank God no one was shot, but it wasn't for lack of trying!

For the next several weeks, there were several attempts to steal my four-wheeler, and one night while I was sitting in the living room, I heard a round being chambered into a shotgun right outside the window, I dragged Abigale upstairs and posted up at a point to be able to shoot anyone coming up the stairs. No one was shot, but I felt that it might be prudent to move on before we had to kill each other, so we moved to an apartment in Newark. Apparently, the whole thing was a beef between Ray and this other fellow. Years later, we all sat around the bar drinking and laughed about the whole thing, though it doesn't seem nearly as humorous today!

Around this time, my father realized that he could make nearly the same amount of money leasing the farm out as farming it himself, so he did. So, my employment started in earnest. I had several jobs around this time. I worked for a while in a plastic injection mold company, I worked for Lane Bryant as a picker/packer, I worked as a roofer, I worked for a lawn care service mowing yards, I also spent some time as an armed security guard working in liquor stores and patrolling apartment complexes. My jobs lasted various lengths of time, but I was usually let go for missing too many days of work. Even though getting high or drunk took money, I would eventually be hungover or trying to find something to use, and I would call off. About this same time, the truck I had always driven on the farm was wearing out, and dad found a 1970 Oldsmobile Cutlas Supreme on his mail route, so he bought it for me. It was probably my favorite car. It was that old 1970s green and was in remarkably good shape. We were living in Newark when I celebrated my 21st birthday.

7

TWENTY-ONE AT LAST

I'm turning twenty-one and can finally legally buy alcohol. I'm a drug addict and an alcoholic so how am I going to celibate my birthday? Abigale and I drive out to Mort's place and invite him and Gloria back to our apartment in Newark. On the way back, we stop at the liquor store and buy a liter of 151 rum, a fifth of dry gin, and a bottle of vermouth, then we stop by the grocery store and pick up a bag of lemons. Somehow, I had heard about a flaming lemon drop and decided that would be the perfect birthday drink. There was likely a bottle of whiskey in the car for the ride; I distinctly remember jumping a set of railroad tracks on the way back to Newark and seeing Mort and Gloria in the backseat with the sides of their heads smashed into the roof of the car.

So, we are at my place cutting lemons, and I'm not even sure that the drink we are about to make is with the ingredients I've purchased, but we're going to make it work, so we put some gin and vermouth in a glass, lay a lemon wedge across the top, pour the 151 over the lemon drop, and light the whole mess on fire! It took several tries before we started to get it right, and by about my fifth lemon drop, I forgot to blow the fire all the way out, I did the shot, threw the lemon in my mouth, then spit the flaming lemon back onto the table still on fire. I break into laughter and say, "Hey Mort, try that!"

The rest of the night is a blur. Mort woke me up the next morning and said I had to take him to work, as he was about to be late! Now in normal circumstances that would have been easy, however I had just woken up on my back on the couch, and apparently, I had vomited after I passed out and my hair being to the middle of my back had caught and held the vomit. Mort said we had to go, he couldn't be late, so I grabbed a towel, wrapped my puke-soaked hair in it around the top of my head, tucked it in, and we were off. On the way down the stairs, the little old lady that lived under us came out her door and asked why in the blue hell were we carrying on for over half the night. I with a towel on my head apologized and explained that it was my twenty first birthday. Out the door and in the car, we head across town.

Mort's boss is standing on the loading dock when I drop him off. Later Mort tells me around lunchtime his boss asked. "Was that Ray that dropped you off, and was he wearing a towel on his head?" to which Mort replied, "Don't ask." Thus, I became legal to drink, not that it was hindering me much before. I should say here that I have absolutely zero business living in the city, alcohol and addiction aside, as I am country at heart, I'm loud, and I want to pee in the yard.

By this time, Abigale had been promoted to a studio manager at her job and she was a little put out that I showed no signs of getting serious about a career or even a long-term job. We argued about money quite a lot, again virtually everything I made was used for drugs and or alcohol. When it came down to having to produce money to help with bills, I ran to dad and told him a sob story and he gave me some money. This is really close to when I had my first brush with the law. I had went to Columbus and ended up eating by myself at a bar I had a few drinks, before I had left, I bought a bag of weed and I hadn't even smoked any yet, because I had had a few drinks. On the way home from Columbus, I was pulled over for changing lanes without using a turn signal. I stuffed the weed between the seats and when I was asked to get out of the truck, I locked the door. The officer asked me to empty my pockets and a pack of rolling papers fell out, so stuffed and cuffed I sat in the back of the cruiser waiting for the inevitable the officer had already arrested me for O.M.V.I. Operating a Motor Vehicle Impaired of course he found the weed and then he took me to the Granville police station. I called dad after midnight and asked him to come and bail me out. I remember telling him not to tell mom, "Like that was possible, I just woke them both up" because I thought she would let me sit in jail. Dad later told me that mom sent him to get me although neither of them was very happy about the whole thing. While I waited on dad to bail me out, the officer told me that if I took him to where I bought the weed, they would drop all charges. I had bought the weed from a friend of Mort's, and he was a really nice guy, so I told the officer no. I did give a urine sample, and when I showed up in court, I was charged with possession of marijuana, possession of paraphernalia, and O.M.V.I. I plead guilty to the two possession charges and no contest to the O.M.V.I. When the judge asked me if I would like to say anything, I said that I would accept the responsibility for my actions, and I tried to remember some program lingo so essentially, I slung some serious bullshit. They threw out the O.M.V.I. and fined me for both possessions and put me on non-reporting probation. So, a little money owed was really the only consequences.

When Abigale found out she was pregnant, she decided that we should start going to church. We were still living in Newark at the apartment, and we started attending an Apostolic church in town. I had stated much earlier that when I read the second step "Came to believe a power greater than ourselves could restore us to sanity" my interpretation was that I needed to find the right religion to have the best contact with God. So, to church I went with Abigale, and I was usually sober until after service. Usually. We stayed in Newark for several years.

I would like to say that having a job that was satisfying made my life better, however I never made enough money and I often missed work because I was hungover or still using, so in reality a satisfying job really didn't mean much at all. I also would like to say here that I was again haunted by the feelings of inadequacy. I never had enough, I couldn't make enough, I was never satisfied or content. I really hated myself and was quite sure that the world would be a better place without me in it. As long as I stayed high or drunk, I could keep these feelings at bay and continue to function. That's a tall order it's hard to always be high or drunk 24/7 but I gave it a hell of a try! Abigale, unfortunately, got to experience the worst of me, she was the one person that was always around when I would be experiencing my worst feelings and behaviors, we would fight and argue about almost anything. I became a fair carpenter because I would have to fix the doors and cabinets, tables and chairs that always seemed to get broken when we argued. I had no more control over my anger than I had over my using, and unfortunately, it's always the ones closest to us that get the most abuse. At my best I might have behaved like a twelve-year-old, but I was usually closer to two. If I didn't get my way there was surely a fit to be had and my way was to stay drunk or high as long as I was awake. That was the only excuse I ever needed to use, that I woke up, but I created a great many more excuses for the benefit of others.

8

BECOMING A FATHER

I actually just talked to Judd and asked him what year he was born. Guess I'm not getting a father of the year award this year either! That's ok I'm just happy to be able to draw a sober breath, but we will get to that later.

On February 7, 1994, my son Judd was born. I was working as an armed security guard then. It didn't pay a lot, I usually patrolled alone, in my Cutlass, so I could use all night while I worked. There were several times while I was patrolling apartment complex's that the police were called; they would show up and ask me if I had seen any gang members driving around, I always had the same answer that no I hadn't. Turns out that my 1970 Cutlass was thought to be a suspicious car in the neighborhood. Being a good addict, I found this just hilarious.

Abigale was up for another promotion at the Kmart portrait studio. During Abigale's pregnancy, I would like to say that my using slowed down, but that wouldn't be the truth, Abigale stopped drinking for nine months, and I used the same as always. On February 7, we ended up at the hospital in labor; I was excited to have a son, but I was also greatly inconvenienced because there was a ton of family around and I had to portray a family image. I waited with everyone else, I would go from Abigale's room to the waiting room to give updates. All I really wanted was to leave and get high. Finally, Judd arrived, and he was perfect when I saw he was 8 pounds, 7 ounces and 23 inches long. The doctor flopped him onto Abigale and said, "Congratulations, you've had a three-month-old!" I remember looking at Judd and thinking, "I'm responsible for this life, and I want to be a good dad." I was again sure that I could be a better person and a good dad for Judd and a better husband for Abigale, that my life was going to change, I just knew it.

The time to take Judd home came the next day. We got the car seat in right and the baby strapped in, there was an ice storm hitting, and I was driving my 1970 Oldsmobile Cutlass, I was very nervous driving, so I lit a joint and got high for the ride home! Well, I was a good dad for a few minutes; at least I was only a little high when I got to the hospital. It was some ride home, and I'm sure Abigale was less than pleased. After Judd was born, I held him up in front of the church and introduced him, and I really wanted to be a good father and a good husband. I also wanted to get fucked up every day, and I really had convinced myself that it was ok. Again, I wasn't headed for any father or husband of the year awards.

Up until around that time, I was still mainly using weed and whiskey and, of course, pharmaceuticals. I wasn't opposed to taking anything that gave me a buzz or changed the way I felt, so I also ate acid and mushrooms, but I was about to find something new to me, and it would be like finding a lost love! In 1995, I got hired at a mom-and-pop marble shop. I was hired to sweep the floors; the owners had immigrated from South Africa. I had only been at the job for about a month, and I hated it. The shop was split into two halves; on one side they made the cultured marble bathroom sinks, tubs shower surrounds, and shower bases - all of the products were custom made - and on the other side of the shop the owner did all the finishing work on the products. While I was sweeping the floors, I watched him working. I was dreadfully bored at work. One day, the boss got called away from a large order of sinks he was working on and while he was gone, I went over and finished what he was working on. When he came back, he stood for a long time looking at the sinks and he called me over and asked me if I had finished these sinks. I told him that I had. He asked me how I knew what to do, and I told him I had been watching him do it for a month. He asked me if I would like to continue to finish sinks, and my job at the marble shop became exceptionally better. I went from $5 an hour to $12 an hour in about six months.

One day at work at the marble shop, a coworker asked if he could ride to lunch with me. I said sure. After we left work and headed for Burger King, he asked me if I could drive him across town to pick something up from a friend. I had just bought a new Dodge Dakota pickup and was willing to drive it just about anywhere, so I said yes. We drove across town and ended up at a little convenience store that looked like it used to be a gas station. My coworker went inside and was quickly followed out by another man. They walked over by my truck and were talking, some money changed hands, and something was handed over. On our way back to Burger King, I asked my coworker what he got. He flipped out a little baggy that had something white in it, smiled, and asked me for a CD. I ordered a sandwich and was eating while he chopped up a few lines. I was more than willing to try the cocaine he had bought; it was my first time! I snorted the line with the rolled-up bill that he had. A few minutes later, I threw up my hamburger, but I didn't mind. I was in heaven. I felt better than I ever had.

The next day at work, my coworker didn't show up. I was really bummed I was going to ask him to take me back across town so I could buy some for myself. By lunchtime, I had decided to go to the little store by myself. I asked the man if he remembered seeing my truck yesterday, and he had, I asked him if I could get the same thing my friend got. He just looked at me for a long time and then asked his wife who was also behind the counter if she heard what I just asked for and she said she had. He finally said he would sell me the same thing, and a rather long friendship was started. Almost immediately after doing coke, I was no longer interested in smoking weed; however, it didn't effect my drinking, which was usually Crown Royal. I went home and shared my newfound friend with Abigale, and she liked it too.

This seems like as good a place as any to say that in writing about my addiction and recovery I cannot recall every experience nor do I want to, especially when it comes to my sexual escapades for one, as I would be writing about others, and this is a story about me. I also am attempting to keep ego and opinions out as much as possible. I am human, and I am affected by a wide range of feelings and emotions; before I write I ask God for guidance and I open my mind to my memories.

This seems like a good place to also say that being fucked up every day takes an enormous amount of work; the hunting and searching just to get the next high can consume hours. There is also an element of scheming and lying to get the money needed. In the latter, my family took the full brunt of the fallout; I never found myself having to steal from strangers to support my habits, however, I would and did steal from my family in many ways. It was all tied up in my feelings of entitlement, I felt like I deserved to feel good, and I was entitled to whatever money it took to make that happen. Just before Judd was born, we moved from Newark to Kirkersville into a two-bedroom apartment. It was an old funeral home converted into four apartments, though we didn't find this out until after we had been living there for a while.

Abigale had been promoted at the portrait studio again and was making good money - money that was spent supplying my habits. I was also spending my own paycheck staying high and drunk.

After we had moved to Kirkersville, one afternoon I was in line at a little convenience store and two guys behind me were talking and joking. One of them points at me and says look how thin he is he probably has AIDS. Well, I was embarrassed and hurt by the comment, but I wasn't going to show it. That comment manifested in my mind, and I began to worry that maybe I did have AIDS, so I went to a specialist and had all the tests ran a few months later I was given an all clear by the doctor. I went back two more times to be tested because I guess I believed that I deserved to have AIDS because of how I lived. On my second trip to the specialist I got the same results after a few months of waiting an all clear.

My third trip to the same specialist, however, was a little different. I was working at the marble shop full time and I was always covered in white powder from sanding sinks, the doctor asks me if maybe I'd like to see a psychiatrist because I was the healthiest person to ever be in his office. He did suggest that I got some help with the drug problem because it was as bad as he had ever seen! A bit confused I asked him what he meant, and he pointed out the powder around my cuticles and around my ears and nose! I broke down laughing I almost fell out of my seat, I had to explain that I worked with marble and that I wasn't covered in drug residue. Who did he think I was - Scarface? I laughed off the whole thing and promised not to bug him again! The truth was that I had a terrible drug and alcohol problem, but I sure as hell wasn't going to admit it!

While I was working at the marble shop, I had a real, not imagined, medical issue. We had made a giant shower base for a builder, and they wanted it installed so that they could build the bathroom around it. This thing was big enough to wash a Volkswagen in. I went with my boss to deliver it, and the builder was there with a helper. The shower base weighed around 500 pounds. The builder was on my side of the base, and it was too heavy for him and he let go. Instead of dropping a very expensive shower base that we had worked on for hours, I gritted my teeth and we carried it into the house! That night at Judd's crib side while saying our nightly prayers, it was like someone held three feet of rope slack at both ends and snapped it taught in my groin. I blew out two hernias, while saying my sons' prayers. One of the hernias was pressing on my sciatic nerve, causing me to flop around like a fish out of water. Work paid for the surgery to fix it. My boss's wife used to be a nurse, she referred me to a surgeon, and I went to see him. I was given a very large prescription for Percocet. The next day, I went back to the doctor and said I didn't like the way the Percocet made me feel, so he gave me another very large prescription for Vicodin. The next day, I went back to the doctor and said the Vicodin made me itchy, so he gave me another very large prescription for Demerol. Now being as happy as a pig in a poke, I went to the liquor store and bought several bottles of Goldschlager. I would take one or two of each of the pain pills and a shot of Goldschlager and so it was that I blacked out for a whole 30 days, losing a month of memory. I was no stranger to blackouts, but a whole month I was sure it had to be some kind of record! I have zero memory of that month, but I was told many things that I did that was surely embarrassing, I spent a lot of time in a wheelchair training a puppy to be a service dog. I threw a friend of Abigale's and her three kids out into the street because they pissed me off. I built a dog door and attached it to our screen door; it was so heavy that you had to kick the dog through it. And I'm sure there was more, but as you can see, I had a lot to clean up after I came out of the blackout. I can say I didn't remember any pain before or after the surgery.

With the coke came a whole new level of debauchery. I was already addicted to sex, and adding coke to the mix was like a flame to gas. I will simply say that my levels of immorality reached an all-time low. I was unfaithful in my marriage, I frequently went to prostitutes, I went to strip clubs, and I became hopelessly addicted to pornography. The last might have been a subconscious attempt not to be unfaithful in my marriage, but it might have been that I just liked porn. I was probably far enough gone by this point to not have a conscious or subconscious feeling about morality. A kind of pattern had developed in Abigale's and my marriage. We fought and argued regularly, but at least once a month it was very bad. At this point, I would rather say it wasn't that bad, but it was; I would punch walls and break furniture, I would choke Abigale and drag her around the house until I would get my way. I was unyielding to anything other than what I wanted with absolutely no regard to how it affected anyone else. My mode of operation was if it felt good do it and if I have to spend rent and diaper money, so be it. During one of these particularly bad fights, the police were called. No one was arrested but Abigale and Judd were escorted to a shelter where they spent the night. I remember being worried sick. The house was empty, and I didn't know where my wife and son were. The next day when Abigale came home, I apologized and promised that it wouldn't happen again and that I would do better...a promise that already had been made a million times and would be made a million more.

While we were living in Kirkersville, I bought a new truck a Dodge Dakota. It was the year the Dakota changed to look like the Ram. I was really proud of my truck. I was invited to a bachelor party that my brother-in-law was hosting. I got up early the day of the bachelor party and went to the liquor store and bought a few bottles - a fifth and a liter of Crown Royal and a fifth of vodka. The vodka was for Abigale, as she had a friend coming over for a girl's night while I was at the bachelor party. I started drinking before 10 a.m. I spent the day washing and waxing my new truck and drinking. I went to the bachelor party around 6 p.m. and started drinking the liter of Crown Royal; it was a pretty good party it was like a high school reunion. I knew almost everyone there. I don't remember leaving the bachelor party, but I remember playing cards and drinking and laughing and the next thing I remember I was coming to in the back of a police car! Apparently, I had been to the hospital before I had come to. I remember asking the officer if anybody was hurt and he replied no. I asked if I had wrecked my new truck. and he replied no. I was just sitting silently trying to remember why I left the party, and the officer said, "You know, Ray, everyone makes mistakes." I replied that I knew I would be paying for this one. When the officer says, "We are going to charge you with drunk and disorderly," I was shocked. Later I found out that I had stopped in a parking lot, and a neighbor had called the police thinking the place was being robbed. I called Abigale and she came the next morning and bailed me out. She told me I had called her from the bachelor party and told her I was coming home and then I never showed up. From the perspective of a using alcoholic, I was very lucky not to have been charged with a D.U.I. From the perspective of a recovering alcoholic, maybe I wasn't lucky at all - maybe if I had gotten into more trouble, I might have stopped sooner! Now, a good hard look at that statement and a thought of what's to come, and I have to say that it probably didn't matter one way or the other, it was going to take what it takes before I would one day be willing to truly admit what I was. Another good way to look at this is that everything happens for a reason; absolutely nothing happens by mistake. So, I was left making more promises to be better and to act better and to never let it happen again and of course, it did.

Abigale was offered another promotion at work, but if she accepted, we would have to move to Mansfield. I'm sure I said all the right things like "I'm proud of you for doing so well at your job," but I really was only concerned with more money. Another promotion would mean more for me, and I liked that. We moved to Mansfield, and I drove 78 miles one way to go to work at the marble shop. A funny thing happened while I was driving so far to go to work. I would drink a cup of coffee in the morning and then leave as soon as I lit up a cigarette. I then would have to find a bathroom. Didn't take very long for this to become a real inconvenience, so I stopped drinking coffee.

Now I can look at this and say I guess that using didn't bother me, but it did. I knew it was coming between me and Abigale, but not using was never an option; it was never even a thought that if I wasn't using things might be better.

While we were living in Mansfield, Abigale kicked me out; she said that it was either her or the drugs and alcohol. I chose the drugs and alcohol and left. I went home to the farm. Mom was away in California helping her parents sell their house so they could move back to the farm; grandma had Alzheimer's, and grandpa couldn't care for her on his own. I was thoroughly miserable; I was more alone than I had ever been. I missed Abigale and Judd, and I knew she was right, but still I couldn't stop doing what I was doing. If I wasn't at work, I was in the bar drinking. I hung out with other female friends, but my head wasn't in the game. I tried to go out on several real dates. I met a really nice college girl who happened to be a vegetarian; I took her to Damon's Ribs, ordered drinks and a rack of ribs, and dug in. I was usually too drunk to give much effort to looking for a girlfriend. Abigale was dating a guy who owned a couple car dealerships, and he lavished her with presents and trips. I was in total misery, and the thought of being alone consumed me.

The day before Halloween, I was fixing on going on another date when my dad told me Abigale had called and wanted me to call her back. I called Abigale and she told me she was having brake problems with her car; it was all I had to keep from suggesting that she tell her boyfriend who had two dealerships and surely he could get a brake job done. For maybe the first time ever I kept my mouth shut and told her I'd be up tomorrow and would look at her brakes.

The next day when I got to Mansfield and looked at the car, it did need brakes on all four wheels, so I changed them for her. Abigale asked me if I would like to walk with her and Judd around the neighborhood for a little trick or treat, and I did. We spent the rest of the evening together, and I helped put Judd to bed; it was getting time to head back to the farm and Abigale said we should talk. As I was about to leave, she asked me to stay and I did. The customary promises were made - it would be better, I would try harder, and I wouldn't drink and use as much. Of course, I might have tried to hide it for a while but that was about as hard as I tried.

We only lived in Mansfield just over a year, and Abigale was able to transfer back to the Columbus area. We rented a townhouse in Little Turtle on the ninth green of the golf course. Living in Columbus, it seemed like all of my friends were into cocaine as much as I was. My house was a party hangout, and it quickly got out of control. I spent everything I made on coke and whiskey and often dipped into what Abigale made too. I would take Judd with me to my dealer's house to pick up, they were always very nice to Judd and usually gave him a toy to take home. When Abigale would get home from work, Judd would show her his new toy, and I would be busted. Abigale was rightly pissed that I would take Judd to my dealer's house; she knew that if I would go pick it up with Judd then I was also using it while he was in the car with me. My best line of defense was to get her to do a line with me, then I felt like everything was smoothed over.

That year at Christmas, I had a house full of people partying, and we wrapped presents for Judd while the party went on. The next morning when Judd got up, we all stopped partying to watch him open presents, and then we went back to it. It lasted for several days. My using continued to progress to where I was eventually not paying our rent or my truck payment, and this went on for several months with me hiding it from Abigale. Finally, the townhouse complex issued an eviction notice. Having dug myself into a fairly good size hole, I went to my parents and told them what I had done. Of course, I lied outrageously, but I did have to admit to spending the rent and truck payments on drugs and alcohol. I agreed to go to a detox center in Newark, and dad found a place for us to rent in Somerset. Now the detox center was pretty adamant that I needed to go to treatment, but I assured everyone that I was all right and only needed to clean out for a few days and get my head right. The truth was that I was very aware that I had a problem, but I justified and rationalized my behavior and actions. I simply just got a little too deep and overextended my budget, living in the big city was offering me too many opportunities to party, everything would be better once I was moved back out to the country! I did a lot of fast talking while I was in detox; I even used a little of the program lingo that I knew to convince everyone that I could do better. The truth was I had absolutely zero intention of going back to meetings and recovery. I was sure that having learned this valuable lesson I would be able to be better.

Around the same time that we were moving back to Somerset, my boss called me into his office for a talk. My boss informed me that he was very confused by me, said that he couldn't hire two people to do the work I did for him. He then said that I had absolutely no responsibility toward my job, that I called off and came late and left early with no regard for anyone else. He also informed me that he believed that I had a very serious drug and alcohol problem and that if I ever wanted to go anywhere in life, I had better get it under control! I thought, "Wow, what is this, everyone climbs on Ray's ass week?" I guess that it didn't help that the day before I had been in a pretty bad argument with my boss's wife. My boss's wife had called me to the door of my bathroom while I was working. She then said I want to ask you something; she took me into my bathroom, opened the mirror on the medicine cabinet, pointed to a small clear bottle full of something white, and asked me what I had to say about it. Well, as it turned out, I had quite a lot to say about it being that it was salt that I used to gargle with. She didn't believe me that it was salt, so I told her to taste it. I got madder and madder - this woman was accusing me of being a drug addict and of using at work, both of which were quite true, I am a drug addict, and I was using at work every day but still how dare she! So, I asked her if she had any idea how much that coke would cost and if I were a drug addict did she really think I would leave it where anyone could find it? And then the argument really got started. She yelled at me for a few minutes before I finally had had enough, and I told her to stop. I informed her that I didn't let my wife talk to me like this, and I'm fucking her! She looked at me like I had slapped her and walked away! I just thought, "Finally, she shut up!" Hence the visit to the boss's office where on top of several things he informed me that he didn't appreciate the way I talked to his wife. I will say here that these were two of the nicest people I would ever work for; they genuinely cared about me and wanted to see me get help. I, on the other hand, genuinely hated me and didn't care one whit about what they thought! That year approaching Christmas break, I was informed that the boss was selling the business to one of my coworkers and that my services would no longer be needed. Translation: My coworker also knew I was a drug addict and an alcoholic and didn't want the headache of dealing with me. So, I collected unemployment for the first time in my life.

9

UNEMPLOYABLE AND REHABBED

Christmas 1999 was upon us, and I was hopelessly lost in addiction and alcoholism, I lost my job that I had had for over five years, I lost my truck because I was putting the payment up my nose, and I lost our home because I was putting the rent up my nose. I was pretty sure that I was a piece of shit and deserved everything that was happening. Still, Abigale had been working her way up in her company and was making very good money, so with unemployment we were going to be all right. I knew deep down that I had a very serious problem and that I needed some help, but there were more important things to worry about. Y2K was quickly approaching, and everyone knew the computers were going to fail, the lights were going to go out, and it was quite possibly the end of the world. I told all of our friends that we had moved home because we didn't want Judd to go to a city school, which was an outrageous lie, and I was afraid everyone would find out that I had taken my family's rent money and put it up my nose. Now these were seemingly very important issues to worry about, so my addiction and alcoholism took the back seat. Of course, we passed Y2K without a hitch, my problems being deflected I settled into a pretty good depression. How do you cope with depression? I'm an alcoholic, so I drank, I became a regular at the three bars in town, and I often showed up at

8 AM when they opened. I would try to be home for dinner and for Judd's bedtime. I would go back to the bar after eating and or saying goodnight to Judd. Abigale and I were experiencing some problems in our marriage she wasn't as affectionate and loving, as I thought she should be. She was likely so pissed at the situations I had created who could blame her. Well, I did; a good wife should be loving and supportive, and I felt like I was being shortchanged on the whole marriage thing. Notice again it's all about me. I thought everyone should just get over my mistakes - they happen "for God's sake" - so as my depression grew so did my drinking, funny how that works.

I would like to say here that a metamorphosis in my addiction was beginning to happen, as I was switching more to alcohol than drugs. Now that's not to say that I stopped using drugs because I didn't, but a change was starting to happen. I knew I couldn't afford to do coke the way I wanted to, and the small farm town I lived in was quite accommodating to the alcoholic. A beer mug half full of Crown Royal and half full of Coke was only $2.25, so staying drunk all day was fairly affordable. I helped dad out around the farm a little, and sometimes I worked for other farmers but not much; I mostly just drank.

One morning on the way to the bar, I ran into an old friend, and he had a bag of mushrooms to sell. Naturally, I thought mushrooms and whiskey seemed like a capital idea, so I bought them, ate them, and went to the bar. That afternoon, as all the farmers came in for lunch, they found me drunk as a lord, watching Willy Wonka and the Chocolate Factory laughing my ass off and falling off of my bar stool. Nothing to look at here, everything is right as the U.S. mail! After a day of tripping and pickling myself, I apparently blacked out. We had an old toilet in the basement that wasn't even hooked up, and Abigale found me after dark passed out in front of the toilet with my pants open. Evidently, I needed to piss. She couldn't wake me up, so she called my dad. I woke up getting the shit slapped out of me on the floor of the basement; my dad was not as gingerly about trying to revive me. When I came to on the cement floor, I was still as drunk as a lord and still tripping. Dad walked me out the back door, and I took off after a skunk in the yard and dad took off after me trying to keep me from getting sprayed. Well, he caught me before I caught the skunk and then got me into the house. I promised not to leave and to go to bed so everyone would leave me alone, and the whole incident went down in the books as more of my shenanigans.

Come April 2000, I was still fighting depression and still sitting on the same barstool. Abigale was working full-time and pregnant with our second child, supporting a drunk husband who thought she was rather unaffectionate. One of my normal days at the bar, I received a phone call from Abigale who wanted to know if I would be home for dinner. She told me that she loved me and she missed me. I was a little shocked but promised that I would be home for dinner and that I loved and missed her too! I was really quite pleased Abigale still loved me and thought maybe she was going to try to be a little more affectionate. I was so pleased, in fact, that I really started to enjoy my drinking, and being a good drinker, I spent time playing pool, throwing darts, and putting money into the jukebox (I always played the best songs), and the night flew by in a blur. I only lived about a half a block from the bar, so about midnight I staggered home.

When I walked through the back door, I found Abigale sitting at the table with a spaghetti dinner on the plate cold. She was pissed that I didn't come home for dinner and accused me of not loving her and Judd. I naturally accused her of not understanding how bad I felt for letting down my family and losing my job and that she just didn't understand how depressed I was. Well, that didn't help my case any, and the real fight started almost immediately there was name calling, throwing furniture, slamming doors, altogether a pretty good fight, and finally the climax, I grabbed the plate of spaghetti and flung it across the room plate and all. I informed Abigale that I had heard enough and that I was taking the car and going to the farm to go fishing. Now how and why I came up with going fishing at midnight is beyond me, but that's what I did. Abigale informed me that if I took the good car and not my beater that she would call the police, so naturally I took the good car and headed for the farm.

When I got to the farm, I went into the shop where I had a couch that I had been storing and heaved it onto the back of a brush hog. I then loaded my fishing pole and tackle box onto the couch. Down over the yard I went headed for the gate to the pasture where the pond was. I'm sure my parents probably thought, "Ray's up to his shenanigans again." I dragged the couch down to the water's edge and tied my favorite Rapala to my fishing line and settled in for some fishing. Now, fishing is a good place to think, and I was very pissed off and had a lot to think about. In fact, I was so pissed off that I remembered that I had a joint in my cigarette pack, and I got it out - to hell with the fact that I was already drunk, and it was likely to make me sick. So, I lit up and fished and wondered why Abigale couldn't understand how embarrassed I felt over losing my job just because the new owner didn't want to employ a drug addict and alcoholic. How could she not understand how worthless I felt? Mind you, I wasn't looking for a job and had zero intentions of stopping using. Still, why was everyone so unreasonable? As I lay there fishing getting high and bitching and moaning in my head, I saw a police cruiser coming down the driveway with its lights flashing. I thought, "Why did that bitch call the police, all I'm doing is fishing!" Well, the police pull down through the yard to the closed gate of the pasture field and get out of their car. I cast out again and take another hit and start reeling in my line, when they call out over the P.A., "Ray, we need to talk to you." So, I put the joint back in my cigarette pack, leave it on the couch, climb back on the John Deer 4020, and drive across the field to the gate. I climb down off the tractor and over the gate and ask the officers, "What can I do for you?" They proceeded to arrest me for domestic violence. Then they had a fifteen-minute discussion between themselves trying to decide if they could give me a DUI for driving the tractor drunk. Finally I pointed out that I was on private property and was pretty sure I could drive whatever I damn well please! I'm not sure, but that might have started a bad relationship with the officers, but I wasn't sweating it at the time. This was going on at around 1 AM Saturday morning it was well after 4 AM by the time they got me to the regional jail in Nelsonville.

Around 6 AM, a CO kicked my rack and told me breakfast was being served, but I was much too sick to think about getting up, so I rolled over and went back to sleep. Later when I finally woke up before lunch, I was confused about where I was for a minute. I was in a little room with a couple of cots, and I could hear a lot of people talking. When I got to my feet and did a little investigating, I was told I was in an observation room off of general population in the regional jail. I had never been to jail before, and I was a little intimidated, but I wasn't going to show it. I felt like I was going to die I was so sick; I was sick from all I had drank the day before and even more sick from not being able to get a drink to settle my stomach. I saw someone I recognized and bummed a smoke, and that helped a little. I asked the CO what I had to do to get out, and he told me I was charged with domestic violence and couldn't be released without going in front of a judge for a bond hearing. I sat down on my rack and prayed, "God, if you will get me out of here, I promise I'll do whatever I have to do to get better – I'll even stop drinking!"

After lunch, which I just picked at – I was still too sick to even think about eating - a CO called my name at the door to general population. I walked over to see what he wanted, and he told me to come with him, as I was having a video hearing to bond out. The CO asked me who I knew to be getting a Saturday bond hearing. I had absolutely no idea. I faced the judge on a video arraignment and was given a $10,000 bond, which $1000 had to be put up to get me out, and a hearing date was set up for about a week away. I was also told that a protection order was in place and I couldn't see or talk to Abigale. A few hours later, a CO came and got me and told me I was bonded out.

When I walked out of jail, I experienced a feeling of freedom, I looked around, and there was my dad waiting by his truck! Turned out dad made some calls and was able to talk the judge into going in on Saturday to give me a bond hearing. Not only did dad talk the judge into going to work on Saturday and pay my bond, he also cleaned up the couch at the pond and put away the tractor. I only just now today as I write this realize what all my dad did for me. At the time, I was just glad to be free and to get a pack of cigarettes. I was really a self-absorbed ass.

Dad told me he thought he saw a pack of cigarettes on the couch. I remembered the joint in my cigarettes, relief I'm saved and that quick I turned my back on the promise that I had made to God, which he obviously delivered on his side rather promptly. I wasn't allowed to go home because of the protection order, so I went to the farm with dad. I immediately called Abigale and apologized and told her I loved her and Judd! There is nothing like having someone tell you it's illegal to see each other to make you want to spend every minute together. We talked every day, and it wasn't long before we were seeing each other every day also. I went in front of the judge a few weeks later and plead guilty to a misdemeanor domestic violence, I was sentenced to 90 days in the Community Transaction Center (CTC); it was a treatment facility plus a transition center for people being released from prison. I was also told I had to complete anger management to have the protection order lifted.

So off I went to CTC for another three months of treatment. CTC helped people get their GED and driver's license, so about four hours Monday through Friday were spent in school. I already had my diploma and license, so I didn't have anything to do during class. Instead, I studied to take my CDL test. I already knew how to drive CDL vehicles from working on the farm, but I was never licensed. I did attend recovery classes and meetings, and I said all the right things and showed interest in recovery, but I had no intention of going back to meetings and working a program. I can only say that I believed that if I just tried harder, I could control my using and drinking. I also believe that I had a resentment to the program; from my viewpoint, it obviously didn't work. Of course, the fact that I didn't work the program was sort of overlooked; I mean, this couldn't be my fault. So, I showed the proper enthusiasm to all of the staff and my counselors and kept my preconceived ideas about recovery to myself.

About fifty days into my treatment, I was allowed to start looking for a job. I applied to a few places, and at sixty days in treatment I started working for a plastic injection mold company. It didn't pay much, but it was my first job since the marble shop. I was only on the job about a week when they found out I could operate equipment, and I was promoted to shipping. I was only on the shipping job a few days when one of the drivers came in - it was a friend I had made while I had been working a real program for four years. I was a little embarrassed to tell him I was back in treatment, but I did. We talked a little, and I saw him a few more times over the next week. I was still living at CTC, but I was working full time. One of the other companies I had applied to called and offered me a job; it paid almost $5 more an hour and had an opportunity to become a CDL driving job after I passed my driver's test. So being a proper impulsive alcoholic, I switched jobs with no notice to the plastic outfit. Besides, more money meant more gooder, more better!

While I'm in treatment and getting back to work, Abigale is working full-time, taking care of Judd, and about to give birth to our first daughter. We made arrangements with CTC that if Abigale went into labor my mom was going to come and get me and take me to the hospital so I could be there! I was doing well at Lumbercraft and was in my last week at CTC when Abigale went into labor. I made it to the hospital in time and was there when Alice was born. I remember being in awe when I first saw her, and I felt like my life was surely changing for the better. I remember being afraid that I would forget and wipe the wrong way when I changed her diaper, being that wiping a girl is the opposite as a boy, and wanting to be a good father. That was my deepest fear - not using again or being unemployed or getting a divorce and being separated from my family. My worst fear was wiping the wrong way. Again, I was positive that I only needed to try harder, and I would be able to control my using and drinking. That my friends, is insanity - "doing the same things and expecting different results."

I completed CTC with a successful discharge. I had a new job at Lumbercraft making custom ordered trusses, and they even gave me several hours a week and a semi to practice for my CDL test. When I left treatment, I moved back in with Abigale and the kids and started my anger management classes that I had to complete to have the protection order dropped. I was also on probation, so I had to report once a month to a probation officer. When I saw him, I told him that I was doing everything I was supposed to be doing; I left out that I was living with Abigale who I was supposed to have no contact. Life was going better; I don't remember how long I made it after treatment before I started drinking again, it might have been a week or two but definitely less than a month.

I took my CDL test and passed the pre-trip and maneuverability on my first try. However, I failed the road test, which I didn't understand, as I had performed I thought perfectly. The test was in Columbus, and we drove through city streets and I didn't hit anything or rub any curbs. When I asked how I failed, the instructor told me I didn't look in my mirrors enough. So, the next time I took the driving test I made sure to move my head from side to side when I looked into my mirrors, this seemed to satisfy the instructor and I passed. I got promoted at work to a driving position, and I started my career as a professional driver hauling wide load trusses.

10

INSANITY

Let's take a few minutes to take a look at what was really going on. For starters, going to CTC was in lieu of a jail sentence; I was sent to treatment instead of jail. I had no intention of working a program to stay sober, I was thoroughly and completely convinced that if I just tried harder, it would be better. I'm working a new job as a professional driver and I'm sure life is about to blossom into the dream I thought I should be living. Reality was that I was driving a new route to work and had new coworkers and that seemed to equal new bars and new liquor stores. After I got out of CTC, I might have made a half-assed attempt to stay sober, but really all of my eggs were in the "I will control it basket" so I was set up for failure from the rip! I will say that Abigale had been sober for her nine months of pregnancy with Alice and when I came home from CTC she was drinking. I say this to point out my own failings because among other things I am also a jealous alcoholic; seeing someone else drinking affected me greatly. I was full of preconceived notions that were completely false, but I believed them nonetheless. Among them was "If everyone else can drink and control it, then so could I."

A few years earlier, I was drinking with my best friend Mort one night, and he told me he felt a little guilty. He felt like he was drinking a little more than he should be, and he also felt like he should be taking his mother to church. When Mort was very young, his dad passed away, and Mort was the last kid living at home with his mom. Well, me in my infinite wisdom I said, "If you want to take your mom to church, then take her!" I watched Mort's life change in the space of a few months, he started going to church, he got an incredible job, he started building a house of his own, and I saw this as he was coming into his own, he had matured and was living a good life. In my mind, I believed that all I had to do was grow up a little, stop drinking so much, and be an adult. It was just that easy it must be because I watched my best friend do it like it was nothing.

Now, I had been around the program clean for just days away from four years, and I heard talk about alcoholism and drug addiction being like an allergy of the mind and body that once taken in any form created the phenomenon of cravings and once the cravings started there wasn't much other than jails, institutions and death that could stop them. I also had heard that a great many alcoholics and addicts follow the belief that they will someday be able to use and or drink like a normal person, to the very gates of insanity and even into death! Hell, what do millions upon millions of recovering alcoholics and addicts possibly know that I should listen to them? It might have been said best by George Costanza in *Seinfeld* when he said, "It isn't a lie if you believe it!" So, there it is, I was living by my own preconceived ideas, and the fact that many of them were outright lies didn't really matter.

The job at Lumbercraft was kind of fun. I was hauling wide load trusses to residential homes and apartments that were under construction. The job had a lot of challenges, and for the most part was interesting. I delivered to a lot of rural homes being built and would have to back down driveways because there is usually nowhere to turn a semi around. Sometimes the driveways would be tree lined and have lots of turns, I quickly learned to unstrap the load so I could shift it around on the trailer to get past trees. After I would get off, I started stopping at a bar close to work to have a few with coworkers and in the blink of an eye I was drinking and or drugging everyday again. It was definitely the phenomenon of cravings, but I was in denial, I wasn't willing to be honest with myself or anyone else. When I had a drink in my hand, I was already thinking about the next one. Drugs were the same way; I was always concerned about the next high, did I have enough, where to get more, and what to get. There was literally never enough! I was never capable of saving more for later when it came to pills, coke or meth, beer, and liquor; I used whatever I had until it was gone and often until the money also was gone. I would have to suppose that there was a gradual shift away from drugs and toward alcohol because financially I could get drunk every day and not run out of money. There were however times that I would go on a spree and use and drink for days until there wasn't enough money to get more. When I was without alcohol and or drugs, I was left to face myself and that was a terror beyond imagining. I hated who I was what I did and when I had no way to self-medicate, I was in complete and total despair. The severity of depression and mood swings was greatly affected by what I was using, the worst times being when coming off of coke or meth. I was surely unbearable whatever I was coming off of and if I was forced to be without because there wasn't enough money I was enraged on top of miserable. Unfortunately, it was my wife and children that were around the most, so they inevitably got the worst of me and during those times I was more like a tiger in the room than an elephant!

I only worked at Lumbercraft for about eleven months. I was coming to work drunk and calling off a lot. I remember going out after work and drinking until the bars closed then going back to work and sleeping in front of the security gate. The gate had to be opened for Lumbercraft employees to have access to the property, so they had to wake me up to move so they could open the gate. I felt this was a pretty good example of a symbiotic relationship, but I don't think they felt the same way at all! It really worked out well for me; the boss showed up to open the business, woke me up so I would move my car, and I was at work early. It so happens that I was at work early a lot. One snowy winter morning, I was particularly hung over and feeling peevish, I complained to my dispatcher that I didn't think my truck's brakes were operating well enough for snow-covered roads. We argued for a while, and I really don't remember if I quit or if I was fired, but by the end of the argument, I no longer worked at Lumbercraft. I had been talking to Abigale's brother, Ray, and he was working for an Atlas moving company and told me they were always hiring drivers. I drove over to Atlas the same morning I left Lumbercraft, and they so happened to have a crew waiting for a driver. I was hired on the spot, and I got almost another $5 on the hour more than I was making at Lumbercraft. You know my motto - more money, more gooder, more better!

As a driver for Atlas, my responsibilities were to drive the truck and manage the moving crew, and also to be a packer, mover, trailer loader and to deal with the customer. I had a lot to learn, but it was a pretty relaxed atmosphere. Everyone I worked with seemed to party just about as much as me, so I fit in immediately. I was later trained to pack expensive stuff like China and crystal, so I went on a lot of high-end jobs. I worked mostly intrastate jobs, which means I didn't leave Ohio. The job was usually fun because I was almost always high on something, and we started drinking as soon as the job was done usually before we were back to the warehouse. When we showed up in the morning to start packing, we raced to see who got the master bedroom and master bath, as that's where all the good pills were. Eight out of ten master bathrooms had some kind of narcotic medication, and we liberally helped ourselves to what we found. If we finished a job early, we would park the semi behind a bar and go in and drink on the clock for a few hours, I was in heaven, as I was quite sure I had found the perfect job!

Abigale and I were looking for a bigger house to rent, as the one we were living in was only a two bedroom, and Judd needed a room of his own. My parent's church had a house for rent that was a three bedroom and right beside the elementary school. So, we decided to move. My parents and several of the church congregation helped paint and replacc carpet to get the house ready. We moved out of a house that was built in 1812 and into a house that was built in 1890, so it was a move up. I tore the front porch off and built a new one, and we had the house looking really nice. There was a screened-in back porch that Abigale and I could smoke in; we never smoked inside after Judd was born. We had a much bigger yard and more room for the kids to play. I'll say here that I helped with the kids the best I could, and they were always hugged and told that I loved them. I spent Saturday mornings watching cartoons with them, and I played in the yard, I was almost always using or drinking, but I did do normal things with my family. Abigale liked to go to church on Sunday, and I would usually go although I had a bottle of whiskey under the driver's seat that I would drink on the way to church, then I would chew a few sticks of Big Red gum before entering. I chewed a lot of Big Red gum; I believed that it covered up the smell of alcohol. I probably should have invested in Big Red I might have got some of my money back. I picked up the kids from the babysitters through the week, and I usually had them all weekend to myself because Abigale worked weekends. So, I would drag Judd and little Alice to the bar for lunch, I'd get Judd a hamburger and a Coke and be feeding Alice a bottle while I drank a few Crown and Cokes. There was a bottle of whiskey at the house, so essentially I drank all day while I watched the kids. When Abigale would get home from work, I would have the kids bathed and ready for bed and sometimes already in bed when Abigale came in. When she got home, I would leave and go to the bar for a few hours. This is a great place to point out that living life is like standing on a ladder - you can always look down and find someone under you, and you likewise can look up and see someone above you. I spent a fair amount of time looking both ways, I would look down and think, "At least I'm not that bad" or "It could be worse, I could be doing that!" Looking up, I often felt like "Why can't I be doing good enough for nicer cars or my own house? Someday I'll have those things too. I spent a great deal of time looking up and down that ladder, and I used it to great benefit to use or drink more because I didn't have what those above me did. Then there was always the excuse that at least I'm not as bad as those below me are. The truth is this disease is one of perception and all of these preconceived ideas are, at their core, deadly. So, I used this ladder to make myself feel worse so I could use more, and then I'd justify it because I could always find someone worse.

On September 10, 2001, we were hauling store furnishings into a new Nordstrom store at the Easton shopping center. I was in a warehouse close to work supervising my trailer being loaded, and I'm sure I was loaded. The forklift driver was pushing crates full of glass tabletops into my trailer, and he was having trouble with a crate, as it kept spinning sideways. So, he stopped, and I walked past the lift and put my left hand on the crate to hold it steady so he could back up and get straightened out. The forklift driver came forward instead of backing up and crushed two of my fingers on my left hand. I stumbled out of the trailer and fell to my knees and looked at my hand - my middle finger and pointer finger were bent backwards. I pulled them straight and felt the black circle closing in. I was already taking pain pills, but it was still extremely painful; one of my bosses drove me to the hospital. There is nothing like a real excuse to make an addict want more. After about two hours, I snagged a doctor walking by and showed him my hand. He cringed and said "I'll have some pain medicine sent right out." A few minutes and a shot of morphine later, and I was feeling much better about the whole thing. I sent my car keys back with my boss, and one of the packing girls drove it to the hospital, she came in and gave me my keys and told me where my car was. About six hours later and another shot of morphine and a few pains pills I assured the hospital I had a ride, I went in search of my car. Took me two solid hours to find it, but I was fucked up enough not to be too aggravated. I finally realized that there was more than one parking garage, and after I broadened my search, I found my car. Now I had to collect myself and make plans for the ride home, which was more than sixty miles. First, I had to decide what pharmacy I was going to fill my pain prescription and then what bar I was going to stop at for a drink. There was a lot to figure out, and it was getting late, so I headed for home and hoped all this important stuff worked itself out. I made it home several drinks and one pharmacy later, I can't say I really remember much of the drive!

The next morning, I got out of bed, took a couple pain pills and a shot of Crown, and was sitting in front of the

TV flipping channels when I thought I saw a plane hit a building, I flipped back and watched the second plane fly into the World Trade Center live on TV. I called Abigale and we both sat transfixed to the TV, I was in shock at what I saw I believed we were being attacked, I was angry, I was scared, I was confused, all the things that made a great excuse to get fucked up and that's just what I did! Abigale took the kids to the sitters, as she knew I wasn't going to be able to watch them. Well, it was a time for community action, so I went to the bar and drank and watched the news with everyone else. The truth is the only excuse I needed to use was waking up, but it was convenient to have a new one that was to me a perfectly legitimate reason.

A few days later, I had reconstructive surgery one my two fingers. I used my old faithful ploy of not liking my pain meds to get as many as I could. I was off work with pay for a couple months.

When I got back to work, my fingers hurt, so I ate more pain meds. It was nice to have an excuse to be doing what I was! So, I worked and ate pain meds until I got off, then I started drinking on the way home. I was usually pretty well lit by the time I got home, and then Abigale would want a drink, so I'd drink more. Sometimes I mixed it up a little - Xanax and drinking or Valium and drinking - there were so many different buzzes available it was good to spread them around a little. I even went back to smoking weed for about six months; a connection of mine was getting authentic opium-dipped Thai stick, and it was really good. I learned that if I did some coke, I could drink and smoke weed without feeling like I was going to spin off of the planet. I wondered if that's how everyone had been doing it all along.

Abigale and I were still arguing, but it was only really bad about once a month. One night after work I was at the bar drinking, and Abigale called and asked if I was coming home to put the kids to bed. I said I would but kept drinking and talking. I was pretty well drunk, and I left half a beer mug of Crown and Coke sitting on the bar. I told the bar maid that I'd be back and went home. Before I got out of the car, I noticed my hunting knife in the center console and I decided to take it into the house. I walked in the back door and into the kitchen, Abigale was there and obviously pissed off that I wasn't home before she put the kids to bed. Evidently this was going to be our bad night out of thirty, so we got right to arguing. It didn't take long for me to have had enough and I said, "Fuck this, I'm going back to the bar." Now I had the checkbook sticking out of my right back pocket and my hunting knife in a leather sheath sticking out of my left back pocket. When I said I was going back to the bar Abigale decided to try to take the checkbook away from me. I kept turning sideways so she couldn't get it, I was a little afraid she might get ahold of my hunting knife, so I pulled it out of my pocket and tossed it underhanded across the kitchen. Abigale stopped dead in her tracks turned her right foot ninety degrees, stuck her hand on her hip and sneering at me said, "Are you trying to intimidate me with that knife?" Abigale turned and walked through the dining room into the living room and sat down on the couch. It was like someone had flipped a switch, I got madder and madder the more I thought about what she said, I walked over, picked up the knife, and walking to the living room door I dropped the sheath and turned the knife around so I was holding the blade. I walked to the living room door and looked across the room at Abigale scowling at me and said, "Bitch, if I wanted to intimidate you with this knife I would." I threw the knife across the room, and it stuck into the wall about a foot away from her head! For a split-second Abigale looked at me in complete terror, and I thought, "Yep, sufficiently intimidated." Then she rabbited out the front door. I was pretty well drunk but not so drunk as to realize that what I just did was fucking stupid, so I rabbited for the back door. The look in Abigale's eyes was a pretty good indication that the police would be showing up, and I didn't particularly feel like being readily available when they did. As I was heading for the back door, I tripped up and fell toward the door; our back door was made up of little panes of glass, and when I tripped both of my hands and arms went through a couple of the panes of glass. I finally made it to the car and away I went! The rest of the night is a blur; I'm sure there was more using and drinking, but I don't remember it.

I woke up the next morning to Abigale's brother Ray banging on my driver's window. I was parked behind the warehouse at work. The first thing Ray said was, "Did you hurt my sister?" He was looking at me kind of crazy, when I looked down, I saw I was covered in blood; I looked like I had just come from a murder. After a brief moment of panic because I was a little foggy on the last part of the night, I remembered falling through the back door. I looked at my hands and arms, and they were all cut up from the glass. With a little relief, I told Ray that I hadn't hurt Abigale. Ray agreed to tell dispatch that I couldn't make it in due to a family emergency. That sounded better since I looked like a stoned killer and didn't have a way to clean up without everyone seeing me. I left work and found a pay phone and called dad, who informed me that the police were in fact looking for me and I had better come home.

By the time I had made it the hour back home, dad had talked to the town police chief and the town police chief had called the sheriff's department and had talked them out of serving a warrant on me. He gave his word that I would be in court on the appointed court date...Just another example of my dad trying to clean up after me. As it turned out however, it worked, and I wasn't arrested even though I was being charged with assault with a deadly weapon and felony domestic violence.

A couple days passed before I called Abigale. I was pretty sure this whole thing was mostly her fault; I just wanted to drink, and she wanted to fight. I was completely blind to the fact that my drinking was what she was fighting about. So, after some serious reflection, I came to the conclusion that I didn't get in trouble every time I drank, however every time I got in trouble I was drinking - a harsh realization that I'm more than sure that I'm not the only one who can relate to. After hiring an attorney, a decision was made that some form of treatment was in order. I called my old friend Ian and told him I was using and in trouble, and I needed treatment, and he suggested a recovery house that was running a ninety-plus-day treatment in Sidney, Ohio. So away I went for another treatment. I was properly motivated knowing I was being charged with a felony assault with a deadly weapon, and I was more than a little afraid of going to prison. I put myself back into a recovery state of mind, and I started going to meetings and even working with a temporary sponsor while I was in Sidney. I lived at the halfway house and after the first three or four weeks I was allowed to have my car and find a job. By this time, I was driving Abigale's Dodge Intrepid, and she was driving a Chevy Blazer that we had inherited from Grandpa O'Malley. There is a kind of important backstory about Grandpa O'Malley so hold on and get ready for a flashback!

About nine months before my "assault with a deadly weapon" debacle, my parents had planned an extended trip to Hawaii with friends. While they were gone, Abigale, the kids, and I were going to stay at the farm to take care of Grandpa O'Malley. Grandma O'Malley was in a nursing home with Alzheimer's, and my mom took care of Grandpa O'Malley. Now, I will just quickly say that Grandpa O'Malley was in pretty good health, but he had always been taken care of by Grandma, that is always cooked for and someone did his laundry. I guess you could say it was a generation gap kind of thing. Grandpa had been a high-power lineman and had earned a very good retirement by working his ass off and Grandma cooked and cleaned so he never had to learn how. About this same time, Grandpa went out and bought a brand-new Chevy Blazer; it was a really nice truck, and Grandpa was very proud of it. The first couple of weeks went fairly smooth; we cooked meals for him and did laundry, so he always had clean clothes. There were, however, some challenges like Grandpa would follow us around and turn lights off after we turned them on, and he would complain if we were on the phone for more than a couple minutes, but we were able to deal with these challenges up to a point. About the middle of the third week, Grandpa was becoming more and more agitated and his demands about electricity and phone time was becoming a little tiresome. Now I'd like to state for the record that I was still drinking and drugging, but I was trying to moderate a little more than I normally would because we were staying with Grandpa. I was a little aggravated because I wasn't using as much as I would at home, and I thought Abigale should be even more sober than I was, so she was aggravated too! To get to the crux of the problem, come the middle of the third week everyone was aggravated, and I had a pretty big fight with Grandpa O'Malley. He was literally walking behind me and turning lights off after I turned them on and he was yelling at me to get off the phone because he was expecting a call, and I snapped. I told him for the thousandth time that we had call waiting and if someone called for him, he would get the call. I further went on to explain that he didn't pay the fucking electrical bill, so he could shut up about the lights being on. It went downhill from there. We had a huge fight, he threatened to take me out of his will, and I told him he could go fuck himself and his money for all I cared. These were the last words I ever had with Grandpa O'Malley.

Mom and dad got home a few days later, and Grandpa was still pissed. The fight was dragged back up, and he left. Two days later, he was found in a hotel bathtub suffering from an attempted suicide. He lived in the hospital for a few days before succumbing to liver failure and dying. Come to find out when he had gotten so aggravated it was his wedding anniversary, and he was waiting for Grandma to call; of course, she never did, thanks to Alzheimer's. I didn't know, but the truth is I didn't care enough to ask; all I knew was Grandpa was acting like an ass, and I reciprocated by acting like a bigger ass! I was so consumed with myself and my problems that I had no room for anyone else's; my problems were paramount. Was I getting enough to drink, was I high enough to face the day, was there going to be money to stay drunk and or high tomorrow? You know, real world problems, not some kind of feelings shit like, "Is my wife of 35 or 40 years going to call on our anniversary?" After we buried Grandpa O'Malley, mom and dad gave Abigale and me his brand new Blazer as inheritance. The first time I drove it, a rock hit and chipped the window, and my first thought was "Grandpa O'Malley probably threw it at me from the grave!"

11

ANOTHER REHAB

During treatment at Sidney, Ohio, I got to look for a job. One of the guys in the halfway house was working for TNT Logistics, a cross dock for Honda parts, so I went in and applied for a job driving yard truck and docking trailers in the terminal. I was asked why I was applying, and naturally I lied and said my wife was going to be transferred to this area, and I came ahead of her to look for work. I had no intention of telling the company I was in a halfway house for drug addiction and alcoholism and needed a job to pay to stay. I was hired and stayed at TNT for several months while I stayed in treatment. I excelled at the job; it was really easy to me and it paid pretty well. While I was in Sidney, I worked the first three steps again; it wasn't a real leap of faith for me to admit that I was powerless over drugs and alcohol, but I sort of glossed over the "my life is unmanageable part." Clearly it was, but I don't think I saw it that way! I also started praying some and life started to change a little. Now let's remember, I was there because I have charges to face in court and I'm afraid of going to prison, but nonetheless life started to look up a little. I was sober, I went to work on time, I went to work every day, and I went to meetings every day.

Now, I do recall an incident that happened while I was in Sidney. Being one of the only guys in the halfway house with a car, I took a lot of other guys to work and to outside meetings. One afternoon I had a carload of guys from the halfway house, and we were pulling into a shopping center. I didn't really know the area very well, and I had pulled into the exit by mistake. A car was coming out of the exit, as I was driving in and the driver gave me a dirty look, so I hit him. There was plenty of room for two cars to pass, but I crowded the other car and tore off his mirror and left a scratch down the whole driver's side of the car. The driver stopped and pulled over into a parking place, and I swung around to confront him. When I got out of the car, a mother and a new driver got out of the other car and I instantly realized that what I had mistaken for a mean mugging was actually just fear in the eyes of a new driver. I immediately apologized and took full responsibility for the accident. I gave them my insurance and promised to tell my company that I was at fault, which I did. I guess I remember that story just to remind myself that perception can be a funny thing and the way I see something doesn't make it so.

I made new friends in recovery in Sidney, and when it came time for me to graduate and go home, I went through a ceremony that the treatment center had come up with. They picked a rock and passed it around to everyone and they all said something nice about you and wished you well in your recovery. You got the rock last and said goodbye to everyone then went home to continue your recovery. Well, me being me, I told them I already had a rock I'd like to use, and I brought an arrowhead from the farm and passed it around for my farewell ceremony. I later had it made into a necklace, and I still have it to this day. There must not have been enough mojo in it, though, because that necklace didn't keep me sober!

So, I'm back from treatment, I go back to work for Atlas with all of my drinking and using friends, but I'm really serious about staying sober this time. On June 13, 2002, my youngest child, Ophelia, is born, and after her birth Abigale goes back to drinking. I finally face the judge on my latest charges, and miraculously the felony assault with a deadly weapon is dropped. I am, however, charged with a misdemeanor domestic violence (my second one). I'm sentenced to 180 days in jail but 150 of that is suspended and held over my head while I'm on probation for two years. I have to do 30 days in the county jail and another six months of anger management, and I have to report to a probation officer for two years! Not too bad for all the worrying I did, I told myself, I believe I can live with it.

I do my time in the county and my anger management class (again) all the while I am attending meetings in Zanesville. I get a sponsor and start reworking the steps with him. My sponsor is an older African American man named Kenneth. Kenneth and I get along pretty well; we go to a lot of meetings together and talk almost every day. My only complaint is Kenneth seems a little pushy about the steps - I mean I've got the rest of my life what's the big hurry anyhow? Kenneth and I argue a few times about the steps and their importance; he even goes so far as to tell me that if I don't buckle down and get serious about doing the steps, I'm at risk of losing my job, my family, and my house! I argue back and say now let's not get carried away here; I'm sober, I'm going to stay sober, and I'm in no apparent danger of losing my job, family, and home! Now, let's take a few breaths here and not get hysterical!

I found a local guy that needed rides to meetings, and we started going to them together. One night we were on our way home after a meeting; it was around 9:30. My friend that was riding with me lived out in the sticks, and we were almost to his house when we saw a red glow in the sky. It looked like the neighbor's fields were on fire, so we set off through the woods to investigate after about a half a mile trek through the woods all uphill. We came out into the neighbor's field and what we found was a spectacular view of the northern lights. The whole sky was red; this was a fairly rare thing to see in Ohio and we stood and watched the sky for quite some time! It was a great reminder that there was more to life than my wants and needs, and I'd have to say I experienced this same feeling every time I spent some time sober.

I'd like to say that from this point my life only got better, but that isn't my story.

12

HOPELESS

My sobriety on this particular try lasted a little over seven months. On my way home from meetings, Abigale would call and ask me to pick her up a bottle of wine or sometimes a six pack of beer, and since I found her much more friendly at bedtime after she drank, I would stop and pick up what she wanted. I was also working with only using people, but you know I thought myself different than everyone else in recovery. I mean, I heard them talk about changing people, places and things, but I was sure that was for them and not for me. I heard Kenneth's warnings that I was on the way to losing everything dear to me if I didn't buckle down and get serious about working the steps, but again life was already getting better; besides, Kenneth grew up in the city - surely, it's different for me, I live in the country. I was raised a farmer; there's no way I'm going to really let alcohol and drugs take away everything, that's not really possible anyway! I continued to do things my way, and I started feeling a little jealous about Abigale drinking while I was going to meetings and living sober. Work started to become an irritation also; everyone was drinking on the way back to the shop after we finished a job. All the while I am acting like a "teetotaler." This whole thing was starting to get a little out of hand, as these people I'm going to meetings with are trying to convince me I'm something I'm not. My sponsor who should be my friend has threatened me that if I don't do what he says I'll lose everything, and I know that's bullshit. The more I think about this whole thing, the harder it is to figure out why I was even doing it!

I was on the way home after a hard day at work and the word *teetotaler* is bouncing around inside my head, and it's really fucking pissing me off. Abigale calls and asks me to pick her up a bottle of wine, and I say, "Sure honey, I'd love to." I get off the phone and think *now you have got to be fucking kidding me!* I swing into a liquor store and buy myself a fifth of Crown Royal, and miraculously the whole world gets better. I'm no longer aggravated, everything is starting to make since again, and so what if I know what a teetotaler is. This whole thing has been a huge misunderstanding, I just have to show life that I've got this! I mean really, it's "legal" to drink, I'm not buying an eight ball of coke! Now somewhere in the dark recesses of my mind I was aware that I was skipping a few commitments that I had made; I had promised my sponsor Kenneth that I would call him before I took a drink as well as a few others who I went to meetings with. Let's be very truthful here - I wanted to get drunk, and I was pretty sure that talking to any of my program friends let alone my sponsor would possibly have a negative effect on me getting drunk so after about a second of thinking about it I decided that again I've got this! I also didn't find it necessary to call and inform my probation officer that I had decided to drink because technically speaking it was illegal for me to drink because I was on probation but really, we're splitting hairs here, it's only "illegal" for me because I got into trouble and I'm sure if I only try harder, I will be able to stay out of trouble. Even Abigale was an easy sell on the whole idea, so I mean what the hell, right? Oh, to be so young, dumb, and full of cum again! If I only knew then what I know

now...trouble is, I knew a pretty good bit then I just didn't want to believe it!

Let's recap a little, because we have learned a couple very valuable things in the last few paragraphs. One, if you want to use or drink, under no circumstances do you want to call your sponsor or your program friends, as no good will come of it. And two, if you ever hear me or anyone else in recovery using the phrase "I've got this" know that It's code for "I bet I can really fuck up my life watch this!"

Needless to say, I started drinking and using again - and again there was a peculiar phenomenon that I experienced, I turned my back on recovery and my friends in recovery, I went back to lying and trying to hide my alcoholism, and anything I had learned in recovery was so far out of my mind it might as well have been on the moon. Once every nine- or ten-days, Abigale and I would have a severe fight, and if I weren't physically abusive to her during these bad fights then I was abusive to a table or chair or kitchen cabinet; someone or something was going to be broken. On this account, I will say again that I became a fairly apt carpenter because I had to rebuild chairs and tables, cabinet doors, coffee tables, and the list just goes on! There was no distinction between human and inanimate when I was enraged. Wow, what fond memories.

There was an incident about this time that bears looking at; I really don't remember if it happened before or after I relapsed, as it's hard to wade through so many years of using memories. It often feels like I was always drinking, but there were several times that I spent sober. Anyhow, one day as I'm walking in the door coming home from work. Abigale and Judd are arguing over what, I had no idea; apparently Abigale has told Judd that no he isn't allowed to do something. I'm not three steps in the door and I hear Judd say, "You're a fat fucking cunt!"

Now I'm shocked - where could this seven-year-old have possibly heard such language? Abigale looks like she has just been slapped, so I put on my best good dad face and step into the fray, "What did you just say, young man? There will be none of that in this house!"

"Bullshit!" is Judd's reply.

"Go to your room, you are grounded," I say.

Up the stairs Judd stomps to his room where he slams the door so hard the house shakes, and then he has a meltdown. He starts breaking his toys and screaming at the top of his lungs that he hates his life, and he wishes he were dead. I'm at the bottom of the stairs looking at Abigale like *where has this kid learned to act like this?* And I can see in Abigale's eyes that she expected me to put a stop to it at once. So up the stairs I go, thinking *what the fuck did I do, I just got home from work, why do I have to handle this!* I put my game face on, and I open the door and a toy truck flies by. I'm not sure where this kid learned to act like this, but I can recognize pure artistry when I see it.

"Judd, stop breaking your toys," I say. "What happened?"

Another truck flies by; guess I'm going to have to get his attention.

He had a plastic garage shelf in his room to put toys on; it was in two pieces with round plastic legs holding the shelf up. I kick the shelf nearest me, and it exploded into pieces, and I yell, "I'll break everything in this fucking room if you don't stop!"

Another truck flies by.

Guess I'll have to be a little clearer, so I grab up a leg off of the shelf and swing it like a bat a few times and yell at Judd that he had better stop. Judd is still screaming he hates his life, and he is about to grab another toy to throw, and I step up my game a little more. "God damn it, Judd! I said stop breaking your toys!"

As I'm swinging my club, I can see Judd is following the shelf leg with his eyes. Now being a good showman myself I decide that if I throw the shelf leg surely, I'll get his attention, so I throw the shelf leg at the wall. I can see that shelf leg flying at the wall still to this day! The leg flew from my hand and hit the corner of the wall at full speed. It ricocheted of the corner and hit Judd right on the top of his head. Two things happened instantly. One, Judd quit breaking his toys and screaming, and two, blood shot out of the top of Judd's head at an alarming rate!

I grabbed a towel out of the bathroom across the hall and I held it to the top of Judd's head. With everything getting quiet, Abigale came to investigate. She walks into what looks like a murder scene!

"What have you done?" she screams.

Now I'm literally in shock, so I miss my usual smart ass come back; it would have been perfect if I had said, "I bet he doesn't call you a fat fucking cunt again." However, the truth is I couldn't say anything; I was just trying to stop the blood. All I could see is my son dying in my arms looking at me like *what happened?* After a while, I composed myself enough to talk and I told Abigale that I threw the leg at the wall and it ricocheted into Judd's head. She looked at me like I was a liar, and Judd says, "Really Mom, he didn't throw it at me." We finally had Judd lean over the tub and ran cold water over the wound until the bleeding stopped. Abigale wanted to take Judd to the hospital to get stitches, but I was sure no one would believe it was an accident. I had just recently been convicted of a domestic violence, and I was sure if we showed up at the hospital that Child Services would be getting involved, and all I could hear was the *clang* of a prison cell, so I convinced everyone that it would heal up on its own, and it did. Judd has a nice J-shaped scar on his head that is clearly visible when he wears his hair short.

All right, I'm trying to decide where to go from here. And I must admit that it's a little difficult to proceed, as there is an overwhelming feeling of shame knowing that I would rather risk my son's life than take him to the hospital because I was afraid of being accused of child abuse. The truth is at the time, I only felt my fear, so I drank the problem away. This is probably a good time to thank my creator for being there when I wasn't. I also would like to state that I am not writing for redemption nor am I writing for sympathy. I am attempting to write my memories and show that I was truly on a road through hell, and much of what I have written and will write really does bring up feelings of shame and embarrassment, remorse and even shock! Now it's obvious that I am not drinking, for if I were, I would drink all of these feelings away because at the heart of the problem I can't face, process and or handle feelings, good or bad, and my only defense was to drink them away. Now, there is hope and life did change, but we aren't there yet! I also would like to say I thanked my creator for being there when I wasn't because at the end of my story my children are still alive and part of my life. I have friends who have not made it, I have friends whose children did not survive the road through hell. So, it is with true thanks that I acknowledge that it is nothing short of a miracle that I haven't killed anyone in my family or outside of my family; it surely wasn't for my lack of trying!

Thinking about splitting Judd's wig has brought up another memory that had to be around the same time. It was a good day - that is, no fighting - but I was most definitely using and drinking we went to the grocery store as a family, and we were shopping. Abigale had Ophelia in her car seat in a shopping cart, and she was doing the actual shopping. I had Judd and Alice, and we were racing around the store just playing. Alice was in the seat of the cart and Judd was standing in the front and I being a good dad was running a few steps and jumping on the back of the cart and we were flying down the aisle having a ball. Alice wanted to ride inside of the cart like a big girl so she could see where we were going instead of where we had been. Being a good dad, I said, "No it wasn't safe." (Wow!) Alice started to have a fit, and it was putting a real damper on the fun, so I caved and let her into the front of the cart. Again, I was at no risk of getting the father of the year award. I told Alice that if she was going to ride in the cart like a big girl then she had to stay sitting down. I might as well be discussing the molecular breakdown of an atomic bomb! It was clear to me as a good father that the risks of a child in the cart could end badly, however the thirty second fit that she had seemed to defeat all good judgment in my possession. So away we went, zooming through the store laughing and annoying other shoppers with our general shenanigans. Now if you have children or half a mind for that matter, you know what's coming! As we are rounding a corner, Judd hollers stop just as Alice is standing up in the cart, and as I stop the cart, there she goes! Alice flips over the front of the cart and her head hits the floor with the sound of a cantaloupe being hit with a batt! Oh my God, I'm 90 percent sure I just killed my oldest daughter. Abigale comes running from several aisles over, having heard the whole thing, and I pick up Alice and she has a goose egg on top of her head, and she is screaming like she is still being murdered, and my feelings kick in. I'm embarrassed and ashamed, and I feel like I'm on fire from people looking at me, so I tell Abigale we are going to the car, and away we went. Now just for clarification, I will say that Alice lived. Ophelia usually gets better grades, but Alice still makes the honor roll, and to be truthful after that hit, I'm surprised she can spell her name. Now another truth of this story is that I remember it as being Ophelia that fell out of the cart; Judd and Alice have corrected my memories and Ophelia would have been too little. Oh, what a great dad I was - I can't even remember what kid I almost killed.

So, the next few years are kind of a blur, but there are some very important things that happen in this blur. I will say that I was drunk every day and had a connection with a friend who cooked meth and so I was also using regularly. It was a mixture of whatever was available, as "More was More Better." My relationship with Abigale was starting to unravel (I don't know what could have caused that). We were fighting more than not, and she would beg me to stay home and not to drink so much. I would continue to make promises that I would indeed stay home, and, of course, I'd love to slow down on my drinking and using, but I never did. At one point, Abigale threatened suicide if I didn't stay home. Looking back, I can see this as an act of desperation. One night Abigale actually took a handful of pills in front of me, and I responded by dragging her up the stairs to the bathroom and sticking my fingers down her throat until she threw up. After she threw up all that she could, I carried her to the bed, threw her in it, and went back to the bar. The next morning when I woke up, Abigale was in bed beside me. That's another proud moment in the life of an alcoholic! Our relationship seemed to be spinning out of control and my dumb ass had no idea why.

A few weeks later, I showed up to home with a liter of Crown Royal about a quarter of the way drunk with the expectation of spending an evening at home. Abigale was angry, and we began to argue (I didn't understand why -I was going to stay home), and during the argument Abigale grabbed a full bottle of Benadryl and threatened to take it. I had one of my light switch moments (took me years to realize that when this happens shit's about to get fucked up). I wasn't really angry. I was definitely not suicidal. but when she threatened to take the bottle of Benadryl, I asked her if she would like to see what suicide really looked like! I took the bottle from her, opened it, and dumped the whole bottle into my mouth and washed it down with another quarter of the Crown Royal. "There, you ignorant bitch, now you can see what suicide really looks like," I said then turned and walked out the door. I took my bottle of Crown Royal with me. If I was going to die, I was going to go happy!

They found me several hours later laying on top of Grandpa O'Malley's grave. I have a very vague memory of hearing my mother's voice and seeing the flashing lights of the squad and then nothing. Now what do I say for myself? I'm gone but obviously not finished. I died on the way to the hospital, and they revived me evidently, I had finished my liter of Crown Royal conversing with Grandpa O'Malley, and apparently I had no intention of dying with honor. Every time I died and they revived me, I was insanely violent. I tore out IVs; I bit the squad personnel. Evidently, I was a ball of laughs.

My next coherent memory was coming to after several days in a coma. There was light - it was very bright - and I could hear people talking, and as I concentrated, it began to be a clear conversation. A doctor was talking to my wife and my mother; he was explaining how high my levels of drugs and alcohol were and that I had done permanent damage to myself, and there was a real possibility that when I woke up I wouldn't even know who they were. I heard Abigale ask the doctor, "You mean he might not know who we are when he wakes up?" As I'm listening to this conversation, I want to communicate that I can hear them, and I know who they are, but all that came out of my mouth was a whispered "biiiiitch," and Abigale says with confidence that "He knows exactly who we are!" I had been in a coma for four days, and they were not sure I would recover. The doctors told me I had done permanent damage to my body, and I likely would never work again. There were several counselors that came to see me to talk about the attempted suicide, but how the hell do you explain to someone that you killed yourself and you aren't suicidal?

A nurse showed up to take out my catheter, and she was a friend I had graduated with. We can add this to the high embarrassment list, but I was still to fucked up to realize it. As she is taking out my catheter, she tells me I would be missed if I died. I tell her thanks and ask "Would you mind unstrapping my hands and feet?" She smiled and said, "No, the doctor would have to make that decision." Apparently, I was very violent. On the weekend, I saw a new doctor who was happy to unchain me. He asked me some questions like what year it was and who was president, to which I answered correctly. He then asked me what I wanted to do, and I said, "Go home," so he discharged me. Abigale and the kids showed up for a visit and I was dressed and said, "Take me home." She wasn't sure that was the right thing to do, but after some fast-talking, home we went.

For the next two weeks, all I could do was lay on the couch. The kids would take turns lying beside me; we watched cartoons, and I slept. After a couple of weeks of rest, I was myself again. I went back to work and back to drinking and using. Abigale was at her wit's end with me, and we continued to drift apart. I remember an argument in which I was complaining that I wasn't getting enough love in the bedroom, to which she replied that if I wanted more maybe I should go and find it. So, I did. Now to be honest, things get said during arguments that are not meant, but I took this one quite literally and started sleeping around. I wasn't trying to hide it either. My defense was that she told me to! I was in several short relationships. I stayed above the bar for a while with the girl who had been my first kiss. I had a short fling with one of the packing girls at work. But I always ended up back at home with Abigale and the kids. I stayed in the bar on my days off and after work. Abigale and I talked about going to a marriage counselor, but it never happened.

One day in the bar I ran into an old friend from school and her husband. Marilyn and I had known each other forever, and her husband left her in the bar to drink with me while he went and ran some errands. As we were drinking and talking, Marilyn asked me if I had any weed, and I did so we went to the back parking lot where I rolled her a joint. As we were getting high and talking - mostly she was getting high, as I still couldn't smoke much weed while drinking without becoming violently ill - she looked at me and asked me to kiss her! My heart fluttered, and my mind raced - could this be the one? Could I finally find the Walt Disney Love I've been looking for? So I kissed her to find out! There were bells and whistles, my heart nearly beat out of my chest with excitement, and that was it, just one kiss, which happened to be the one I had asked for under the bridge many years ago. We went back inside to our drinks, and when her husband came back, she went back to her marriage. I started looking for Marilyn when I was out drinking.

Abigale and I had been talking about divorce, and the decision was made over an incredible argument. Abigale had the rent and bill money in an envelope, and it was in the drawer of her computer desk, and it turned up missing. Abigale accused me of stealing the rent and bill money from her desk, and I told her I hadn't taken it. Now to be fair, I had only stolen money and lied about it a million times, but I swear this time I was telling the truth! Abigale didn't believe me, so she filed for divorce, and I agreed. I was done and had been for a long time. I was totally and wholly lost in drug addiction and alcoholism. and I was happy so long as I could drink and drug the way I wanted!

On March 17, 2005, I'm out drinking up Saint Patrick's Day I'm headed for a divorce and I'm facing my deepest darkest fear of being alone, and I run into Marilyn. We spend the evening drinking and listening to music, playing pool and maybe darts, and come closing time we are still together so I invite her to spend the night with me at the farm, and she agrees. We consummate the beginning of a relationship together. I'm sure that I show her that Disney love is real, and boy is she in for a treat! I'm going to woo her with love and tenderness (I'll be doing good to not throw up on her in a fit of drunkenness), so the next morning we wake up together, and I'm as pleased as a pig in a poke that I'm not waking up alone, and Marilyn is waking up, and we hug and kiss, and I'm sure it's real, there really is Disney Love, and I've finally found it. Now Marilyn starts talking about her Uncle Steven and her cousin Dewy, and I say that's funny I have an Uncle Steven and a cousin Dewy. She smiles at me and says, "They are the same ones, dumb ass!" Uh oh! Houston Horizon, we have a problem. I'm pretty sure that for it to be Disney Love, cousins aren't supposed to be doing it together! So, we immediately get into a long discussion about our heritage, and I'm glad to inform you we are not cousins. As it turns out, Marilyn's father's sister married my father's brother before either of us were born, so we do have family together, but we are not blood-related. That was a near miss, Disney Love is back on!

Now, I am still for the most part living in a house with Abigale and the kids, and I am also seeing Marilyn on a regular basis. One night on the way out, Abigale asks me to bring Marilyn over, and in my drunken state I say, "Maybe later." Not being overly bright, I decide later that evening to take Marilyn home with me, and we all three sat up drinking and talking together. I was karate kicked off my bar stool twice that night, which I found quite impressive because Abigale didn't know karate. Now there was one or two reasons why I didn't respond to being kicked off my stool - one, I was drunk enough not to care and just laughed it off, and two I was in a new relationship with Marilyn, and I didn't want her to see my violent side. Hell, it was probably both. Regardless, the next morning Marilyn and I woke up together in the house I shared with Abigale and the kids. Marilyn was uncomfortable and thought it crazy that we were there. When we came downstairs, we found Ophelia drawing on the white sectional with Marilyn's red lipstick; it was adorable, Ophelia was only two, and she was quite proud to show us her masterpiece. Abigale didn't find it quite so cute, but we all lived through the ordeal!

As to the white sectional, there is a bit of a back story, so let's have another little flashback! Abigale had a friend down in Athens who was moving, and she had an amazing white suede leather sectional and she sold it to Abigale, I don't remember for how much, but that's not really relevant. So, Abigale asked me to go to Athens and pick up said suede sectional, and I called her brother Ray and asked if he would like to come along. Now this is a recipe for disaster, as Ray and I like to drink and drug together! So off we go, headed to Athens, we borrowed my dad's S10 to haul the large sectional. We stopped at the beginning of this trip, and we each bought a bottle of whiskey. I'm quite sure we were using drugs also, but what exactly we were using I don't remember. Needless to say, we reached Abigale's friend's house in Athens we were completely fucked up. Abigale's friend was incredibly attractive, and I had warned Ray before we got there to be prepared, as she didn't usually wear many clothes. I don't think he believed me, but he found out for himself. Anyway, we were both drunk as lords, and we were in the basement looking at a huge sectional that we had to fit into the back of an S10. The sectional was loaded down with clothes and hangers, to which Ray just swiped the clothes off the couch against the wall and there happened to be some glass, hopefully ashtrays, but I'm not really sure. It sounded like we were tearing down the house when everything hit the wall Abigale's friend hollers down the stairs, "Is everything all right down there?" "Yes," I reply, and Ray and I can barely stand up from laughing and general drunkenness, so we carry the sectional out to the truck and being two professional movers, we proceed to load the whole thing into the bed of the little S10. We strapped it all down and headed for home. About six miles out of Athens, we run out of gas. In my drunken stupor, I forgot to get gas. Now we are on the side of the road stranded with a six mile walk to the nearest gas station. When we made it home several hours later, we were still drunk, but Abigale loved her new sectional. It was pure luck that we weren't pulled over; we looked like the Beverly Hillbillies with that sectional strapped in the back of the truck, and it was nothing less than dumb luck that a police officer didn't happen by while I waited at the side of the road for Ray to get back with gas. I don't remember how Ray got to be the one to walk for the gas; he must have drawn the short straw. Ray and I worked together, and we got into a fair amount of trouble together, we were pretty much thick as thieves. So that's how we got the sectional that precious little Ophelia is using as an art tablet with Marilyn's red lipstick.

Marilyn and I stayed with Abigale several more times before we all moved. Abigale decided to rent a house in Thornville with her parents, and I helped her pack and move what she wanted to keep. As I was disassembling her computer desk, we found an envelope with $1400 dollars in it! It was the envelope I had been accused of stealing. I told Abigale, "I told you I didn't take it. Now give me half of it." She did. I moved Abigale to Thornville with her parents, and I was proven to have not stolen the money that we blamed for our divorce, yet we didn't look back, it was over, and enough damage had been done. I will quickly say that at one point Abigale's boyfriend and Marilyn ganged up on us and told us we weren't to be talking to each other all the time - and we did talk a lot. We were friends before we were married, and we were apparently still friends after we divorced.

13

NEW HORIZONS

Now on to my new relationship with Marilyn and the overwhelming love that I was sure to show her. I was going to treat her like the princess she really was, and I would shower her with kisses and roses, and she would be a believer in Disney Love just like me. Well, that all sounds nice, but what she was really getting was a mean fucking drunk with little to no responsibility and absolutely zero ability to deal with real feelings and or emotions. I spent a very long time with Marilyn portraying myself a gentleman or so I thought. The truth was when Abigale and I got together, I was sober and there was no fighting; when I started using, we had one bad day for every thirty, but by the time we separated we had one bad day every 10 and that is where Marilyn steps in. Unfortunately, she inherited one bad day in every 10, and to this I will say that I tried to keep my hands to myself but inevitably I failed. I would like to state here again that I am trying to tell a story as honestly as memories will allow, and I'm quite sure that when Marilyn reads what I'm about to write I will probably get a smack on the head and may be dodging flying crockery, but this is my story and I'll tell it as it comes out. Marilyn and I had a bad night one in every ten, and I had accumulated several slaps and a few pushes before I finally yoked her up by the neck, slapped the shit out of her, and told her not to hit me if she didn't expect to be hit back. After that, I'd like to say that we didn't hurt each other, but the drunken truth is we were very mean to each other when we were drunk on our bad days. It obviously was a hell that we were both willing to live in because we stayed together. Now, don't get me wrong, it was only bad one out of ten nights, so I guess the other nine made up for it. Truth be told, I don't know how she was able to put up with me; I was a living nightmare, and I wasn't bashful about sharing my misery. Staying drunk and or drugged up was my top priority, and I've heard Marilyn recall living on hot dogs because I spent everything on alcohol and/or drugs.

One fine day we awoke and decided to spend the day at the truck and tractor pulls in Glenford, so in preparation we went out and bought a liter of Crown Royal and a couple twelve packs of Budweiser then went to the pulls early and started drinking before 10 a.m. We visited with friends, watched the pulls, and were having a great day. Around 1 p.m., I suggested that we go over to Abigale's house and see if Judd would like to come to the pulls with us. Marilyn thought it was a good idea. So we stopped in at Abigale's, and we were invited to sit on the porch and drink a beer with Abigale. We were talking when Alice walked over with a kitten and said, "Daddy, Daddy, look at my kitty." She set the kitten in my lap, so I picked the kitten up by the back of the neck the way a mother cat would, and the kitten curled up into a ball as it should, and as I was setting the kitten on the ground I say, "The only good cat is a dead cat" (ok I'm a drunken idiot). Alice thought I was hurting her kitten and started to scream and cry. Abigale leaps from her chair and immediately starts cussing me like a dog. "You piece of shit you are never going to change, what the fuck is the matter with you?" Well, Drunk Class 101, I can see this isn't going to turn out well, so I tell Marilyn, "Let's go." Marilyn gets up and gets into the passenger side of her car.

I get up and am trying to head for the driver's seat and Abigale is poking me in the chest with a finger and telling me I'm the biggest motherfucker on the planet. I don't even respond, I didn't hurt the kitty, and it was all just a misunderstanding; the fact that I was drunk was just well part of life, I guess. I'm trying to sidestep Abigale and get to the car and she is still poking me in the chest and cussing me like a dog when uh-oh, one of those light switch moments hits (this really isn't going to end well). I push Abigale onto the ground and standing over her I explain that if she pokes me one more fucking time, I'm going to kill her. I turn around and get into Marilyn's car and see Judd looking out a window just shaking his head, as I leave. We go back to the pulls and we stay until the Crown Royal and all the beers are gone, then we head back for the farm. Marilyn is passed out in the passenger seat, and evidently, I pass out behind the car in the gravel because that's where I am when a police officer wakes me up and with a smile informs me that I'm under arrest for felony domestic violence and with the same smile he informed me that it would be a felony this time because it was my third domestic violence with Abigale. The squad was called because they suspected that I was suffering from alcohol poisoning, and I was transported to the hospital. I refused treatment at the hospital with the hopes that I would be able to walk away, but when I left the room, I was in, a police officer rearrested and transported me to the jail. The long and the short of it, I don't remember how I got out of jail, but I did, and I was able to hire an attorney to represent me for the hearing. I continued drinking and didn't experience the same desire to stop because I had gotten into trouble again.

When I went in front of the judge, I was offered a plea bargain - if I pled guilty to a felony three domestic violence, I would be sentenced to two years in prison with the whole sentence suspended with five years of community control probation, and I would only serve ninety days in the county jail. In the judge's words he was only willing to except this plea bargain due to the non-egregious nature of the crime. I was missing another opportunity to go to prison, I accepted the plea bargain and my ninety days in the county jail was postponed until my divorce hearing was held only about a month away. So now I am officially a felon and I'm on community control, which came with all kinds of stipulations. I wasn't to be around any alcohol, or anywhere that served alcohol. I was to pay my fines and probation fees. I was to report twice a week to my probation officer. I was to be evaluated for drug and alcohol counseling. I was to complete a six-month anger management class. I'm sure I'm forgetting a few; I literally didn't follow through on any of them. As a matter of fact, when I left court after being sentenced, I went to a restaurant that was rumored to be where the judge and court officials ate, and I sat down and got drunk.

There was absolutely zero recognition that alcohol, not to mention the drugs, might be causing me a problem. In my eyes, life was just unfair, and apparently everyone was out to get me. It's more than a little possible that I was completely insane, and my life was totally out of control, but I truly couldn't see it! I was convinced that I was just suffering from bad dumb luck and surely it was to get better!

So, I continued to drink every day, and if I was going to use drugs, I stuck with ones that only lingered in your system for three days, like coke, meth, and most of the pharmaceuticals. I suppose that I can mark this as the time in my life that I pretty much quit smoking weed, and I'm also pretty sure that in my delusional thinking I was complying with my probation regulations by doing so. I quickly learned that if I showed up at lunch time, I could report by signing a book without having to see my PO, so that's what I did. A fair amount of the time, I reported drunk and or while drinking, and no one ever noticed. Again, I should have bought stock in Big Red gum; I always had a pack in my pocket, and I was sure that's all it took to cover up the smell of whiskey.

The day of my divorce hearing finally came, and I woke up still half-drunk and more than a little nervous about going to court. I asked Marilyn to go with me, as I didn't want to go alone. Who takes their girlfriend to a divorce hearing? Apparently me because that's exactly what I did. Court went pretty much as was already discussed and planned, we were only there for a few hours. After court, I saw Abigale on the sidewalk and told her I was sorry for the way things turned out. She also said she was sorry for how things had turned out. Marilyn and I left, and I started drinking immediately after court. I drank the remainder of the day and by dark Marilyn and I were in the shop at the farm. I was drinking whiskey and she was drinking beer, we were listening to music and talking. In the shop, I had all of the house furniture that Abigale didn't take with her - a buffet and several marble end tables that I had made, a marble kitchen table I had made, stereo equipment, chairs, and a few odds and ends. I was overwhelmed with emotions; I was hurt that the divorce was finalized. I was in fear that I wouldn't be seeing my children as much, and I was fairly sure that it was somebody else's fault. As the night crept on, I drank to hide and or suppress my feelings so that I could live with them. I became angry with Marilyn and in an argument I chased her away, and she left, I'm sure knowing that in my drunken state I wasn't going to improve any. After Marilyn left and I finished my bottle, I became angrier and angrier. I sat looking around me and all I saw were memories of my life with Abigale. I became so overwhelmed with emotions that all I could show was anger and rage! I destroyed everything, I grabbed a sledgehammer and I smashed everything to pieces. I destroyed the tables that I had made, I destroyed the buffet, I destroyed the chairs, and after everything was in splinters and pieces, I destroyed the stereo equipment then I smashed the speakers. The inside of the shop looked like it had been hit by a tornado! After everything was completely destroyed, I cried, it's possible that I started to cry, as I was demolishing everything. I realized that I had lost my family, and the pain and emotions were too much. There was absolutely no way I could live with this pain. Kenneth had warned me that this was going to happen, and I didn't believe it was possible. I put my face in my hands, and I cried and cried. It was all too much. I was suffering from my own doing, and I couldn't take it. I was sure I couldn't live with this pain, and I had a solution - it just came to me - I *didn't* have to live with this pain.

So, with purpose I got up off the floor, and I walked from the shop to the hay barn where I decided that I would rather die than have to feel this pain. So, I got a rope, and I tied a perfect thirteen-loop hangman's noose (I had watched many old westerns and knew a hangman's knot was to have thirteen loops); apparently, I'm just a plethora of useless information. I tied my perfect thirteen-loop noose then threw it over the top rafter in the middle of the hay-barn. I was pleased with myself, as my solution was perfect. I couldn't live with the pain I was feeling, and I wasn't going to but for a few more minutes. There was a boat trailer on one side of the barn, so I adjusted the rope so that I could stand on the boat trailer and get it around my neck. After everything was set to my satisfaction, I stood atop the boat trailer and put the rope around my neck. Now you would think this would be the time to say, "Goodbye cruel world, I've beat your injustice once and for all." That's not how this played out. I was so overwhelmed with pain, fear and selfishness that after I put the rope around my neck I stepped of the trailer - and was quite literally snapped back into reality at the end of a rope! The physical pain of hanging was a little more than I was prepared for; it was like having fire rapped around your neck and as my feet dangled in the air, I thought, "You have fucking got to be kidding me, this really hurts!" I reached above my head, grabbed the rope with both hands, and shimmied up It. I was slowly able to work lose the noose and I fell free to the floor of the barn where I proceeded to roll around in pain and agony, the likes of which I had never felt before! When I was finally able to get myself up off of the barn floor, I had officially had enough, so I went down to the house and to bed. Luckily, I hadn't paid enough attention to details - had I wetted or oiled the noose, I wouldn't be writing today.

The next few weeks, as I waited to turn myself in for my ninety days, I was forced to where turtlenecks to hide the rope burns and scars left from hanging myself. Now we can look at this for what it is. I hid what I had done because embarrassment was debilitating to me. When I experienced embarrassment in any form, I was put on feelings overload. One of the worst feelings I ever experienced is to be told that I'm talking too loudly, it causes an overwhelming feeling of embarrassment and can result in a light switch decision and we all know those don't turn out very well for me. So, the truth is I am maladjusted to dealing with my feelings and embarrassment throws me straight into overload. So, I spent several weeks living in turtlenecks, I'm sure it was seen as some kind of fashion statement!

I turned myself in on the appointed date to do my ninety days in the county jail, my longest stint behind bars so far. I showed up early in the morning only a little hung over. It was to date the soberest I ever showed up in jail! When my first visit was available, mom and dad brought Judd to see me; I knew they were coming and I was very conflicted about seeing Judd while I was in jail. When I was called for the visit, it was in a long room with little booths, and there was glass separating your visitors. The only way to communicate was through a telephone that went to the visitor through the glass. As I sat in a cubicle waiting for the visitors to be let in their side, I couldn't believe how much I was looking forward to seeing Judd and my parents. I felt like I had been severed from my family. You would have thought I had been gone for years by the anticipation I felt, but I had only been in jail for a week. When the visitors were let in, my mother sat on the other side of the glass with tears in her eyes. We picked up the phones, and she said that Judd wasn't allowed to come in and that dad had stayed outside with him. They required a legal guardian to accompany a visiting minor. I was very let down, and I teared up watching my mom cry and apologize for me not being able to see my son. I decided right then that it was probably best for him not to see me in jail. I tried to control my hurt not wanting anyone to see me with tears in my eyes; I was in jail and was pretty sure crying wasn't a good idea. That was the one and only visit from my parents, and I only saw my mom. Marilyn came and visited every week, and we wrote to each other and talked on the phone, so I settled in and did my bit. It seemed like forever. Marilyn saw to it that I had money on my books (commissary account) so I could buy cigarettes and snacks. I saw people that I knew and met people that I didn't. I watched people get released and show back up a few days later with new charges. I just shook my head in disbelief; once I got out, I wasn't ever coming back, I vowed.

I was only there for a couple weeks when a CO asked me if I would be interested in working in the kitchen. He said that if I took the job, I would be moved out of general population and placed in a much smaller cell block with more privileges, so I said sure, why not. So I'm a kitchen worker, and we cook all the meals for the entire jail, which happens to be a tri-county regional jail that held somewhere around 500+ inmates. Needless to say, my time went a lot quicker after I started working in the kitchen, and the perks were worth it -

we got ice cream, and who doesn't like ice cream? Sometimes we got pop and lots of free snacks. Before I knew it, I was being released, and Marilyn was waiting for me in the parking lot. It's incredible the difference free air tasted after being locked up for three months; I was happy to be out!

Marilyn and I rented a house in Groveport. Moving back into the city, I found new bars and new liquor stores. We rented a really nice little house right across the street from the police station in Groveport, probably not the best location for a drug addict/alcoholic to live. I don't really remember everything from the two years we lived in Groveport, so I asked Marilyn last night if I was still working full-time at Atlas when we lived there, and her reply was "You worked when you needed money, but I wouldn't call it full-time." I was also still reporting twice a week for my five years of community control. I do know that I have heard Marilyn talking about those two years we lived in Groveport, and she claims to remember living on hot dogs because all our money was spent on alcohol and drugs. There were several memories from the years that we lived in Groveport that do stand out. I was drinking whenever I was not at work and sometimes when I was. I strictly followed the bad night one out of ten schedule like it was religion. I remember those early years with Marilyn; we were not always very nice to each other, and when we were out drinking in bars we often drank until we were seeing double and acting single! We did a lot of apologizing to each other but not much effort was put toward being better to each other. There were several times the police became involved in our arguing and drinking. Marilyn and I were both charged several times with domestic violence, and we would fight the charges in court. One time I was forced to accept an attempted domestic violence as a plea bargain. I am still not quite sure how you do attempted domestic violence. I was adamant that I couldn't have another DV charge; I already had two years of prison time over my head, and I was sure that another DV would mean I would be going away for a long time.

Late one night we ran out of cigarettes, and I jumped in the car to go get more. I had been drinking all day, and some of it outside, so the police across the street were more than aware that I was drunk, and we were well acquainted with each other. I no more than backed out of the garage and put the car in drive and a squad car was behind me with its lights on. I remember one time after being arrested that I felt like I was being watched so my solution to evading any more trouble was to shave my head completely bald. It was sound, reasonable thinking that if I changed my appearance then I would not be noticed. Somehow in my drunken stupor of a solution, I missed the fact that I still lived across the street from the police and still drove the same car. Evidently drunk reasoning left something to be desired. I went in front of the Columbus court system several times, and on one occasion I was sentenced to 60 days in the workhouse, which as far as jails go is by far the worst place I have ever been.

14

THE WORKHOUSE

I have already said that I found The Workhouse in Columbus to be by far the roughest jail I have ever experienced. It was by far ten times worse than prison , which I had yet to experience. To explain, The Workhouse was an intercity jail and Columbus has a population north of 900,000 people. Needless to say, a white farm boy stood out a little! The Workhouse was so bad that if you were not willing to fight for your food, you didn't eat. So, as it was, I was sentenced to sixty days, and it's sixty days that I'm not likely to ever forget! After being processed, I was taken to a pod on the first floor; the felons were on the second floor. In this particular case, it might have been better to be with the felons, as the first floor had a tendency to flood sewage during storms. As luck would have it, it was wintertime when I went, and we didn't have any heavy storms. The pod I was taken to had twenty beds and around thirty inmates. There were eleven people sleeping on the floors. There was one empty rack, and it just so happened to be above the biggest man in the cell!

What happened next was really an accident. Had I known any better, I would have put my mattress on the floor, and my nightmare would have begun, however I didn't know any better, so I strolled up to the empty bunk set down my mattress, sheets, towel and soap. I took all the books and magazines off the top rack and handed them to my rather confused bunkie. With a smile, I said, "Hello, you don't mind if I borrow one of those books, do you?" I proceeded to place my matt on the top rack, tie my sheets in the proper jail house style, and make my bed. I climbed up with a book and laid back and started reading.

My more than dumbfounded bunkie got out of his rack and says, "You've been here before?"

I answered, "Yeah, a couple times but I'm usually upstairs with the felons."

He replied, "I can tell."

I laid back and closed my eyes and proceeded to take a nap. The truth was that I was terrified, but I had enough common sense to not show it and by taking the bunk above what turned out to be the guy that ran the pod, everyone saw something else. So, I spent my sixty days, I made friends, I told stories, I listened to stories, and I witnessed several fights the likes of the gladiator bowl! About a month into my sixty days, I overheard a cell mate telling a new guy, "We don't know who the little white guy is, but don't mess with him, he's crazy!" In that pod I saw several brutal fights, a drug addict died on the floor, and a scared cell mate who was afraid to shower, get stripped, put in the shower, and then had bars of soap thrown at him like baseballs. It was a very educational sixty days. There was normally only me and one other white guy in the pod; at one point there was three but the third only lasted a couple days. The guy wouldn't listen - he took three showers a day and walked from his rack to the shower naked. No one cared how many showers he took, but no one wanted to see him walking naked to the shower. He was asked to quit, so his last trip naked to the shower turned into a beating, and he was holding his own against three when a C.O. stepped into the pod, tased him from behind, and dragged him out the door. That was the last we saw of him. I told a lot of drinking stories, and the guys nicknamed me Paul Masson, a liquor I wasn't familiar with, and they thought it was just hilarious.

With about fifteen days left, they put another drug addict in the pod with us. He was suffering withdrawals terribly. The guys in the cell were particularly tormenting; they wrapped him up in toilet paper while he was passed out. They threw soap at him and told him to take a shower. This kind of stuff went on for a few days, until my bunkie got a good look at him. To me, the guy looked like he was already dead, he had wasted away to just skin and bones, was a perfect poster child for why not to do drugs. Once he started to come around, however, my bunkie saw something else and told everyone to stop. My bunkie sat on his rack and had tears in his eyes! I asked him if he was ok. His response was "I know him, he took care of my family after my dad died when I was little." He told us how this man had taken care of his family for years. After my bunkie told his story, everyone was nicer to the junkie; they gave him food from their commissary and made sure he kept all of his food on his trays. I learned several things from this incident. First, everyone has feelings, even the hardest gangbanger in the system. Secondly, addiction and alcoholism have no boundaries, it affects people from every walk of life, and it kills indiscriminately. Third, human compassion and empathy are not viewed as a weakness. And fourth, if you have any sense at all, you will stay out of inner-city jails.

When my sixty days were up, I said goodbye to a few guys and left. I hoped never to go to jail again. Marilyn was waiting for me in the parking lot, and we went out to celebrate by getting drunk.

A few months later, I had to go back to Nelsonville for thirty days for a probation violation. I don't remember what it was for; it could have been a good number of things. Regardless of the reason, I was sent for thirty days to the regional county jail; it was like church camp after being in The Workhouse. Nothing much happened during my thirty days other than a day or so before I got out, I scraped my knee on one of the metal bunks. It didn't seem like a big deal at the time." When I got out, Marilyn was waiting for me, and we celebrated by getting drunk.

A few days later, we went to one of our local hangouts in Groveport and we were drinking and talking. I told Marilyn that I didn't feel well, and I wanted to go home. Now this was totally out of character for me, but we went home. The next morning, Marilyn went to work, and I still wasn't feeling good, I stayed in bed. I woke up a few hours later and needed to pee, but I hurt so bad I couldn't get up. I finally had to make the decision to get up or wet the bed. I rolled out of bed onto my hands and knees and worked myself into a standing position. I made my way downstairs and used the bathroom. After the trip down the stairs, I was completely wiped out. I called Marilyn at work and asked her to come home for lunch because I was really sick, then I fell asleep on the couch. Marilyn woke me up when she came in, she took my temperature, and it was just under 105. I felt like I was dying, Marilyn gave me some Tylenol, and before she left to go back to work my temperature had come down to 103. Not long after she left for work, I started hurting again and eventually called the ambulance. I was quite sure I was sick enough to die. When the paramedics arrived, my temperature was back up to just under 105, and they found a hot spot on my side. They figured my appendix had ruptured, and I was raced to the hospital. They were calling for an emergency operation, but before we went, I had an X-ray at which point it was determined that my appendix was fine. After several tests,

I was put into a private room "in case I was contagious" I was diagnosed with cellulitis, and they started pumping me full of antibiotics and pain medications. I was in the hospital for a few days, while Marilyn was visiting , I noticed my knee was bothering me a little - the same knee I had scraped in jail. I looked at my knee, and there was a scab about as big as a quarter. I squeezed the area, and an unimaginable amount of pus leaked out. Twenty-four hours later, I walked out feeling myself again. As I headed for a drink, I realized that jail was an incredibly dirty place, and if you are there it's probably a good idea to remember that. I've seen people in jail with staph infections that leave a hole where the infection literally eats away at you. You would think that I might consider changing my lifestyle so as not to be getting arrested as much; I, however, had a better idea - I would just wash my hands more while in jail. I told you I was a thinker.

***

A few weeks have passed since I've written anything, and I must confess that I have been suffering from the human condition. It is a little difficult to remember the long road through hell and the repetition of what looks like pure ignorance is in fact quite embarrassing and I've already admitted that embarrassment is like kryptonite - if allowed, it can be debilitating. One of life's lessons I've learned is that I can't let my mind, my thoughts, and my feelings control my actions. So, I press on and I face my embarrassment. I say the Third Step Prayer: "God, I offer myself to Thee to build with me & to do with me as Thou wilt. Relieve me of the bondage of self, that I may better do Thy will. Take away my difficulties, that victory over them may bear witness to those I would help of Thy Power, Thy love & Thy way of life."

I'm fifteen days away from being four years sober; that will be the longest period of sobriety in my life, and I am secure in my program that it will be achieved, yet I find I am still affected by the human condition. The true beauty of recovery is learning to live with progress not perfection . I will be forever under the influence of my thoughts and feelings, but I am learning that I don't have to live my life being controlled by them. I very easily could find myself back on the road through hell if I choose to live by my thoughts and feelings, so being aware of that today, my friends, is progress!

So, let's look just a little closer at my embarrassment. It opened the door to self-doubt. I began to wonder why anyone would want to read about my addiction or my recovery, so I've read a few books instead of writing this one. If I face my embarrassment and my thoughts and feelings, it doesn't really matter if anyone wants to read about my life, I wanted to write it! I was willing to face my embarrassment with the hope that what I write might help someone. When I was first in recovery and spoke on drug and alcohol addiction, I would pray before I would speak that if what I said helped just one person it was worth it. I find myself saying the same prayer as I am writing this, and I find myself working on finishing something I started. I also find myself thinking of others and wanting to be of service. In all of this, I find recovery and the principles therein, I have been delivered from a hopeless state of mind and body and rocketed into a fourth dimension. This has been learned and is possible only by working a program of recovery as outlined in The Big Book, and I'll say here that it only took me twenty-eight years to read it in its entirety. If you think or know you have this disease of addiction and would like to find a way off the road through hell, you might consider reading The Big Book a little sooner than I did! I might be a little thick because I was well aware that there was a solution long before I was willing to use it. You also could say I was a fucking idiot, but I'm sure my story shows that for itself. I also would like to say here that I have a few friends that don't believe that addiction is a disease, that it is a choice; I can only hope and pray that they never have to find out. Make no mistake, addiction and alcoholism is a disease and one that when you are in it is quite devastating, I spent a great many years trying to kill myself under the very same idea that I should be able to control this because I didn't want to believe it was a disease. I've seen a great many people go to their death with the same beliefs! So, I prepare to go back to my story and to face my own embarrassment and I think this is a great place for a movie quote from *Young Guns* that seems to me to be very fitting for an alcoholic story, "There is many a slip twixt a cup and a lip!"

15

LYCANTHROPY

I'm living in Groveport with Marilyn; I was just deathly ill from what I believe was a staph infection from thirty days in jail, and I'm back to my fun-loving alcoholic self. Several things happened while we were living in Groveport. First, I lost my job at Atlas. At the time, I blamed the job loss on the fact that I had to report to probation twice a week, so I was missing work. The reality was my drinking and drugging was getting in the way of making it to work. That is the reality because the second thing that happened was I quit going to report to my probation twice a week. I'm sure my excuse for this was that probation was getting in the way of work, but the reality is that probation was getting in the way of my drinking and drugging. So now I don't have a regular job, and I still need to drink and drug. I used Marilyn's money to get what I needed. The truth is that she has made comments to the effect of, "I can't believe we lived on hot dogs for months at a time!" Being a good alcoholic, food wasn't very high on my priority list. I did eventually get another job with a company that made parts for semi-trucks like the air tanks and fuel tanks. In my alcoholic wisdom, I was now essentially on the run from the law; I was aware that eventually they were going to catch up with me. I found it acceptable to live this way for over a year and the decision to stop wasn't mine, I was eventually caught, but we aren't quite there yet.

At some point, we left Groveport and moved back to the farm. There was a full apartment in the basement and living rent free left more money for drinking and drugging, so it was a win-win for me. I got to have my kids every other weekend since the divorce, and we spent them together even though I was usually or always drinking. I'd say that my best parenting consisted of taking drugs away from Judd, who was displaying all the signs of being one of us, when he was caught with them. I would lecture him on why it was wrong and then use whatever I took from him. Marilyn became more and more concerned that I was going to be arrested and have to go to prison. I, on the other hand, just blocked it out of my mind and kept on using.

Marilyn planned a couple of vacations for us one with just her and I, and another with the kids. Both vacations were going to be on Lake Erie; we were going to Put-in-Bay, and then taking the kids to Cedar Point. Looking back, I can't tell you how we saved the money to go on two vacations, but we did. If I had to guess, Marilyn was probably hiding money from me to save up so we could go! Marilyn and I went on our little vacation first; we went up to Lake Erie to Port Clinton and took the ferry across to Put-in-Bay. We set up a campsite at the state park and started drinking at 10 AM. There were a lot of bars and restaurants on the island and hotels with bars in the swimming pools, so we drank all day. When the sun went down, we were still in town drinking, and we started arguing. Somewhere along the line, I left Marilyn at the bar and I went back to the campsite and continued drinking there. I might have passed out or blacked out, but I came to around 2 AM and evidently Marilyn and I were still angry because we set to arguing and fighting. A family camping close to us with young kids called the police! Here we go again! When the police showed up, I was polite. Marilyn was not so polite. I explained that Marilyn had had too much to drink, and I apologized for the disturbance. The police were about to leave when an officer walks up from one of the cruisers and asks, "Do you have a felony domestic violence?" I replied yes, and they quickly decided that I should be under arrest. Marilyn wanted to know why I was being arrested, at which time they decided she should be under arrest too! We were arrested the first night of our vacation and sent on the ferry back to Port Clinton to be held in the county jail to wait until Monday to see the judge.

I wake up in jail on my second day of vacation. It's a Saturday morning or afternoon. I'm sick to my stomach either from having drank too much or not having anything to drink now. I'm overwhelmed with anxiety and fear, I haven't reported to my probation officer for months, and I'm fairly sure there is a warrant out for my arrest for a probation violation. This arrest is another probation violation, so I'm fairly confident that I am screwed! I'm angry that Marilyn and I were fighting again, I spend some time trying to figure out why Marilyn and I fight so often and also why it seems to be worse after dark?

As I'm using all of my available brain power to ferret out this problem, I realize that it's really a simple answer - one or both of us obviously has a touch of lycanthropy, which easily explains why our behavior worsens after dark! Well, that wasn't so hard to figure out! In case some of you don't know, lycanthropy is the disease of being a werewolf. As asinine as it sounds, lycanthropy was a more realistic cause than alcohol; the fact that we were always under the influence when we argued never even registered in my mind. Hell, it was easier to believe that Marilyn was probably simply crazy than to think alcohol might be a factor in this equation!

I'm lying in a bunk and a few other inmates in the cell when they tell me it's time for lunch. Now I'm a little foggy, I don't really remember getting here too well when I start to absorb my surroundings. I'm lying on a real mattress with a real pillow, there is a shower in the cell that might be as nice or nicer than the one at my house; I look into the large one-person shower and there is a soap and shampoo dispenser on the wall. I followed my cell mates out to go to lunch, and I see that we are on the second tier, as I look down to the floor below, I see a basketball ball court off to one side some metal picnic tables. We walk down some metal stairs, and when we reach the ground floor, I see a TV on the wall that actually has a good picture; you can hear it too. Where the hell am I - the Hilton? The floors are all clean enough to eat off of, and as I'm looking around, I realize that the inmates are all on the clean side as well. They tell me that the jail didn't have a kitchen, that all meals are catered in from the old folk's home across the street. Again, I get another surprise, the food is more than edible it is actually recognizable! I could tell what I was eating; there were little packs of salt and pepper too! You have got to be shitting me, I thought, this is by far the fucking nicest jail I have ever seen! If you are ever on vacation at Put-in-Bay and you get arrested, boy are you in for a treat. When you get out, you can get a T-shirt that says "Put in jail at Put in Bay"; they really do have them, but I didn't buy one. I was a little put out over the whole thing really.

So, I'm in jail - a rather nice jail - waiting for Monday to see the judge, mulling over my little problem of how am I going to get tested for lycanthropy without being put into a mental asylum. I spent the next few days playing cards and getting to know my cell mates, not really enough time to start a book, everyone knows if you leave jail without finishing a book you will come back to finish it. Just a little piece of useful info I've picked up along the way.

Monday, we go to court, Marilyn and I are put in front of the judge at the same time. When asked how she pleads to a domestic violence Marilyn pleads guilty and is released with a small fine and a year off non-reporting probation. The judge asks me how I plead to a domestic violence, and I plead not guilty. I know I'm guilty as hell, but I'm not going to say so, so I'm issued a $5000 bond, and another court date is set up.

Back at the jail after court, it's time for a little more worrying about if I have a warrant in Perry County, I won't be able to pay bond, and if Marilyn is still pissed she won't pay my bond. What it boils down to is the odds are definitely against me, I'm probably screwed. So, I worried, and I paced, and I felt the world crushing in on me, I was going to prison and wouldn't get out. A C.O. called my name and told me to get my things, as I was processed out. When I walked out the door, there stood Marilyn. She had walked barefoot to a bail bondsman and posted my bail. On her walk back to the jail, she found a cheap pair of flip-flops and bought them, so she wasn't barefoot. All I knew was after all of that I really needed a drink. Marilyn didn't hide the fact that she thought that was the stupidest idea she had ever heard! We took the ferry back to Put-in-Bay and caught a cab back to our camp site; everything was still there including a cooler of beer. Ahh beer, thank God a drink! Now on this I'll make a little side note here - I hated beer. I was a whiskey drinker, Jack Daniel's Crown Royal, Makers Mark, Jim Beam ,but along the way Marilyn had figured out that I was an ass when I drank too much whiskey, so she converted me to drink beer, specifically Budweiser, like that was going to solve the problem. Evidently it didn't make any difference;

I was just as much an ass on beer as whiskey. Maybe if I didn't think she would tell me I was stupid I'd tell her my lycanthropy theory! I guess I was too scared of being put in a straitjacket, so I kept it to myself.

We finished our little vacation drinking not quite as rowdily then we went home to the farm. We kept it to ourselves that we had been arrested at Put-in-Bay. I did however point out the T-shirt to Marilyn that said "Put in jail at Put in Bay," and her only reply was, "Are you stupid or something?" So, to put a close on the whole Put-in-Bay thing, Marilyn went back and hired an attorney to represent me in a case against her. Eventually after two trips that she made by herself to appear in court, the case was dismissed with the charges dropped.

A week after the Put-in-Bay fiasco, we took Judd, Alice and Ophelia for a camping trip to Vermilion to go to Cedar Point amusement park. The purpose of the trip was family fun and breaking it to my kids that I am inevitably going to be going to prison. That's always a fun conversation to have with your children, with lots of crying and asking "Why daddy?" I handled it as best I could with a lot of hugs and shrugs. I really thought I was going to prison because the judges had it out for me! The probation officers were unreasonable, they wanted entirely too much money. Again, it couldn't have anything to do with drinking. So, we went to Cedar Point for a full day of fun, and again by 10 AM I was searching for a bar inside the park to get a drink! Eureka, I found an adult island swimming pool with a bar, and I started drinking. How does an alcoholic always find a bar you might ask? He looks! So, my kids' big day at Cedar Point involved a lot of trying to get dad to leave the bar long enough to have some fun with them. See, I told you I was in no jeopardy of getting the father of the year award. The day was spent, however, at an amusement park.

On the way back to our campsite to cook our dinner with hot dogs and s'mores, I picked up a bottle and some beers. I had a little anxiety about going back to the campsite, dark was quickly approaching, and how was I going to keep this lycanthropy thing under control? My last memories of the night consisted of my family chasing after me. Somehow, I had come up with the idea that if I jumped a boat on Lake Erie and headed for Canada, I could strike it out on my own and beat this whole prison rap! See I told you I'm a thinker! I remember my daughters crying and Judd telling me I was the biggest asshole he had ever seen! I'm not sure how they got me off of the lake and back to the campsite (maybe a silver bullet), but the next morning I woke up in my tent and the kids were in their tent. The day dawned with me stretching, looking around and opening a beer.

About four more months passed before I was finally picked up and taken in front of the judge for a third probation violation. I spent those months working seeing my kids every other weekend, helping out around the farm when I wasn't too drunk to be of any use and of course drinking at every possible opportunity. My father was very sick with Parkinson's, so I tried to help him with little projects when he asks, he might want to change a breaker, or an outlet switch; he couldn't use his hands anymore. I often find myself being his hands with him standing over my shoulder directing me on how he wants it done. For the most part, I am able to do this for him out of respect and love, even with as little as I know about either. I mentioned helping dad because it was the last time that I got to spend with him, yet all I thought about was another drink. The day they finally caught me I had went into town at eight a.m. when the bar opened, had a few drinks, then went back at the house. Marilyn was at work, and mom asked me if I would take their little dog Shadow down to New

Lex to be groomed? I said sure. I was walking out the door with Shadow on a leash when a sheriff's car came down the driveway. I did an about-face, handed mom the leash, and headed for the basement. I was in my apartment in the basement, contemplating running out the back door heading across the pasture for some cover to hide in. I had given the police the slip more than a few times and thought I could do it again. Mom hollers down the stairs, "Ray, there are a couple gentlemen that would like to talk to you!" Damn that woman and her damnable honesty, all she had to say is, "Ray isn't here" not "Just a minute, he is in the basement." Man, the game here is to allude the police, not invite them in!

An officer calls down the stairs, "Ray, are you coming up?"

Yes, goddamn it, I'm coming up! So, my decision was made not to run, it was over, I was headed to prison, and I was about to walk myself right into the hands of the police.

Dad was talking to the officers when I came upstairs. I asked if we could go out on the porch so I could smoke a cigarette and call Marilyn at work. They said I could if I wasn't going to run. So, they knew I had rabbit in me! I promised not to run, called Marilyn, told her they were here to take me. We talked for about ten minutes while I smoked one after the other. Marilyn promised to have money put on my books so I could buy cigarettes. She also promised to get my kids every other weekend and bring them to the farm so I could call and talk to them. Finally, an officer said, "We need to go." I told Marilyn that I loved her and I hoped to see her soon. I hung up, an officer came over, leaned in close, and whispered that they were not going to put handcuffs on me in front of my father. I looked over, and there were visible tears in his eyes. I told the officer thank you. I hugged my mom and dad and told them

I was sorry. I walked with the officers to the cruiser, got in the backseat. At the end of the driveway they got me out and put the cuffs on. Again, I thanked them, they informed me that it was out of respect for my father that made them do it. I was transported to the regional jail in Nelsonville to await a probation hearing. My attorney was contacted to represent me, but I held little hope of not being sent to prison.

Several weeks passed before I finally made it in front of the judge, and my fears were becoming a reality. My probation was revoked, and I was sentenced to a full two years in prison. I was sent back to Nelsonville to await transfer to Corrections Receptions Center (C.R.C.), basically prison intake where they decide where you will be sent to serve your sentence. I was several months in Nelsonville with nothing to do but wait. During this time, I took an extremely hard look at myself and the bedlam I had made of my life. During a moment of clarity, I had to admit to myself that it was more likely that my problems were being caused by alcohol and drugs than from lycanthropy. I'm not sure if I came by this revelation by means of being honest with myself about my drinking and drugging or if it was the simple fact that I only had maybe three hairs on my chest, which by de facto, had to rule out lycanthropy! This was a powerful revelation to me however I came by it, and I was very near the truth but only touching on the very edge of it. It's quite an amazing thing how jail seems to help so many find a moment of clarity and a fever for religion. I found the latter a little detestable; I thought if they took Jesus home with them, they probably wouldn't be back! In all reality, what I did was really no different; I just didn't claim to find religion in jail. I did, however, make a commitment to myself and my family that I understood that alcohol had contributed to my incarceration, and that I was never going to drink or do drugs again! I spent many an hour in contemplation about every stupid thing I had done in recent years while drinking and drugging. I even sent Marilyn a letter listing all of my realized transgressions. Actually, I was really no different than the inmates that threw themselves into religion; I was just as forcefully throwing myself into what I perceived as reality. I was very sincere and adamant that I would never drink and drug again. I, however, had decided that I wanted nothing to do whatsoever with twelve-step recovery or religion. I was convinced that what I needed was to still myself and concentrate on what is really important in life like Love and Family, Future and Friends. It was more than clear to me that my behavior on alcohol and drugs had landed me here. Now that I knew the problem surely, I could face it and shape it and find a way to put it away like all childish things and grow up. Again, I was right on the edge of it, but alcoholism and addiction are so allusive, cunning, baffling, and powerful. I thought I finally had found the solution, and it was exactly what Nancy Reagan had been saying all along "Just Say No!"

For the next two years of my life, I lived by my commitment to stay sober and drug free. Now, you might say to yourself, "But you were in prison!" Every day I saw people drunk or high I had many offers to use or drink, and I turned them all down I became stronger (so I thought) every time. Jail is such a fun place, let's talk about it for a minute. If I were to be asked what the most important thing is to have in jail (and this can roll over to prison as well), it wouldn't be the Bible, it wouldn't be paper and envelopes (pre-stamped preferably), it wouldn't even be soap and shampoo or even toothpaste and toothbrush, though all of these things do make life more bearable. If I had to pick the number one most important thing to have in jail or prison it would be shower shoes. If you shower in a community shower barefoot, your feet are going to start to rot within a few weeks, and athletes foot medication is expensive on commissary, and you would rather spend your money on food than medicine. Oh, and shower shoes double very nicely as a toilet seat once you learn to balance your ass on them! There is also a plethora of other things to learn if you are going to habitually visit jails or prison, such as "mind your own business" and "snitches get stitches." Alas, I wouldn't want to ruin all the fun of learning these things for you more adventurous types. So here I will interject maybe the one and only opinion I give in this book, if you don't want to find out why shower shoes are my number one pick, don't go to fucking jail or prison! Unfortunately for other alcoholics and addicts that are of the similar type that I am, this won't be an option! Jail and prison are a way of life and you will either learn to live by their rules or you will be in misery and very likely pain for your entire stay. I was a little over two more months in Nelsonville before I shipped out for C.R.C. I spent Thanksgiving and Christmas Eve in Nelsonville. On Christmas Eve, a religious organization came in and handed out presents. I know right, presents in jail! There are good people in jail who have done bad things, there are bad people in jail that could do good things. What it boils down to is there are people in jail.

There are also religious organizations that believe loving all people and showing kindness is unto Godliness. Well one of these groups came in and passed out presents, I walked through the line and was handed a little bag with a Christmas scene on it, I returned to my rack to sit down and see what I had been given. I dumped out the contents on my rack and there were a few pieces of candy, a small pamphlet with religious scriptures, and a pair of the nicest thickest black socks I have ever seen! I couldn't believe it, and you may not understand, the first thing they do when you go to jail is, they take your clothes, socks, underwear, everything, and you are given county-issued clothes; they are usually not much better than rags. I hadn't seen a pair of socks in months that you couldn't read the morning paper through. I put my new socks on and felt like I was in heaven. I threw away the religious pamphlet without really looking at it, but man they got me with the socks. I was quite overwhelmed, I'll tell you the truth, I can tear up to this day remembering those socks and how it felt to be treated with human dignity when I felt I deserved none. I sat with my new socks on with tears in my eyes, overwhelmed that this group of religious people spent their Christmas Eve in the gutter handing out presents to inmates it touches my heart to this very day. I have to say I am also to this day a little crazy about socks. I refuse to wear any that are getting thin, I throw them away. My wife thinks I'm crazy because I want new socks every few months; well the truth is I might be batshit crazy, but I can promise you this, I'm going to be batshit crazy with a fucking good pair of socks on my feet. The next morning - December 25, 2008 - I got up, smiled at my new socks, and went for my breakfast. Shortly after breakfast, a C.O. informed me to pack up, as I was being transferred to C.R.C. today. You have got to be kidding me right, it's not bad enough that I'm going to prison but on Christmas Day, come on! Sure enough, ours was the only county that transferred prisoners on Christmas Day, and my day only got better from there.

16

THE BIG HOUSE

There were five or six of us that got into a van and were taken to Orient Ohio to C.R.C. When we arrived, we were taken into a room where they took our commissary, our cigarettes, and our clothes – *all* of our clothes. And yes, they took my new black socks. I never saw them again. They stood us shoulder to shoulder, made us bend over and spread our ass cheeks while they shined a flashlight on it. You might think this a little excessive, but I have to say there was an incredible amount of contraband in prison, anything from cell phones to syringes that came in with dope in cigar tubes. I'll make no mistake in saying that the fact in C.R.C. almost all contraband was likely in someone's ass made my decision to stay drug free a little easier! C.R.C. is the equivalent to solitary confinement; you are in a private cell, let out for breakfast, lunch, one hour of rec, and once every other day to take a shower. The hardest thing to get used to was mealtime; they took your whole pod (somewhere around one hundred men), and you went through the line to get a tray. Then you line up, everyone standing until everyone was ready to sit. Everyone sat at the same time, then you only had three minutes to eat. The food was usually scalding hot. I saw several of the inmates dump their drink onto the hot food then shovel it into their mouths. I finally caught on and was able to finish a meal in the required three minutes. I'm pretty sure they were not overly concerned whether I had a full tummy or not; thankfully I wasn't stupid enough to ask! I was tested for any and all communicable diseases. I was there for about three weeks and from there I was transferred to Noble Correctional facility, the actual prison.

At Noble I was given a number and told I was no longer Ray Vance, I was inmate 596353 when asked by any C.O. who I was, my response was to be "Inmate 596353." When it came time to leave, if I didn't identify myself as "Inmate 596353," I wouldn't be let out. So, it was here that my stay in prison started in earnest, I became Inmate 596353.

As I have stated earlier, for whatever reason I have always excelled in the worst places, and prison evidently was no exception. My second week there, a C.O. told me to get my shit I was moving! I wasn't sure what was happening, but I got my stuff he told me to report to the Honor Dorm. The Honor Dorm was for exemplary inmates, now how I could have stood out? I have no idea, and I didn't ask. There was no curfew, I was able to get my own TV and lay in bed and watch what I wanted. I was given a job in the officers dining room where we had our own kitchen with access to real eggs, hamburger, sausage, bacon, lettuce, tomatoes, and potatoes. I rarely ever saw the inside of the inmate dining room again. We ate like kings; I was able to walk four to six miles a day on the athletic track; sometimes I ran a mile or two. I never did see those new black socks again, but this Honor Dorm thing pretty much made up for it.

I had virtually unlimited access to the library, and I found the best way to get out of being trapped in prison was to lose myself in a book, and that is exactly what I did - I read and I read. I spent 75% of 18 months reading and the other 25% was divided between eating, sleeping, working, exercising, and calling or writing home. I found that I could lose whole days with my head in a book. I could read and experience what I read as if I were watching a movie! I read mysteries, science fiction, fiction, spy novels, murder suspense, I read The Bible cover to cover, and I read The Quran cover to cover. I started a love affair with books, and it is with me still. I read David Eddings, Patricia Cornwell, Vince Flynn, Tom Clancy, J.K. Rowling, Stephanie Meyer, Steven King, Ann Rice, Dan Brown, Robert Jordan, and I'm sure others as well. They were all my salvation, They transported me out of prison every day. Because of them, I found myself living contently in prison. With their books I experienced life, I traveled the planet and maybe a few other planets as well. I found a door that led to anywhere, and I opened it! I spent eighteen months reading, and I am still reading today. When things get a little crazy, I can detach with a book; reading quite literally has changed my life!

The eighteen months that I spent in Noble prison was the best eighteen months of my life! I don't even know how to defend that statement other than to say I had nothing to worry about. I quite literally did what I wanted and learned a great deal. I didn't drink or use drugs, all of my needs were met, I was at total peace with myself! Come January 2010, I was offered the chance to participate in an intense six-month cognitive behavioral treatment; if I accepted, I would have one day taken off of my sentence for every month I participated. So, in a nutshell I'd get out six days early. Well hell, that's a no-brainer, so I spent my last six months in what I consider my fourth treatment program. Now, before we talk about the one event that ruined the best eighteen months of my life (Wow, that sentence could lead to a lot of places.), let's back track a little. Let me clarify that even though my cellmate was definitely homosexual and often had late night visitors, to the point that after waking up to their late night rendezvous, I asked to be woke up before any more such encounters so I could excuse myself from the area. I couldn't quite grasp the whole idea that "It's not gay if you're in prison concept." Anyhow, I was saying, after I found the library, I found a book on Hebrew and using the Hebrew alphabet, I designed a tattoo for myself. It was supposed to say, "Strong Drink Leads to Ignorance and Poverty," and I put a symbol above it. I paid a man $25 to have it tattooed on both forearms. Now evidently, I didn't read enough of the Hebrew lessons to realize that Hebrew is written from the right to the left and I wrote the script from left to right so literally only God knows what my tattoo really says, but I know what it means to me. My whole intention was that I was sure I wouldn't drink again, but if I did reach for a drink with either hand, I would see my tattoos and remember that Strong Drink Leads to Ignorance and Poverty. Again, I told you all I'm a thinker!

So on to the one bad event that happened in prison. We have already established that I didn't get buggered in the shower by six burly inmates. Truthfully, that would have been better than what was coming! That says a lot. I had already been through two riots; one was contained in the chow hall but was still off the hook. The S.R.T.s had to break it up, and that's done with bean bag guns and pepper spray. The second riot was really off the hook; it spread out over the whole camp, and there were several rather bad injuries. The whole prison was confined to bunks for almost a week after the S.R.T.s finally got it under control. We knew it was coming, and a few of us stayed inside while the whole thing went down. I read through it like nothing was happening. All right to the one bad thing - don't be pushy, I really don't like to think about it much. Let's set the stage a little. It was the first week of February, we had a little over six inches of snow on the ground, and there were inmates using cardboard boxes for sleds, and yes, they were sledding down a hill in prison. They had all kinds of inmates cheering them on. There was a rather large cheer section that was almost exactly like "The Longest Yard" with Adam Sandler. Oh my god, I don't know if I've ever laughed harder watching these hardened criminals running up the hill to slide down again with the abandon of six-year-olds! Eventually the C.O.s came and broke it up; evidently you aren't allowed to have too much fun in prison. A C.O. found me and said, "You need to call home."

I called home, and mom answered the phone. She told me they were taking dad to the hospital, and that it didn't look good at all. We talked for a few minutes more. I walked away with tears running down my cheeks, I was stopped by several inmates and asked if I was ok. My reply was, "No, my dad is dying." I was offered truly heartfelt apologies of "Sorry to hear that."

The next few days were like being trapped in quicksand. I knew what was coming, but I wanted to fight against it. I wanted to convince myself that he was going to get better. I had only talked to dad once while I had been gone, and it was only for about ten seconds. I think it hurt him too much to think about where I was! I did everything I could not to face the fact that dad was likely going to die while I was in prison. When I tried to ferret out the problem, I was overwhelmed with guilt and shame for being in prison while my family went through this. When I thought about my dad, I remembered being a little boy and waiting for headlights to shine on my wall so I could get up and see my dad. I remembered that everything I knew about love and being a good person came from my dad. I had to face the fact that it wasn't just my dad dying, it was my best friend and he had been for my whole life! Great, more guilt and shame that I had to face because before I came to prison.

I was always drunk or high and I wasn't really concerned with spending time with my dad. I was concerned with getting another drink! When it became too much, and I was on the brink of going insane, I would open a book and disappear into a story. I found myself on the brink a lot, every thought took me back to dad and prison. I stayed in touch with Marilyn and asked every night, "Is he getting better?" Marilyn was living at the farm and helping mom with dad and I was in prison because I was a stupid fucking drunk! On the brink, everything took me back to dad and back to prison! This went on for almost a week.

On February 12, 2010, a C.O. came and found me and said, "Come with me." I followed, though I was in quicksand, on the brink of terror! We went into an office, and he pointed at the phone and said, "Call your mom's cell phone." I called and mom answered; she was at the hospital, she said, "He is still alive but just barely, he isn't going to make it!" She asked me what I wanted to do. I didn't understand; I'm in prison, what can I do? She said that I could come to the funeral or I could come now to the bed side to see him before he died. I didn't find out until later that she had paid the prison for this service. I said I want to come now. The C.O. took me to another room and told me to wait. It seemed like forever, but two C.O.s came in and said they were taking me to Columbus to the hospital; they explained that I was only allowed to see my dad that I couldn't talk to anyone else or even see them. They asked me if I agreed to these rules, and I said I did. I was then put in handcuffs and shackles with a chain around my waist, hands, and feet, connected by another chain that went through the chain around my waist. I was loaded into a van, and away we went. It was the first time I had seen roads or been in a vehicle in more than a year. I barley even noticed that the whole world was blanketed in snow six to eight inches deep. I was in quicksand; I couldn't believe what was happening. Getting to the hospital seemed like it took forever.

Finally, we made it I was taken out of the van and led to an elevator, up we went, the doors opened, as I stepped out of the elevator, I saw my family at the end of a hall, some of them were around a corner. I thought, "Great, I'm shackled and cuffed." I could only move my feet three inches at a time, so it took an incredible amount of time to walk down the hall to the outside of my dad's room. A nurse was outside the door, and she asked me if I was aware of what was going on, and I said yes. The C.O.s and I walked into the room. One of the C.O.s took my right hand out of the cuff and attached the cuffs and my left hand to the rail of the bed. I looked at my dad, and his eyes were closed, his mouth was slightly open; he looked like a mummy he was so thin. A C.O. said, "You can talk to him." I reached out my hand and laid it on his arm and I knew instantly that he was dead. I asked a C.O. to please get the nurse for me, and he did. I asked the nurse if he was dead. She immediately started apologizing, she said she thought I knew. I said to the C.O.'s, "Let's go, I can talk to him anywhere now." They stood and looked at me, one of the C.O.s said to the other, "Go and get his mother." They brought mom into the room, and we held each other, I told her I was sorry. Mom told me she was sorry that I didn't make it in time; dad had died 30 minutes before I got there. I hugged mom again and told her I loved her, and said goodbye. We went back out into the hallway, and as I was shuffling down the hall, I could see my family peeking around a corner to see me. I felt like I was about an inch tall shackled and cuffed; they could have put me on a dolly and strapped a leather mask across my mouth, and I wouldn't have felt any more like a criminal than I did at that moment! At least I wasn't in orange and wearing shower shoes.

We got back in the van and headed back for the prison. The C.O.s stopped at a Tim Horton's and got coffee and donuts; I guess that made sense being closely related to police and all. On the ride back, I talked to dad, I told him I was sorry that I didn't make it in time, I was sorry for being in prison, and that I wasn't going to drink anymore. I guess it's no different lying to the dead than the living. I really thought I would never drink again, and all of this was why!

My last five months in prison flew by. I went to treatment during the day, I read late into the night. Sometime during my reading adventure, I had read about a book called "The Zohar"; I'm pretty sure I read about it in a Dan Brown novel, one of his Robert Langdon series. "The Zohar" is basically a mystical study of the Torah and the principle writings of Kabbala. I was deeply interested; the book is actually twenty-three volumes; it's written in Hebrew and translated into English. So, I asked Marilyn and Mom if I could have it as a coming home present. Ok, who asks for a present for getting out of prison? I told you batshit crazy! As the date was coming closer to me getting released, I had decided to give my TV and my books to Adam, a friend I had made while I was there. Adam and I still talk every few months just to see how we are each doing. Who goes to prison and makes friends? Apparently I do! One more small note on prison, I was only there for about two months when Ohio decided to take all tobacco out of the prison system (that might have been the cause of the second riot). That was fun.

17

LUMBERJACK

On July 3, 2010, I walked out of prison, and Marilyn was waiting in the parking lot with a pair of my jeans and a shirt. You leave prison in prison-issue sweats, and I wanted my own clothes to wear. We went straight to my hometown Fourth of July parade and celebration. All of my family, neighbors, and lots of my friends were there. My kids were there; my daughters hugged me so long and hard that I thought I would break into tears. I felt enormously ashamed and embarrassed, as I felt like everyone was looking at me. I wanted to be able to lay down on my rack and read. I didn't want to deal with all the feelings and emotions that I was experiencing. I wanted to lose myself in a book so it would all go away. However, I stood tall, shook hands, and accepted all of the welcome homes that I was given. I was like a statue; I was afraid to move, I really felt everyone was watching me. I made it through the parade, and we went down to the park for the customary chicken dinner. As we ate, I was bombarded with more welcome homes and handshakes. I spent the day with my family, and when we went home, I was surprised to find "The Zohar" waiting for me! I was overly excited to start reading it, yet that evening we went back to the park for the town fireworks. I noticed everyone had a beer to drink, but I stood firm I wasn't going to drink again.

Marilyn surprised me with concert tickets in late August to go see Rush. I had never been to a concert, and it sounded like fun to me. I spent time with my kids and started slowly feeling better about being home. The feelings of panic and embarrassment seemed to be fading. I spent the next month and a half spending time with my family, working around the farm, and reading the Zohar. I had grown so used to reading that I couldn't put it down.

When I was released from prison, I was put on parole for three years. I was less than pleased about this. When my probation was revoked, and I was sentenced to my full two-year sentence, I felt I had done the full punishment for my crimes and to further force me on parole was double jeopardy. I had to live with it, though, and truthfully my feelings probably stemmed from another phenomenon that befuddles many an inmate. For reasons yet obscure, many inmates turn into jailhouse lawyers and believe they have a grasp on the inner workings of the law. I must have been mildly thus affected because I wasn't bashful about telling my parole officer that I thought it was bullshit that I was being forced to see him. I was also slightly pissed that they expected $25 every visit!

The week of the concert was rapidly approaching, and I was getting excited. Marilyn had reserved a room in a new hotel, and we were going to make a weekend getaway out of the whole thing. As I have already said, I had never been to a concert before, but that isn't exactly accurate. I had for several years gone to The Grateful Dead weekend at Legend Valley, but I had never bought tickets to the show; a group of us just went to the parking lot and got totally inebriated for the weekend. The day finally came, and we headed for the hotel, around 3 PM. We were planning on spending the late afternoon at The Zucchini Festival on the outskirts of Columbus. We checked in the hotel, and our room was really nice. As I was looking around the room, I noticed a coupon on the end table for three free drinks at the bar. Wow, this is really a nice hotel! I showed the coupon to Marilyn and commented that this hotel had gone all out for Its grand opening. Now let's recap - at that point I have been sober for about twenty-three months, and since I had been released, I was angry about being on parole, I was mortally ashamed of having been in prison when my dad died, I was also very stressed out over not having a job yet, and lastly, I was stressed out over my son Judd who had been getting into trouble at his mother's house and at school for using drugs and drinking. So as a reader I bet you have enough intuition to glean what's fixin' to happen! Well, I didn't. Marilyn and I went to the Zucchini Festival and spent the afternoon eating and walking around. There was a racetrack about three quarters of a mile away, so we walked over and watched some of the races. All this time, my thoughts kept returning to three free drinks at the bar; that stupid coupon was stuck in my head, and it might as well have been in my hand. As it was getting dark, we started to head back to the main festival grounds. There was a stage, a band was setting up, we asked around who was setting up to play? We were told Blue Öyster Cult. Marilyn was thrilled, as she is a real music enthusiast and has been to all kinds of concerts. Me, I was still thinking about three free drinks at the bar! I asked Marilyn what songs they sang; she said "You know, 'Don't Fear the Reaper' and 'Godzilla'!" Oh yeah, everyone knows those songs. So, I ask Marilyn if she thought Blue Öyster Cult would be more fun if we had a beer?

Marilyn just looked at me and said, "You don't drink."

"I know but look around everyone is drinking, and really what is a couple beers going to hurt?"

"Are you sure?"

"Yeah, it's ok, and besides we have that coupon for three free drinks at the bar!"

We had a few beers and listened to Blue Öyster Cult, and it was fun. But from my first drink, I felt whole again. I stopped worrying about everything else and enjoyed the drink. It made me feel warmer and safer, like I was being held tight in a hug. I couldn't for the life of me figure why I had ever stopped drinking. I'm not hurting anyone! A blanket was being pulled slowly over my memory, how could there be anything wrong with this? Why I FEEL CAPITAL!!!

After the mini concert, I insisted that we pick up some beers to take back to the hotel. When we got back to the hotel, I insisted that we use the coupon, and when we ran out of beers in the room, I happily suggested that we go out to a bar! At this point, Marilyn put her foot down, and the funniest thing happened, I got a touch of the lycanthropy back! We had quite an argument and ended up going to bed angry. The next day, we went out to the Brewery District and ate before the concert, and I ordered drinks. We got to the concert early, and I ordered more drinks. Rush was incredible, life was incredible. How could I have ever quit drinking; what kind of absurdity could have made me think this wasn't good? I no longer felt ashamed for being in prison when my dad died. Hell, we are all going to die. It was just a string of bad luck, an unfortunate set of coincidences. If you look at it in the right light it could have happened to anyone! Yep, you guessed it batshit crazy! So now, I was wholly restored to myself.

I was putting a good effort into finding a job, but I kept striking out. I attributed this to being a felon; surely smelling like alcohol wasn't a factor. I mean, I was chewing Big Red so no one could smell the alcohol. I spent a fair amount of time visiting Mort and his family. I usually showed up with a bottle, so it's no surprise that Mort's wife wasn't very happy when I showed up. Mort had a 250 Suzuki quad racer, and I talked him into selling it to me. I was sure that I just wasn't doing enough fun things to be happy, and the four-wheeler was going to fix it. I promised Mort I would pay him for the four-wheeler as soon as I got back to work. I had the quad for a couple months and then sold it so I could have drinking money.

I was doing what I believed was the best I could; I was however drinking at every opportunity. I really liked having a couple Crown and Cokes to start the day at 8 AM when the bar opened; that also quite often turned into a longer stay at the bar than I had intended! So, things started to get a little hectic. Abigale called and said she couldn't handle Judd; he had already been to several treatment centers for addiction and behavioral problems. I put on my thinking cap and tried to solve the problem. We already know that when I start thinking, shit is about to get fucked up! My solution to the problem was Judd obviously needs his dad, so we decided that I should get full custody of Judd. Now because I'm a thinker and quick on my feet I negotiated that if I had Judd and Abigale had the girls that future and past child support should be waived, and we should share the responsibility of the children. Told you I was a thinker. Well, the Judge bought it, and Judd moved to the farm with mom, Marilyn, and me. I fixed up a room upstairs for Judd and had him enrolled at Sheridan High School.

As you can probably imagine, it didn't take to long for things to get out of hand. We tried very hard to make it look like everything was ok, but the truth is the kettle was about to boil over. We decided to rebuild the garage that I had a few years earlier dropped a pine tree on, so we had a project. We also did a fairly large landscaping project at the same time. Uh oh, I feel a flashback coming on...

As the fog of memory clears, I can remember the smell of pine sap and Crown Royal. It all started on fine spring morning. Marilyn and I are staying at the farm alone. Mom and Dad are on what would end up being their last trip to California together. I wake up to the birds chirping and the early morning dew settled over the lawn. Truth is, I think I needed to piss! I'm fairly sure I'm still half-drunk from the night before. Not wanting to ruin such a fine beginning, I find myself standing at the end of the porch with a cigarette in one hand and a freshly opened bottle of Crown Royal in the other. I'm pissing off of the side of the porch, and it looks like it's going to be a beautiful day! As a matter of fact, I feel CAPITAL, JUST FUCKING CAPITAL! As I'm focusing on my surroundings, I look across the driveway in front of the garage. I see quite a mess of pine needles and pinecones everywhere. God damn pine needles are fixing to ruin my day, I thought. I walk out into the driveway and look up into the pine tree that is just off the corner of the garage. It's one hundred and fifty feet to the top; two people can barely touch hands around the trunk. I remember dad saying numerous times that he wished that tree wasn't there! And it hits me, an aha moment, I know what I'm going to do today! I'm going to be a lumberjack and take down this tree, what could possibly go wrong? I take another pull from my bottle and head back inside to tell Marilyn the good news. Now Marilyn thinks I might just be overreacting about the pine needles, but she obviously senses my excitement. I get dressed in jeans, my Red Wing work boots, and a red flannel shirt. If I'm going to be a lumberjack, I might as well look the part. I spend the next few hours drinking and gathering my tools together. Chainsaw, check. Chains to fasten to the tree, check. A tractor to fasten to the chains, check. This is coming together nicely; look out pine tree, your number is up. I climb up the tree, which is a little harder than I expected, dragging a chain, couldn't be the Crown Royal, as that makes everything better. I finally get the chain fastened where I want it.

Then I run into my first real problem – I don't have enough chain to clear the distance from the tree to the tractor. The proper solution would be to go buy more chains. Now hold on here, I'm fairly sure that I will need more alcohol before the day is out and spending money on chains doesn't seem very prudent when it could be spent on alcohol! So, while drinking my bottle I set myself to ferreting out this problem. I go back to the shop to look for more chains that I know aren't there when I stumbled across a goodly sized coil of rope. Well, everyone knows that old rope was made of hemp and is very durable, so hell, problem solved. Now the fact that this rope was likely older than I was made no never mind to me. So, I tied the rope to the chain and to the drawbar on the tractor, and I was ready to go! I went back to the tree, fired up the chainsaw and cut a perfect wedge out of the trunk aiming the tree the direction I wanted it to fall, away from the house and garage. Now I pull the tractor up giving a little tension on the tree for some extra insurance that it falls where I want it. Now this whole time Marilyn has repeatedly asked me if I'm sure I know what I'm doing.

"Of course, babe, look at me, I look like a lumberjack!" I said. "Don't you trust me?"

Everything was set just like I wanted it, so I take another pull from my bottle and head in to make the final cut. Now, let me remind you this tree is about 150 feet tall, it has a goodly amount of tension on it, bowing it out toward the open yard. I step in and start my final cut; this is going to be epic. In my head I'm singing, "I'm a lumberjack, now baby, I'm going to cut you down to size!"

The tree started to creek and pop, almost there, I'm still cutting when the tree snaps one last time, the rope breaks, and the tree vaults ten feet straight up into the air, does a perfect pirouette, and falls flat on the garage roof! This all happens in the blink of an eye; I'm still standing there with a running chainsaw and the tree trunk is about six feet over my head and I mean directly over my head. If the garage would have collapsed, I would have been pinned under the tree. How I didn't kill myself with some of the dumb shit I did I'll never know. Mom must be right - I have something here to do and that's why I'm still alive today. When I pulled the tree off of the garage, it leveled the whole structure. It was, however, covered by the insurance, so we built a new one.

All right, enough of the flashback. It was really all subterfuge if I stayed busy and useful; I thought I could stay drunk or high, and it wouldn't be noticed. The garage turned out really nice; it was a family effort my sisters' husband and kids and several of dad's friends all helped. The garage was attached to the house. Mom could park in the garage and walk on to a side porch to an interior door. Everyone was happy when it was finished. The landscaping project was just Judd and me; there were a couple places in the yard that flooded and a center island that was inside of a driveway circle that needed some major work. We moved around a hundred tons of topsoil and filled in all of the low areas and then reseeded the yard. Again, everyone was happy when we were done.

Now, I mentioned that doing these projects was a form of subterfuge and it was, but it was also a personal form of subterfuge. I was still unemployed, and I felt defeated and was embarrassed that I hadn't found a job. I was also under an enormous amount of stress trying to be a full-time dad to Judd. I was trying to hide my drinking and using from others and myself. It seemed like the more I did and could accomplish the more this helped me to feel some sense of being normal and productive. Even though I was completely miserable suffering a self-made depression. I was a master at deflection, justification and denial. Marilyn and I drank almost every night and our past scheduled one bad night of every ten was quickly becoming our routine. On one of our bad nights while we were fighting and arguing, my light switch flipped, and I decided that she must be the problem (it couldn't be my drinking) so I told her it was over and that she needed to leave. So that added to my misery and depression, so how do I cope? I drank more. Seems logical doesn't it?

I started painting one of the tractors, a John Deere 4430. I spent every night in the shop working on the tractor and drinking. I was doing the best I could at being a dad, and for a while when I caught Judd with drugs, I would take them, I don't remember how when or where. I started using with Judd. We would both work on the tractor every night, and it turned into a party every other night with people showing up and bringing beer. We spent as much time playing beer pong as working on the tractor. This went on for months, and I will say the tractor looked incredible when we were finished. I also don't remember exactly when Marilyn and I had our big fight. I do remember her being there when I started the tractor project. I was a mess; I no longer read at night or anytime, I had what I needed in alcohol and drugs. I was seldom if ever not under the influence of something. It's hard to remember how trapped I was. I couldn't stop drinking, and I was so far in denial that everything that happened was someone else's fault. The only thing that seemed to help was to drink more. At some point, it was becoming obvious that Judd was using every day, as he was getting in trouble at school and at home.

Now, for some masterful deflection, that is on the verge of an art form. Let me clarify, Judd is my son, I love him, I didn't want to see him die from a drug overdose, and he showed an incredible knack for mixing the wrong drugs together to the point of pure insanity. With Judd I could honestly see that there was a problem. But this isn't about Judd or his disease of addiction, it's about me and mine.

Let's flashback a little. Before Judd came to live with me, my family was focused on my disease and my drinking and drugging. They had almost broke through the barrier and reached me. Mom had some friends of the family that were also members of her church that were both involved with recovery. They had come to the farm and talked to me (It was as close to an intervention as I would ever have.); they knew of a religious treatment program that I could go to for a year. Evidently, I was in a little hot water with the family, though I couldn't imagine why. In the end, I agreed to go the following day to this treatment program. To make a long story short, the next day I went with the two fully well-meaning church members to an enrollment evening at this treatment facility; they had made sure I had everything I would need, including a new bible.

During intake, a preacher came out and started preaching. During his little sermon, he said above all that we would learn and believe that masturbation and premarital sex was of the devil and we would be having none of it! Uh oh, Houston, we have a problem. They lost me right there. I got up, excused myself, and went outside. Our two friendly church members came out to talk to me, and I calmly apologized and said there is no fucking way I'm going to stay here. You can either take me home now, or I'll get there on my own! Evidently, I was convincing enough because they took me home. Then Judd came, and I was able to use his addiction to take the focus off of my own.

The Bassett House is the juvenile treatment center that my friend Ian worked for, so I already knew it was available and fairly close to home. After a few family meetings, we decided that Judd was in dire need of treatment. Now let's look at something here! I had absolutely no problem recognizing that Judd had a problem with addiction. I knew that he needed help because his condition was possibly fatal. Let's also remember here that I had spent almost four years in recovery, three of which I spoke in an educational capacity about drug and alcohol addiction and awareness. I was, to say the least, very aware of the problems involved in addiction and was scared for Judd. However, I was totally unable to see myself caught in the same addiction; I was unable to bring to bear any of the knowledge that I had on alcoholism and addiction when it came to myself. Furthermore, I was unable to face reality about addiction when it came to Judd. I wanted Judd to go to treatment, get fixed, and stop using! I knew that was an impossibility without working a program of recovery after treatment, but if I would have admitted this, I would have been able to admit that I needed it also. I was completely lost to the disease of alcoholism and more willing to believe a lie than to face my own reality. In an attempt to be a good father, I convinced Judd to go to rehab and the day for him to go was here. What followed next was very near a re-creation of my trip to Athens with Ray.

I left with Judd, and as we were talking, he said, "I don't want to go to treatment sober." I could relate to this feeling. I asked him what he wanted to do. Judd told me he had a friend that had some Xanax and a little weed if I would take him by his friend's house, he could pick it up. Well, seemed reasonable to me, so that's what I did. After we had picked up the Xanax and Judd had smoked a little weed, we were back on the road. Now I had no intention of using on the way to take Judd to treatment, but as it turns out I am a jealous alcoholic and I really hate to see someone getting fucked up alone! Everyone knows Xanax works better with alcohol, so I stopped and bought a bottle of Crown Royal, ate a few Xanax, and headed for Athens. By the time we reached the treatment center, we were both pretty well hammered beyond repair. I justified all of this by thinking letting Judd use on the way to treatment made him a little more pliable to the idea of going. We reached the Bassett House, even liquored up and Xanaxed out I was emotional about leaving Judd at treatment. Now I'm sure I was chewing Big Red so no one could possibly know I was using and drinking, I thought that we looked and acted quite normal, there's no way anyone could tell that we were totally fucked up. Unfortunately, what the treatment center saw was akin to the scene in "Fear and Loathing in Las Vegas" where Johnny Depp walks into the casino on ether. It didn't take me too long to start picking up on the vibes that if I didn't disappear real soon the police were likely to show up. I hugged Judd told him I loved him and to behave and listen to what he was told, and I split! I was so convinced that the law could be on the way that I took a different way home than I came; you can never be too safe when you're driving, and you can barely walk. Again, I was so far down the rabbit hole with my own alcoholism and addiction that this time in my life is a little fuzzy or lost in a haze. My main goal at the time was to keep my using and drinking a secret from everyone; unfortunately, I was the only one who I was keeping the secret . Judd was in treatment for about two months but after he ran away then came back, they threw him out.

During spring of 2011 after having thrown Marilyn out, I had met a woman at a friend's house, and we had started seeing each other. Now I might point out that I was using and drinking so heavily that I really don't remember her name, and I don't believe I'll ask Marilyn if she does, so we will just call her Trudy. Trudy didn't seem to mind how much I drank or used, and I found this to be refreshing considering everyone else seemed to have a stick in their ass over the whole thing! So, it came about that Trudy was talking about her son who lived in Panama City Beach, Florida, who had an Audi sports car that wouldn't start. Trudy asked me if I new anything about cars, and I replied that I did a fair amount of mechanicing on my own vehicles, though I owned none at the time; I was driving my dad's S10 and hadn't owned a vehicle of my own in years! So, I talked to mom and asked her if I could take the truck to Florida and then asked Judd if he wanted to go to the beach. As it turned out, I got a yes back to both questions, and mom even threw in a credit card to make sure I had enough gas money and whatever else might come up!

Now is a good time to point out how I had been drinking and partying since I had got home from prison, I hadn't worked a job in several years so where was the money coming from? Well, I found myself doing a lot of shopping for mom picking up groceries or getting salt for the water softener or any number of meaningless little things that I would pick up for her. I almost always had one of the credit cards, and I wasn't above hitting the cash back button when I bought stuff. By the time it was finally taken away, it had a tune of around $13,000 unexplained charges on it, and that was just around a year and a half. We aren't quite there yet but getting close.

I told Trudy that I could take her to Florida if she didn't mind if my son came too. That's how Judd and I ended up in Panama City Beach, Florida, for college spring break 2011. Really, I had no idea it was Spring Break; well, I might have had a little idea that it was. What followed is an unexplainable week of pure bedlam. We hit the beach with a mission, and it took Judd about two minutes to be lost in the crowd. I was looking around for him, and I spotted him in the middle of a crowd of college kids with a beer bong in his mouth. At that point, I had a slight premonition of jails and police, both of which never came true, though I'm not sure why. What happened was a week of partying that I find it hard to believe myself that it was real. We hit the clubs on the beach every night and partied all day on the beach. We snuck Judd into Club La Vela, we rode the mechanical bull at Coyote Ugly, and we played volleyball at Sharky's; essentially, we partied like it was 1999! At some point we spent about thirty minutes with the hood up on Trudy's son's car. My professional opinion was it was a computer issue and needed a real mechanic, at which point Judd and I went back to the beach. Judd was buying K2 (fake weed), from the head shops, which was still legal in Florida, it had already been outlawed in Ohio. One day Judd's Uncle Ray came over with his wife from Mobile, Alabama, and spent the day drinking on the beach with us. In the end, we spent an entire week completely fucked up. I drank to my fill, which was all day every day. We ate seafood and had the time of our lives. I didn't draw a sober breath until we were on the way back to Ohio. That was a road trip from hell - out of money, out of drugs, and out of my mind. By the time we had made it back to Trudy's house, I had come to the realization that she was likely a worse drunk and drug addict than I was! Quite frankly, that was a terrifying reality and when I said goodbye when we dropped her off, I was quite sure I didn't care if I ever saw her again. Forced out of fear of being alone, I decided to re-evaluate my relationship with Marilyn. We had been together for over five years, and we were still talking to each other. Maybe I had been a little hasty in blaming her for all of our arguments. Slowly, over a couple months, we started seeing each other again. We still argued and had a really bad night about every tenth night. We also held hands and talked to one another, and we held each other at night, and we weren't alone.

During the summer of 2011, I got a call from my old friend Vladimir; he was working for a lighting company that did factory refits on lights inside of commercial buildings, and they were looking for help. I was ready to go back to work, as over three years had passed since I had last held a job. I had to do a little creative adjusting to my resume, like being self-employed for the last three years instead of unemployed and in prison, but after a few weeks of waiting I was hired. We were going to work a large job in Pittsburgh doing a five-story building and would be there for a month or more. I was so excited I couldn't stand it; working in Pittsburgh was going to be great. I would be gone a week at a time and back only for the weekends. I really believed the job was going to solve everything. I wouldn't feel like such a loser, therefore, I wouldn't drink as much, and if I were in Pittsburgh, my family wouldn't be watching me as closely, and I wouldn't be under all this pressure; surely, I wouldn't have to drink as much.

We showed up on the job on Monday and started work, it was a relatively easy job. After the day was over, we went to our hotel, which had a restaurant and a bar. The only thing that was much different in Pittsburgh was I drank Yuengling instead of Budweiser, and I didn't drink in the morning. I had to work two weeks before I would get my first check. Every night I would call Marilyn and check on Judd. My family was very proud of me for being gainfully employed again. It felt great to be working, and it felt great to have everyone telling me how happy they were that I had a job. My first weekend home was really good; I could hold my head up again, and I felt like everything was going to get better. My second week in Pittsburgh was just as good, I could tell Marilyn good night then go to the bar and drink until I was ready to go to bed. I was even moderating my drinking, only having six or so before turning in for the night. Friday came, and I collected my first paycheck in over three years.

When I got home, I told Marilyn we have to go out and celebrate! We had a small argument when she found out I was planning on going straight to the bar to start celebrating; she thought we would at least go out to dinner first. I'm not sure who won the argument, but if I had to guess, I'd say we went out to eat before we headed to Buckeye Lake, Scooters was where I wanted to do my celebrating! At Scooters, everyone congratulated me on getting a job and we commenced to celebrating, we played pool, shot darts, listened to music, and we drank. It was close to a perfect night; we had a great time with only one little argument at the very start. We stayed at Scooters until after midnight when we finally decided to head for home. I decided to head the back way out of town and to stick to county roads and state routes instead of taking the Interstate. As it so happens, that night there were a couple local police cars parked on the corner of the back way out of town, and one of them jumped out behind me.

Now let's have a little backstory. Before I get my first DUI, I have always been very lucky when it comes to driving under the influence and let me say from the start, thank God I've never hurt anyone while driving drunk, at the time I considered this as being from skill. Again, I was very delusional, I really believed that I was as good a driver intoxicated as I was sober. I had already had many experiences with the police while driving and had gotten out of all of them so instead of trying to recount all of them I'll tell you about the worst one I remember. I use the word "remember" rather lightly because I was in a black out for the whole experience, the police were not involved in this particular incident. I had spent the day drinking at one of the local bars and after who knows how many beer mugs full of Crown and Coke, I decided switching to Jager bombs would be a good idea, now if this makes perfectly good sense to you, too, you might be an alcoholic.

So, anyway, I woke up the next morning to my phone ringing. At least I think it's ringing something is ringing and it's possible that it's my head. My mouth feels like a litter box I'm not real clear on where I am or how I got here. After a few seconds I realized, I was in my bed in my house, and the phone is still ringing. I answered, "Hello?" It's my cocaine dealer from Columbus! This is kind of odd, I don't remember him ever calling me, I always call him. He asks am I alright and did I make it home ok. "What are you talking about?" I say, "I'm in my bed, I was here all night!"

"You were at my house around 2 AM," he said.

"I was not. I was at the local bar and then I came home."

"Check your pockets."

I think this is a pretty bad attempt at a joke but what the hell I'll check my pockets. I pull out a sack of coke. Uh-oh what did I do? So, I decide I better listen.

He tells me he is glad I made it home ok, but I better go out and look at my car.

I told him I just woke up, let me call you back in a few minutes. I got up, brushed my teeth, did a line (Can't look a gift horse in the mouth), and went outside to look at my car. The back end looked fine, I walked around to the passenger side and there was nothing. I thought, "Now what is really going on?" I walked around to the driver's side, and I couldn't believe what I was looking at. There was guardrail rash from the front bumper to the rear bumper all the way down the driver's side! I called my dealer back and asked what happened.

He told me I was on the phone with him, I had decided I was too drunk to go home, so I headed for Columbus to get some blow to sober up. Hmm, seems legit, I think. As we were talking, I said "Where are all of these sparks coming from?" He said I was laughing and told him I'd be there in a few minutes.

As near as we could put together, I must have hit the guardrail as I was getting on 270 on the east side of Columbus; that was the only thing that explained why it was on the driver side. So again, I'll say thank God I never hurt anyone while driving, and I was fully delusional in thinking it was because I was a good driver. The truth Is I drove many times when I wasn't even present at all, so I thought it was skill that kept me safe. Now I know it was really divine intervention.

Back to Buckeye Lake, out celebrating my first paycheck, finally back to work after being out of prison for over a year! Damn my luck, I should have taken the Interstate. I was pulled over on a back road leaving the lake and am being charged with my first DUI. Little do I know it but the shitstorm that is coming from this DUI is going to change my life; in fact, it was a turning point! Marilyn and I were both arrested and taken to jail in Newark. I hadn't been in jail in Newark and found the whole experience not to be to my liking.

I woke up the next morning and spent most of the day waiting to be bailed out. Marilyn posted my bail and took me home to the farm. My fathers' truck that I had been driving was still in impound in Newark. I made a humble apology to my mother and was fairly sure everything was going to be smoothed over. Well, it wasn't! A couple of days later, I received a call from my parole officer, and he informed me that my mother and sister were in his office as we were speaking. He then proceeds to tell me I have one hour to get all of mine and Judd's clothes and leave. I was told that he didn't care where I went but I wasn't staying at the farm anymore. To say the least, I was a bit shocked, it was only a DUI. I hadn't murdered anyone. I felt being thrown out was a little extreme. The DUI was just the icing on the cake, though. My parole officer told me I had ran up my mother's credit card and had been stealing scrap from the farm and that I was no longer welcome there. I was shocked. and I had an explanation for everything I was being accused of. Finally my parole officer broke it down, so I understood just where I was at - he said either leave the farm or go back to prison! Well, I wasn't going back to prison, so I packed my shit, Judd packed his, and we left with nowhere to go. We ended up living in tents behind one of our friends' houses, in a couple of old barns. I lost my job; I lost my class A driver's license, and I lost our home at the farm, all over - in my mind - a DUI.

Mom put the farm up for sale, and it started to sink in that I really did lose the farm! It was to be my inheritance from my father. I decided that I hated my mother and sister for doing this to me - they made me homeless, and they took my inheritance. I was so angry I wanted to go back and burn it all to the ground and dance drunken in the ashes. Luckily, someone pointed out that arson probably wasn't going to help my situation. I had to settle for stealing the realty signs from the end of the driveway, which I felt wasn't nearly as satisfying as dancing in the ashes would be!

My next several months were lost in hate and anger. I stayed drunk and or drugged, and I was exceedingly violent. All truth be told, I should have been back in prison because I was a danger to myself and everyone I was in contact with. It was a very dark time; as they say, though, it's darkest before the light. I don't remember seeing my daughters during this time really; I don't remember much other than being full of hate and rage. As winter approached somehow, I talked Judd into going back to The Bassett House for treatment. I think I used a warm bed and three meals a day to convince Judd to go back to rehab. Marilyn talked her mother into letting me move in because I was living in a tent. Her mother agreed, but it was probably more to do with the fact that Marilyn was staying in the tent with me more than she was at home. So, I moved in and did what I could to help out, but unfortunately, I made their life a living hell. I continued to drink, and Marilyn and I stayed on our routine of one bad night every ten. There were times the police were called; there were times I walked off and slept in the woods. It wasn't pretty. I did, however, resume my visitation with my daughters; they would come every other weekend and stay with us. I was still so consumed with drinking that I don't remember much. At some point, I called my ex-brother-in-law Ray; he was living in southern Alabama and working at a steel mill, he told me that they were always looking for equipment operators and that if I wanted to come down, he could get me a job. Now a job and money seemed like a good idea, and the more I thought about it the more I realized that all of my problems would be solved if I had a good job, I would have money and I wouldn't feel like such a loser therefore I wouldn't need to drink as much. The more I thought about it, the better it sounded; all of my problems would be solved if only I had a good job! Yep, delusional and batshit crazy! So, I went to see my parole officer; as it turns out my parole officer quit his job, and I had a new one. I explained that I had an opportunity to go to work in Alabama and asked if I could go. My new parole officer thought I was being very responsible to have come to him and ask, so he submitted paperwork to have me released from parole a year early. I soon was free to go to Alabama and apply for a job. Wow, I thought, this must be the right thing because it was happening, so I bought a Greyhound ticket and on February 12, 2012, left Ohio for my new life in Alabama.

18

GEOGRAPHICAL CURE

Marilyn, Alice and Ophelia took me to the Greyhound depot in Columbus. On the way there, I picked up a bottle of Crown Royal for my carry-on bag; it was going to be a twenty-four-hour Greyhound ride. With a bottle, I started my trip to a new life where I wouldn't have to drink anymore, and that made perfect sense to me. Luckily, I was already a touch on the drunk side before I got on the bus! Leaving wasn't the easiest thing I have ever done; my daughters were very emotional at the bus stop. I think Marilyn was just glad I was leaving. I really hadn't behaved well for the last year, and I was the cause of a lot of misery for a lot of people. After a tearful farewell, I climbed on the bus and was sure I was as ready as I could be for the next twenty-four-hours of chaos.

What a trip! At one point the bus had to stop on the side of the road and wait for the police to come and arrest several people that were fighting on the back of the bus. The only other thing worth mentioning was I had a three-hour layover in Atlanta. I was warned before I got off the bus to not leave my luggage or it would disappear. Now my bottle had ran empty by the time we reached Atlanta, so I was already nervous and on edge, but I was in no way prepared for the big city! Several blocks in every direction around the Greyhound depot was like a tent city; there were homeless people everywhere. While sitting in the depot guarding my luggage, I saw a transsexual with a monkey on their back leading a Rottweiler! Uh-oh Toto, we aren't in Kansas anymore! Now, I had been in the inner city in Columbus many times, but I ain't never seen the crazy shit I saw in Atlanta. I really needed to go to the bathroom, but I didn't want to try to carry all of my luggage with me, and I was quite sure if I left it, it would be gone before I made it back. Luckily, a young Asian couple asked me if I would watch their luggage while they took their children to the bathrooms. I said yes if they would watch mine so I could go after they were done. An agreement was made, and we watched each other's luggage so we could go to the bathroom. Greyhound in Atlanta was no joke; it was by far the most dangerous place I ever hung out in for three hours.

I finally reached the depot in Mobile, Alabama just after 9 P.M. Ray was at work, but he took off an hour to come and pick me up. Ray drove me back to his trailer, which was about five miles from the mill. The next day, I met with the boss in the parking lot, and after talking to him for about five minutes I was hired pending I passed a drug test, which I did. All of my eggs were in this one basket; I was sure that a good job was just what I needed to quit drinking. Some of you may recognize that I was trying a geographical cure, moving away, and hoping I was leaving all of my problems behind. The fact is that no matter where you go, there you are! Being that my problems were of my own making, they traveled with me. I had been sure to convince Marilyn that Ray didn't drink, and I was headed for a better environment. Now Marilyn had heard stories of some of Ray's and my shenanigans, so she knew I was lying. I think I knew I was lying, but I'm not so sure, I had really convinced myself that everything would be different, that I wouldn't need to drink or drug anymore if I only had a good job. Batshit crazy!

Training started at the steel mill, and I was a quick study. The mill had just changed its computer system, and the guys who worked on the old system were really having trouble adapting. I, on the other hand, didn't know the old system, so I picked up on the computer right away. We worked twelve-hour shifts with two weeks day shift then two weeks night shift. It took some getting used to, as I hadn't worked full-time for quite a while. Now as far as my drinking, nothing changed other than I didn't have anyone complaining about what I was doing, which I thought was quite nice really. Hell, maybe I didn't really have a drinking problem, just a people problem because people were always telling me I had a drinking problem and since there was no one there to complain, *voila!*, no problem. Told you guys I was a thinker!

My job was to run a ninety-ton forklift. I moved slabs of steel that weighed anywhere from twenty-five to fifty tons. It takes the average person three to six months of training before they are ready to fly solo and be turned lose on this type of equipment; it took me three weeks! On a night shift, at the end of my third week, I broke a fork. A fork costs $55,000 to replace, oops. There was an investigation, and it was deemed an accident. The fact that I had been eating Lortabs all night didn't play any part in my mind. The fact that I'm a drug addict and an alcoholic, I knew if I drank several bottles of water before anyone showed up, I could pass a drug test. Which I did, and I passed the drug test. I was a little nervous that I was going to lose my new job, but I didn't. In fact, because it was deemed an accident and not operator error, I wasn't even given the mandatory suspension. Always been lucky, that's why I play the lottery!

The week after I broke the fork, Ray quit his job at the mill and decided to go back to Ohio. Ray was the only person I really knew in Alabama other than my coworkers that I had just met. I had been driving Ray's hunting truck to work, so we worked out a deal on the truck and some tools and a Benelli shotgun that he and I had bought years ago during some of our shenanigans. I had lost all of the guns that I thought were to be mine when my mom sold the farm. Oh, I still hated my whole family and occasionally considered taking a drive with a few five-gallon gas cans and heading for Ohio. Yep, I was still quite pissed off, and when I was drunk, I could imagine myself dancing in the ashes. I also assumed the rent from our landlord, who we will call Harry. I became good friends with Harry, I didn't know it then, but I would be renting off of him for the next five years.

Now I had figured out where the good bars were at and all of the liquor stores. Oops, I'm in the South now so they are A.B.C. stores - in Pennsylvania they are Package stores, don't ask me, but I could tell you some things about Pennsylvania that would make you scratch you head. Things just get different south of the Mason Dixon Line, and Pennsylvania isn't even south of the line, but they don't know it! So, I spent as much time drinking with my new job as I used to, maybe a little more because I was earning a regular paycheck. I was alone, so I worked any overtime that was offered, which made the checks even nicer. The reality was that the new good job didn't really help matters with my drinking in fact it was probably making things worse.

One of my favorite bars was called The River Pub. It was a private bar - you had to be a member to get in - on the Tensaw River. The bar was almost always open, and there was music and pool, everything a good bar needs.

On one particular day off, I had spent a good part of the day drinking at The River Pub, and it was beginning to look like a good part of the night as well! I knew I had to work in the morning, and 4:30 AM gets here really fast, but what's another game of pool going to hurt? I was winning a lot of drinks. I remember leaving the pub and thinking maybe I should just lay down in the truck for a while and get some sleep. I thought, "Naw, I've always made it home; I'd rather sleep in my bed," so down the road I went. At one point I remember being off the road to the right in the ditch and just getting back on the road and straightened out in time to drive over a bridge that crossed a creek. Wow that was close, I thought, guess I'm a little more fucked up than I thought. Another five miles down the road, the rear driver's side wheel broke off of my truck and passed me before disappearing into the woods. Uh-oh, Houston, we have a problem! I immediately turned on my four-way flashers, the ass end of my truck was just over the double yellow line, and just before I got out, a car came over the hill and clipped the rear end of my truck. I thought, man that was close, I got out. The car that hit me came back and said that I hit them. What's wrong with people? I told them, "Fuck off, I was sitting still broke down in the middle of the road with my four ways on, and you hit me." A truck pulled along side and asked if I needed any help, I said, "Yes do you have a chain or tow rope? I need to get this truck off the road. They did have a tow rope. As we were hooking up, a state trooper pulled up behind us and flipped on his lights. Great this is going from bad to worse. We pulled my truck on to a side road - a red dirt road. I jumped out of my truck, unhooked the tow rope, threw it in the back of this guy's truck and jumped in the passenger door beside his wife! I said, "Get me out of here; I've been drinking, and if I talk to that state trooper I'll be arrested."

Evidently my newfound friendship with this fella wasn't cemented firm enough to get him to flee and allude an Alabama state trooper. It was, however, enough to get a smile and a stick of gum before he threw me out of his truck. "You seem fine to me," he said. Oh yeah, I'm sitting down, when I stand back up shit's going to get real, I thought. It did. I was arrested for DUI and taken to the Bay Minette jail and booked. I couldn't believe it; I was only just over a month on the job, and I'm in jail for another DUI.

I was quite pissed when I woke up the next morning and realized I was going to lose my new job that was going to fix me so I didn't have to drink anymore. As I tried to figure out how I got in this situation, the more I thought about it the more I realized that this wasn't even my fault; it was the truck that broke down that caused me to get a DUI. Really, it had nothing to do with the fact that I had been drinking for half the day and night; if the wheel wouldn't have fallen off, I would have made it home. I was driving much better after the ditch - it sort of scared me sober - and I'm sure I would have made it home. Just wait until I talk to Ray, that son of a gun sold me a defective truck, I mean, if you look at it in the right light, it's really all Ray's fault!

I sat in jail, and I couldn't believe my luck. I was going to lose my job and then what? I didn't know anyone here. Later that day, one of the deputies told me to get my stuff I was being bailed out. I asked, "Are you sure?" As I was being let out, they told me I needed to go across the street to the bondsman and sign some paperwork. I walked across the street and met the bondsman and signed the paperwork, there was a number of the person who bailed me out; it was a coworker. I called him up and asked if he could give me a ride home, as I had no other way to get there.

My coworker, who asked to remain nameless, took me home and, on the way, I asked him how he found out and why he bailed me out. It turned out that when I didn't show up, Harry called Ray, and Ray started calling jails, and bingo there I was. As to why, he told me that when he was younger a few of his family members were killed by a drunk driver. I was shocked; for fuck sakes, why the hell did he bail me out then? "You are a nice guy, and you deserve another chance," he said. Little did I know it at the time, but that one act of selfless kindness was going to have almost as much impact on my life as my mother throwing me out. However, right then I was stuck in the grips of alcoholism and I was cuckoo clock crazy on top of batshit crazy! My coworker dropped me off at home and picked me up the next morning for work. That afternoon, I asked him if I could borrow the money to get my truck out of impound and the money to get it towed home. He agreed to loan me the money, and I spent the day getting everything lined up. On a side note, I did pay back all of the borrowed money including bail, it was one of the first times I had ever paid someone back, though it probably took me longer than it should have.

Marilyn was pissed that I got another D.U.I., but she relented a little when I convinced her it wasn't my fault, as the truck broke down. I never told her how drunk I really was. I asked Marilyn if she wanted to quit her job and move to Alabama. She said, "What are you, stupid or something?" I told her that I loved her and missed her and that if she moved to Alabama, I wouldn't be so lonely I wouldn't drink as much, things would be better, we would get along better and we could have our own place instead of living with one of our parents. Evidently, I started making sense because Marilyn started talking about what it could be like. Meanwhile, I set to fixing my truck. I found the rear end I needed and asked Harry if he would take me to pick it up.

We went and got the parts I needed and I fixed my truck, so I had wheels again.

I had a few more bad experiences drinking - you know, just normal stuff blackouts, a head injury from being pulled of a bar stool backwards, just normal drinking stuff. At some point, I had a premonition that maybe I really did have a drinking problem, so I called the Alcoholics Anonymous central service office for Mobile, Alabama, and I talked to a nice young lady I told her that I was a struggling alcoholic that needed a meeting I asked her if there was anybody that could take me to one. I was informed that she had a list of numbers for just this very thing that she would get back to me and let me know. When she called back, I was informed that she had indeed found someone to take me to a meeting, so I got his phone number and gave him a call. The first time I talked to Franklin I had absolutely no idea that he would eventually be my sponsor and have a huge part in changing my life! Looking back now I can see it was like pieces being moved around on a chessboard, there wasn't just one thing that happened that brought me to the willingness to change it was a combination of many things, all of which I was blind to as they were happening; at the time, my perception was that I was a victim of terrible circumstances of which I had no control, when in fact I was receiving blessings in disguise! But we aren't there yet, so let's get back to Franklin, the first person in AA that I met in Alabama. In fact, he took me to my first AA meeting in Alabama.

I didn't know it at the time, but Franklin was recuperating from a stroke and wasn't supposed to be driving after dark. On his way to pick me up, he pulled into the wrong driveway, backed into a pole, and messed up the rear-view camera in his wife's car. This man came and picked me up when he really wasn't supposed to be driving at all and took me to a meeting because I said I needed help. So started a long road toward recovery in southern Alabama.

I don't remember that first meeting; I must have picked up a beginner chip because before this is over, I would have an ashtray full of them! I met several people at the meeting, and they all said come back again, and I did. I hadn't really accepted the idea of quitting drinking or that my life was unmanageable, however, I didn't go to meetings when I was drunk. I went several times hungover but never while I was drinking. Let me clarify here that it wasn't because it isn't allowed; I didn't go drunk because I was so ate up with guilt, shame, and pride, that I couldn't bear the thought of people in meetings seeing me drunk. If you think about it, that's really kind of fucked up - I couldn't stand the idea of a room full of recovering drunks seeing me drunk. I told you I was batshit crazy, and I was! Also, the idea that I was better than everyone else was probably somewhere mixed in with all the other fucked up ideas I had. So, I started going to some AA meetings when I could stop drinking about twelve hours before a meeting.

Marilyn was finally on board with moving to Alabama and finding a new job so we could be together and start our life anew with me working and staying sober. I was doing really well at the working part, but the staying sober was a little more in theory than reality. I should note here that my entire family, as well as Marilyn's, told her she must be off her rocker to move to Alabama with me, but evidently love is blind. I had a month to prepare for Marilyn's arrival. The trailer I was renting was a small two-bedroom, and it was livable for two bachelors; I, however, didn't think Marilyn would be very impressed. There was a three-bedroom trailer beside mine, and the renters had just unexpectedly moved. I asked my landlord if I could switch trailers and if he minded if I did a little repair and painting on the inside.

We agreed on making the switch now. I'll say here that the trailers were furnished by the landlord. I had a storage unit in Ohio with Marilyn's and my furniture, but the thought of getting it to Alabama seemed an impossibility. So, for the next month I worked on the three-bedroom trailer and went to work. I might have gone to a few meetings but getting ready for Marilyn to come was my priority. Harry the landlord got used to seeing me with a beer in my hands; if I stepped outside, I almost always had a beer in my hands. The work on the trailer kind of got away from me. I wanted Marilyn to be happy when she got there, so I went a little overboard I stripped wallpaper and sanded walls to get ready for paint, I filled holes where who knows how many renters had hung pictures. The walls literally looked like someone had used a nail gun like a machine gun and peppered the walls with nails. I filled all of the holes, replaced missing trim, and I painted all the walls and ceilings. In doing all of this work, I did, however, stay out of the bars and only drank at home, which in my mind was an improvement.

Once I had the date that Marilyn was going to fly in, I put in for that weekend off. It was already my weekend off, but I had been working so much overtime that I wanted to cover my bases. Sure enough, the weekend was here for Marilyn to arrive and my boss was telling me that I had to cover night shift for the whole weekend because someone had called off sick. I was still just under my 90 days of probation with the company, so I didn't feel like I could refuse. I was really let down. Still, I was excited that Marilyn was coming; I couldn't wait to show her the trailer that I had fixed up, and I had planned a trip to Gulf Shores. Marilyn had never seen the ocean. Technically I was taking her to the Gulf of Mexico, not the ocean, but the biggest water Marilyn had ever seen was Lake Erie. I was excited to show her the white sandy beaches of The Gulf. When Marilyn arrived, we rented a car for her, and I took her back to the trailer to show her our new home.

Marilyn and I both grew up in Perry County, and we have both lived in trailers before, so I'll tell you the only trailer joke I know. What do you have in Perry County if you have a baby that drools out both sides of its mouth? A "level trailer." I didn't say it was a good joke! Marilyn liked the trailer, and she met our landlord. Harry came right out and told her to be careful of the rattlesnakes and bears. I thought, "Damn Harry, I was going to give it a minute before I mentioned the rattlesnakes and the bears." Marilyn just laughed, and when we went inside, she said, "He was kidding about the rattlesnakes and the bears right?" I said, "No, not really, you should be aware that both are out there and probably closer than you think." I laughed about it, and she decided she didn't think it was very funny! So, I left her home alone her first night in Alabama and I went to work.

The next morning, I asked Marilyn if she wanted to go to see the Gulf. She said she did but we could go another time since I had to work again tonight, but I assured her we had time to go down have lunch on the beach and make it back with plenty of time to spare for me to be able to go to work. Besides, I was really excited for her to see the Gulf, so we headed for Gulf Shores. An hour and a half later, we were pulling up to the Hangout at Gulf Shores, a place where we could have lunch right on the beach. Marilyn was impressed with how white the beach was and how blue the water was. So, we sat down to have some lunch before we did a little swimming. Now I was having such a nice time I figured a few drinks would certainly make it better, so I had a few while we ate. Marilyn had a few too! We decided to go down and get in the water before we had to leave for home. The yellow flags were out, which meant to swim with caution and watch out for riptides and I explained to Marilyn how to spot a riptide. We waded out to about waist deep, and the first wave knocked Marilyn off of her feet and the waves kept coming we were laughing and enjoying ourselves we were only in the water for about twenty minutes. I was helping Marilyn walk out of the Gulf, which isn't always easy when sober as a church mouse, let alone after having a few drinks. She was having a difficult time of it. We were standing on the beach drying off when I noticed a pair of police officers watching us. We were headed for the parking lot when the two officers motioned for us to come over, so we walked over and asked what we could do for them. They asked us if we had been drinking. I replied that we each had had a couple while we ate lunch at the Hangout. They then proceeded to arrest both of us for public intoxication. I thought, "Are you shitting me?" We are standing behind a bar on the beach where you can literally walk up to the bar barefoot and dripping water, and we are being arrested for public intoxication. They handcuffed us both ,put us in the cruiser and took us to the police station where we were both booked and held until the next morning. Neither one of us were even given a breathalyzer. We were released the next morning on our own recognizance and both given a court date and time to appear. We had to walk to the impound lot to pick up our rental car. That turned into a long-drawn-out fiasco, as the impound lot claimed we didn't have the proper paperwork to get the car back, there was some long and tense back and forth, but we finally got the car and headed for home.

I then had to call my boss and explain why I didn't make it to work last night and that went even worse. I was told that I had been fired for a no-call-no-show while still on my ninety days probation. I was floored! I couldn't believe I had lost my job, and I wasn't even drunk! I asked my boss for the site superintendent's phone number when he told me it was out of his hands. I called our superintendent and asked him if he was aware of the situation, and he said he was. I asked him if he was aware that it was my weekend off and that I had put my name on the board a month in advance to be sure I would be off. He asked me to clarify what did I mean it wasn't my weekend to work? I explained again that it was my weekend off and someone called in sick for their shift at which time I was told I would have to cover it. The big boss said let me get back to you in a few minutes. Two minutes later, my boss called and told me I was fully reinstated, that as a disciplinary action I would be left on probation for an extra month. Whew, at least my job was saved, but I was beginning to get a very bad taste in my mouth over the whole thing. I convinced Marilyn that it was completely unjust that we had been arrested after only having a couple drinks while having lunch.

Several weeks later, we went back to Gulf Shores to go to court where we intending to plead our case and ask why we hadn't been given a breathalyzer to prove that we were in fact not drunk in public. Well, our intentions were good, but when we got in front of the judge, he had a full list of my previous convictions from Ohio, and to say the least he was less than impressed. I was told if he ever saw me again to expect to see the inside of his jail for as long as he could possibly provide me a place to stay. When it was said and done, Marilyn and I were both fined $800 each for public intoxication, and to this day we do not go to Gulf Shores to enjoy the beach. We'll go to Destin, Navarre, or Pensacola beach but Gulf Shores is out!

I felt like we had been wrongfully accused, and I used that to justify that my drinking really wasn't that bad, so the overall effects were that I stopped going to any AA meetings and I pretty much drank when I wanted to.

Now remember that I had promised Marilyn that I wasn't drinking as much and that I was getting better, but now that she had moved in, I went back to my normal drinking. As a result, we fell back into our normal patterns of one out of every ten nights being a bad night with fighting and arguing!

I took Marilyn to my favorite bars, and we even found a new bar together; it was a biker bar that was kind of nice. We went into this bar the day we found it late in the afternoon and we stayed fairly late; I don't really remember leaving to go home. The next day, I drove by, and the bar was burnt to the ground. I tried a little harder to drink at home after that, even I can take a hint every now and then. However, I have to say that drinking at home always has the same problem - eventually the alcohol runs out and I'd have to get more!

Marilyn got a job in Mobile, and I bought her a car, an older Ford Thunderbird. I don't remember how I found the car, but the person selling it was willing to take a few payments, so it worked out. I continued to work at the steel mill, and Marilyn was working full-time as well, and life carried on for several months this way. I was still drinking every day, and it wasn't abnormal to still be a little drunk when I went to work. By the time I finally got off work, I was always ready for another drink and usually stopped and got a beer at a truck stop to drink on the way home. Evidently the good job and my girlfriend moving in wasn't going to be enough to stop my drinking, so I guess I decided why fight it, I'll just drink, it's not like I'm hurting anyone.

Marilyn had been in Alabama for about five months when I did just that. I had been drinking at home all day; it was my day off, why not! Later that night, I ran out of alcohol. Marilyn had hidden my keys because she didn't want me driving drunk. I had come up with a logical solution to the problem, why Marilyn could just drive us to the bar, I wouldn't drive drunk, and I could get another drink. Evidently, my miraculous solution to the problem wasn't what Marilyn had in mind; she thought I had had enough to drink, and we could just stay home. As you can imagine, the argument started there! I wanted another drink and Marilyn had hidden my keys, the argument ended when I threw Marilyn on the floor and kicked her in the face for hiding my keys. Marilyn gave me my keys, and I left to go get another drink, I stayed out drinking until early the next morning, I was so drunk when I came home and passed out.

I woke up that afternoon with the realization that Marilyn's car wasn't there, and as I looked around, I realized that all of her clothes were gone. I tried to piece together the night before and remembered fighting about keys but not much else. I called Marilyn; she had driven all night and was back in Ohio. I asked her if she was ok and why she went home. Marilyn proceeds to tell me that I kicked her in the face because she had hidden my keys and didn't want me to drive risking another D.U.I. She then sent me pictures of herself; she had a black eye and a large knot on her cheek where I had kicked her. I couldn't believe it, though it was quite obvious by the pictures and her story that I had in fact thrown her on the floor and kicked her in the face. I couldn't believe that I would do that and at the same time my mind was telling me she shouldn't have hidden my keys! Marilyn told me she was thoroughly disgusted with me and that she left fearing for her life. She also told me she wasn't sure if she ever wanted to talk to me again.

I was devastated, and my only solution was to drink more. I stayed drunk, for if I started to sober up, I would think about how badly I had made a mess of things, and would think about kicking Marilyn in the face because I wanted my keys! In a drunken state, I was able to believe it was somehow her fault and not mine. I stayed this way for the next week somehow not missing any work. On my next weekend off, I bought a case of beer and decided that I would just stay home and drink. I started drinking early Friday morning and passed out somewhere around one in the afternoon. I woke up around six; I should say I was still rather drunk when I woke up! I only had a few beers left and was really lonely. I had a little over $400 in my pocket, so I decided I'd go out for a while. I got a shower, got dressed, and headed for one of my favorite bars. Now, I will say that when I went out drinking, I didn't stay at any one particular place. I sort of made a circuit of going to several places.

I woke up in jail having no memory of how I had gotten there. Sick and very confused, I couldn't believe I was in jail again. Marilyn was in Ohio, I had absolutely no one I could call for bail, and I was certainly going to lose my job. I couldn't believe it! I laid there for hours trying with no avail to figure out how I had got there, I finally looked up, and I asked God why does this keep happening to me? If everyone would just leave me alone, surely I would be fine. No sooner than I asked the question every hair on my body stood up and I got the overwhelming sense of a reply to my question. The reply was "You keep happening, you are doing this to yourself!" I laid there quite shocked at the brutal truth of the answer that I didn't really want. The question was really hypothetical, I hadn't expected an answer, and I wasn't overly pleased with the fact that I had to admit it was the truth. I didn't even know what I had done to be arrested but there was really little doubt that I did it! I laid on my rack and the more I pondered the question the more I had to admit that my problems were of my own making. Seventeen hours after I was arrested, an officer came and got me and said someone was looking to bail me out and that I had to take a breathalyzer to determine if I could be released so I did, I blew a .07. The officer seemed a little shocked; he stated that he was the arresting officer and had I blew when I was booked, I would probably have been transported to the hospital for alcohol poisoning. The officer asked me if I remembered being arrested. I told him that I didn't remember anything. He informed me that I was being charged with DUI, that he had seen me coming down the road, and that I was driving fine until I swerved at him like I was going to run him over. I apologized for swerving at him and told him again I had absolutely no recollection of any of it. The officer told me he was only glad that I hadn't hurt myself or anybody else, to which I agreed. A few hours later, they came and got me and told me that my bail had been posted. When I got my personal effects back, I checked my wallet and there was less than $150, I did a few calculations, and I came up with I must have been really fucked up! When I walked out into the Saraland Police Department lobby, there was my landlord Harry with a bail bondsman who was a bondswoman that looked like she could have been my grandma. I signed some papers, and Harry gave me a ride home.

When I got home, I called the impound lot that had my truck to get the amount I owed to get it back. The person I was talking to asked if I had a driver's license because if I didn't, I couldn't get my truck back, there was a town ordinance that stated they could only release vehicles to a licensed driver. So, I just lost my truck. I should say that calling the impound lot wasn't the first thing I did when I got home, the first thing I did was go to the refrigerator and open the door and lo and behold there were four beers inside. So I opened a beer and then I called the impound lot and lost my truck. As I sat there trying to figure out what to do, I realized that within a week I had kicked Marilyn in the face for hiding my keys, gotten another D.U.I., and lost my truck all due to drinking. Maybe I had a problem. Maybe!

I got the phone book out opened the yellow pages to treatment facilities and put my finger down and called the number it landed on Bradford. I was quickly set up to go to inpatient treatment in Warrior, Alabama, I didn't know how I was going to get there without a vehicle, but I was scheduled to go. I called a guy I had met at a meeting and asked if he could give me a ride to a meeting. We'll call him Hank. Hank came over and picked me up and took me to a meeting. I shared in the meeting that I was going to go to treatment, but I didn't know how I was going to get there. After the meeting, Hank offered to drive me to Warrior, Alabama, a four-hour drive from Mobile. The next day at work, I told my boss that I was going to go to rehab because I had a drinking problem. My boss took it better than I expected and told me I would still have my job when I got back.

19

BRADFORD

Hank picked me up early on Saturday morning to make the four-hour trip one way to drop me off. Just before we left, Harry my landlord came over and gave me a new pair of house shoes; he said he knew I only had boots and he thought I should have a pair of shoes. I was a little overwhelmed that Harry and Hank were each going out of their way for me, as I hadn't done anything for either one of them why were they helping me. I was very hungover on the ride to Warrior, and about halfway there, Hank stopped to get us some breakfast. I was almost too sick to eat, but I forced myself because I didn't want to seem ungrateful. The trip to the treatment center was long, on the way I learned that Hank had almost thirty years sober working the AA program. When Hank dropped me off, before he left, I asked him if he would be my sponsor and help me work through the steps. He said he would. Point in fact is I never worked any steps with Hank, and I ended up in two more treatment centers before I was willing to actually try working the steps, but we aren't there yet so let's get back to Bradford.

I spent five or six days in their detox unit being medicated and watched for alcohol withdrawal. I stayed very secluded during my first week, I spent most of my time contemplating how I had got here. I also spent a lot of time thinking about Marilyn and how I had kicked her in the face because she wouldn't give me my keys. I spent a lot of time on the back porch smoking and thinking. Bradford was in the middle of the woods it was very quiet. I was probably one of the only patients that felt comfortable in the woods, as almost everyone I had met were from cities. There was a guy from Kentucky that was also very country, and we joked that we might be the only two people here that had a chance of surviving if we were to set out across the forest! Most of the time I spent alone trying to decide if I really wanted to quit drinking or not! I had come to treatment on my own, but sometimes I wondered If it was because I had gotten another D.U.I. and thought it would look good to the judge. Was I really willing to give up drinking? Did I really have a problem? Was it really getting that bad? I was moved out of detox and into a cabin to start really focusing on a treatment plan. I was moved into cabin two; we were the Deuces.

Treatment started in earnest with groups and therapy and one on one with a counselor. My first group something happened, I tried to talk but every time I opened my mouth, I became so overwhelmed with emotions that I couldn't talk, believe me when I say this was a first for me, I've always had something to say and if I didn't, I could make some shit up pretty quick! Marilyn had asked me on a phone call if I really knew what all I had done to her, and I didn't think she meant just recently. So, I had been putting forth a good amount of energy toward thinking about all I had done to her. Evidently it had opened the flood gates to all I had done over the course of my entire life and it seemed that every time I opened my mouth it was all trying to come out at once and it was causing a systems overload and I couldn't say a word. Again, I told you I was batshit crazy! So, I grabbed a yellow legal tablet that I had brought with me and started to write and it all sort of just poured out. I wrote for a few days, once I started, I couldn't stop. It was literally like the flood gates had been opened and at the end of a couple of days when I was done writing I could talk in group. I could keep a single train of thought and I could carry on a somewhat normal conversation; I'm using the word normal here in a very broad sense if you will. Because brother, normal I ain't! Now when I had finished writing I put what I had written away and it wasn't meant for anyone to ever see, it was for myself. It was however used several years in the future for my Fourth Step, but we'll talk about that later, it was also read by my oldest daughter Alice some years into the future, I walked into my bedroom where she was watching TV and she had it in her hands reading it. I told her it was kind of private and personal, but she said she wanted to read it anyhow and against my better judgment I let her. But for now, we are in treatment and as I am now able to talk it's time to start my treatment in earnest. I asked my counselor for some First Step material and he gave me a work sheet that I completed and turned back in the same day. I then asked for a Second and Third Step worksheet that he produced. He told me it was rare that anyone ever asked for this material, but he was very glad that I was interested in recovery. Interested? I had a sneaky suspicion that I was going to fucking die if I continued using, you bet your ass I was interested. I started participating in recovery and shared my own experiences; we told war stories about our using, and we laughed at our insanity together. We went to outside AA meetings where I participated in the meetings instead of just going. I started working on my relationship with Marilyn, even though she was back in Ohio. I wrote her a letter outlining everything I could remember ever doing to her while using it was a long and painful letter apparently, we are sometimes referred to as a tornado wreaking havoc in others' lives for a reason. After I mailed the letter, I had to admit that I wouldn't be shocked if she never wanted to talk to me again. I visited the treatment center's long-term facility, it was a six-to-nine-month treatment program that I really wanted to go to, but it wasn't to happen, my insurance wouldn't pay for it, so I stayed for twenty-one days in Bradford.

One of the best things that happened was a seminar about how the drug addict's brain and alcoholic's brain acts differently than a normal person's brain. It was quite insightful, and I'm paraphrasing here - when an addict or alcoholic uses their drug of choice, the brain creates a release of dopamine equivalent to an orgasm, and the addict continues to strive to replicate the euphoric feeling, and as tolerance is built up, they continue to use or drink more and more. **Here is the goodbye to alcohol letter that I wrote while in Bradford:**

You have been there for the last twenty-one years; I have used you in one form or another every day except when I worked a program for four years and twice for six months. White knuckling it on my own, I've had you at parties, I've had you at home to myself, I've always been able to find you when I want you. I've loved you to the point of giving my life away. Your presence is so strong, your memories never gone! I have to say Goodbye. I want my life back. I want to live. I want to see my children grow up. I want to be able to remember my days. I've given too much time to you and I deserve better. I've found a new way to live, one that's proven to work. I don't need you to feel good anymore. I don't need you to hide my feelings anymore. I don't have to live the lie anymore. It's time to say goodbye to every form of you I have ever used because today I realize it's been me being used by you!

No Longer Yours
Ray Vance

I left Bradford feeling like a new man. I was put on a Greyhound and made the trip back to Axis to go back to work.

When I went back to work, I had to rely on a coworker for a ride for a few weeks until I had enough money to buy a car. I saw a 1998 Ford Thunderbird advertised for $1200, I got my landlord Harry to take me to look at the car with $1200 in my pocket. When we got there, the car had a lawnmower battery under the hood, no oil touching the dipstick, no shift handle but an automatic with a hairbrush for a shifter. I gave the guy's wife some money for oil and sent her down the road while I looked at the car. The headliner was falling down, then the owner said the sunroof, power seat, blinkers and brake lights were not working. To a lot of people, the car would have looked hopeless, but it had a 5.0 V8, and I was sure if it ran, then it would run like a scalded dog. With a jump, we fired the car up, and it had straight pipes and sounded great. Harry pulled me aside and said, "Don't look too interested, offer him $800, and I bet he sells it to you. So, I did, I offered him $800 pointed out everything that didn't work and needed replacing or repaired. The guy decided $800 was better than nothing, and I drove the car home. When I got home, I started working on the car, and after a small electrical fire I found where they had wired in an amp to the radio and had a toggle switch to power the amp. The back of the switch was touching metal and shorting everything out. After some rewiring and replacing some fuses, everything worked. I then replaced upper and lower ball joints, inner and outer tie rod ends, had new tires put on, replaced the shift lever, and had a headliner installed, and *voila!*, it was like a new car! I could drive myself to work, I could drive myself to meetings, and that's just what I did.

I soon went to court for my first Alabama D.U.I., and was given a first offense which was only a ninety-day license suspension and a year's probation with a few months of jail time over my head. Now I'm not quite sure how it all happened because I still had a second D.U.I. to go to court for, but we kept putting it off. Somehow, I ended up with a valid driver license, and I was as proud as a peacock. Work was going really well, and my boss told me he was proud of me for going to treatment and admitting that I had a problem, then he gave me a raise! Now things were going really well, but I need to say here that after treatment I didn't work on any step work, I only went to meetings. I did see my sponsor at meetings, but I didn't do any step work with him. I thought everything is going so well it's going to be ok. I went to meetings, and I listened to people talking about working the program and I was pretty sure just going to meetings was enough for me, boy was I fucking wrong!

The next several months went by with me working and attending meetings. I was staying sober. Marilyn and I were talking every day; we were quickly on the path to a reconciliation even after all the things I had done to her. Now while all of this was going on my son Judd had been using in Ohio, and he got into a significant amount of trouble. He had been sentenced to several months in jail followed by six to nine months in another rehabilitation center. Now, I remember talking to Judd just two days before he got in trouble and I could tell he was pretty messed up, and I told him if you keep doing what you are doing, you're going to end up locked up somewhere! Sure enough, that's just what happened, Judd was several months into the treatment facility and was starting to sound like he was going to work a program and stay clean. At about five months sober, myself I had a great idea – what if I could bring Judd down to Alabama and get him a job at the steel mill? We could work together and go to meetings together. I told Marilyn about my idea, and she thought it sounded plausible. Around the same time, we had a visit at work from one of the company's vice presidents, and while he was here, I asked him how old you must be to get hired with the company. He wanted to know why I was asking, I told him I had a nineteen-year-old son that I'd like to get a job; he then asked me if I would be willing to put my job on the line for my son to be hired, and I said I was. The end result: I was told if I could get him here, he had a job. So, I took a few days off work and flew to Ohio to see what I could get accomplished, Judd was court ordered to treatment and I didn't know if I could get him or not.

Because life isn't fun without drama, while I was doing all of this, my ex-wife was struggling with her own alcoholism and had had several near-death experiences, my daughters were afraid if something happened to their mom, they would have to move to Alabama with me. My company also had a mill in Middletown, Ohio, and after talking with my plant superintendent I was given the phone number to the plant superintendent in Middletown, so I called and set up an appointment while I was in Ohio. I wanted a backup plan just in case something terrible happened to my ex-wife. Now just to make the trip really exciting, Marilyn and I had decided I would bring our storage shed full of furniture and household possessions back to Alabama with me, with Marilyn following a few months later when she was ready to come. Wow, I had a lot to accomplish in a few days - try to get my kid out of court-ordered treatment, take him to Alabama and get him a job, go to a job interview in Middletown in case I had to move back to Ohio, and move all of Marilyn's and my worldly possessions back to Alabama. So, to say that I wasn't sure if I was coming or going wouldn't be very far from the truth!

The trip on the whole turned out pretty well, as the judge and Judd's parole officer were willing to let me take Judd. They transferred his parole to Alabama. My job interview with the mill in Middletown went very well; they were so impressed with the different types of equipment that I had experience on that they said anytime I needed to come back to Ohio they would lay-off someone to make room for me. I thought that was a little drastic, but it felt good to be seen as a reliable, useful employee. I also got to spend a little time with Marilyn and my daughters. I visited mom but was still not over the fact that she sold the farm. We rented a U-Haul, loaded up our storage unit, said goodbye to everyone in Ohio, and Judd and I headed south for Axis to a promise of a better life.

On the way south, Judd confided in me that he had just relapsed a few days before I had come to get him. I should have heard bells and whistles and I should have seen huge red flags flying, but I didn't. I told Judd I was proud that he told me the truth. Judd promised that everything was going to be better in Alabama and that he wasn't going to use anymore - at which time I really should have heard bells and whistles because he was saying the same things that I had said a thousand times. I was full of hope, and I totally missed all the warnings. I'll say here that it's that way with me and Judd, I want so much for him to be all right that I look right over what's really going on. It's hard to believe that with as much as I know about addiction and alcoholism, as much experience as I have on almost every drug, that I can't see it with Judd until it's such a desperate case of hopelessness that you can't miss it. It's that way with the ones we love, we want and hope so much for their safety and success that we can't see that the fifty bucks we just gave them is probably going for drugs! I'll say here that having Judd in the house with me or really just having Judd "an addict" for a son opened my eyes greatly to what I had put my parents through. We will revisit this thought later, though, as we aren't quite there yet!

When we reached our trailer in Axis, we moved all of the landlord's furniture out and moved all of ours in. When I had moved in, Ray had left a little nineteen-inch flatscreen TV, and the trailer was furnished with the landlord's furniture. Now a year later I had a fifty-five-inch flatscreen and my own furniture; I thought I was making progress. The truth is, that an idea like how big the tv was being important to me was another blaring alarm that I was probably in trouble. Remember now I'm not working a program, I'm not really changing, I'm just going to meetings, and I am staying sober! Working a program of recovery and staying sober are almost two separate worlds, but again we're not there yet.

Judd was hired at the mill and started work about a week later. I was to be his trainer. A week after Judd started, he was turned loose to operate on his own. To this day, Judd is and was the fastest trained and most prepared to be turned loose new hire we have ever had, Hell it took me three weeks! I will just quickly say three to six months is the normal amount of time needed to train someone for our job; I'll also say here that drug addicts and alcoholics are often times quite amazing workers - it might have to do with overcompensating for feeling like a piece of shit or something! I also will say that training my son to operate a ninety-ton Taylor and to manage our almost always high inventory yard is to this day one of the proudest achievements of my life! It's hard to explain how bad of a parent I had been; I was always using and drinking, I came first. What I wanted, what I needed, I was always first. I was closer to a zombie than a father. I was so proud to teach Judd what I knew, I truly felt like I was honoring the memories of my father who taught me everything that he could. I will say that training your son is much easier than training anyone else; for instance, I could smack him on the back of the head and say, "Shut the fuck up and listen!" You just can't do that with everyone, but really, I was as proud as a peacock with how well and fast Judd learned.

While all of this is going on, Marilyn was still in Ohio, and I was quite lonely. I had gone the longest time in my life without being laid, so my judgment might have been a bit clouded. It really had more to do with the fact that I wasn't working a program and was still exceedingly selfish. I'd rather leave this out, but being a true account of my life, I believe it could be relevant, so here it goes. I was lonely and even though Marilyn and I were talking every day I started getting on dating sites with the hope of meeting someone. I only went on two dates before I pretty much gave up on the whole idea. The first is relevant because as I was waiting in Biloxi, Mississippi, to meet a person of interest, I called home and talked to mom. Mom told me that my little brother Mick had just died. I told her I was sorry and that having just been home a week from being in Ohio I probably wouldn't be able to make it back for the funeral. We said goodbye to each other, and I stood on the beach in Biloxi and cried for the loss of my brother. Then, because I'm a thinker and a risk taker, I went into The Hard Rock casino and dropped $20 into a slot machine to see if I could win the money to go home for the funeral. Well, Lady Luck wasn't with me that day, so I went to meet my date. When she showed up, she turned out to be old enough to be my mom. She could sense my disappointment, and I told her it was fine we should still go have lunch and talk.

While we were talking, I realized that a ten to fifteen year's difference might not be too much as long as it was younger and not older. I know, right! So, after lunch and a walk on the beach, we said goodbye and I headed for home.

I will quickly say I only went on one other date, and that was to meet for dinner in a restaurant up by Atmore and that experience didn't go much better. My date was kind of a larger woman than I had expected. When she asked me what I thought of the dating site my reply was, "It's really kind of hard to tell when people don't use an up-to-date picture." In my defense, so I don't sound as superficial as I was and can be, the whole idea of being with a bigger woman is more of a conundrum. It really stems from the fact that I'm not that big of a guy, and if we are dating and I am responsible for her safety - like if we find ourselves in a burning building and I can't carry her to safety then I must be less of a man. The real truth at that time in my life is, if we are dating, and you find yourself in a burning building there's a better than fair chance I lit the fire!

All right, let's get back to Axis, where everything was going fantastic. Judd and I were getting along at home, we were going to meetings at a clubhouse in Mobile and one in Saraland, and I was almost six months sober. One day while at work, my boss told me he wanted to talk to me. I went into the office and he again told me how proud he was that I was sober and that I was doing an excellent job with my work duties. He told me that I was being promoted to a lead position and I was to run a shift. I was thrilled! I couldn't believe how good everything was going. I told the boss thank you, and I finished the day on cloud nine! Judd and I got home from work right about 5:30, and he laid down on the couch and went to sleep. It takes a little getting used to working on twelve-hour shifts. I headed for my shower; I couldn't believe I'd been promoted, all the bills were getting paid, and everything was exceptionally good! I got out of the shower, got dressed, and drove straight to the bar and got drunk! The Big Book talks about how we can be seemingly defenseless to the first drink. I can tell you that I didn't think about going to the bar, it wasn't something I planned, I just did it, and I did with complete impunity. I had zero thought of consequence, I had zero thought of not being able to stop once I started. I just drove to the bar, sat down, and ordered a Crown and Coke.

20

DUMBASS

I was into my third drink before I realized what I was doing, and by then the damage was already done. I was instantly back to lying, I didn't want anyone to know I was drinking. I avoided meetings altogether, and I suffered tremendously through work because I knew that I couldn't keep working if I drank on nights before I had to work. I met someone with a steady connection for pain pills, and I started eating Lortabs or Percocet on the days I was working. I couldn't bear the thought of going through the day without something to give me a buzz, and on my days off I drank as much as I wanted to.

During summer that year my daughters were invited to go on a trip to Disney World with my mom and sister. On their way back to Ohio from Florida, they made plans to stay a day or two so I could see the girls. I was off the days they were here, but I had to stay sober; I couldn't let my girls and my mom and sister know that I was drinking again. It was two of the toughest days of my life. I was completely miserable when I went to the hotel to see them. They were so excited to see me, they just wanted hugs and kisses, and I just didn't want love. I yelled at them both because they wouldn't stop hugging me. My mom and sister said I had to visit with my girls at the hotel, that I couldn't leave with them, so I was instantly pissed off. I called Abigale and asked her why the girls couldn't spend the night at my house, Abigale said, "They are your kids; if you want to take them home for the night take them." That's just what I did.

We went back to the trailer, and I spent the night with all three of my children. It was a total nightmare. Judd rough-housed with his sister so hard that I was sure one of them was going to get a broken bone and all I could think about was getting a drink and how I had to hide that from all of them. I was completely miserable; I was uncomfortable around my own kids, and I didn't feel like I could do anything right. All they wanted was to spend time together. The next day, I met my mom and sister at a truck stop and said goodbye to them all. As they drove away, I just thought I need a drink, so I went straight to the bar and got drunk. The relief was felt with the first drink in my hand. All the tension left, and I felt like I was going to be ok.

One night while sitting at the bar drinking, a woman who I had met in the Saraland meeting came into the bar. Her daughter was the bartender, and I saw her, and she saw me. She came over and gave me a hug and told me that she loved me and that they were missing me at the meeting. I couldn't say anything, just sat there and drank my drink. I couldn't believe that anyone could love me; hell, I didn't even love myself.

A month later, I was pulled over leaving a bar and given another D.U.I.

In short order, I decided to go to treatment again. I reasoned that Marilyn was about to move back to Alabama, and surely treatment would look good to the judge when I went to court for the D.U.I., so I called a treatment center in southern Florida, The Watershed. I was almost instantly accepted for treatment; they had a plane ticket waiting for me at the Mobile, Alabama, airport, and the next day I left for treatment. I had to tell my boss at work that I was going back to treatment. He wasn't very happy, but he told me to go and get better. The next day, I tried to talk myself out of going, but I had already told work and I was sure it would look better for court, so I went. I was already half drunk when Judd dropped me off at the airport and I went straight to the bar to drink some more while waiting on my plane. There was a small layover in Atlanta, so I went to another bar and drank some more. I flew into Fort Lauderdale, Florida, where I went straight to the bar and drank a final few Long Island iced teas before going to baggage claim where there was a driver waiting to take me to The Watershed. Needless to say, I was pretty much all the way drunk when I showed up in treatment! I figured it's never good to show up for treatment sober. The next day, when several of the patients told me the driver would have stopped so I could buy a bottle if I'd have asked, I was a little pissed off about the whole thing. On the whole, I made it to treatment, and I meant to make a go of it. The Watershed was the nicest treatment facility I had ever been to. All of our meals were prepared by a chef, and the cafeteria had soft serve ice cream available from about two o'clock on. It was all you could eat, and the thirteen-year-old in me was pretty sure we had arrived!

I stayed fifty-four days in The Watershed, and for the most part it was a mostly positive experience. As you all know, it wasn't my first rodeo so I came prepared - I had a carton of smokes, paper, and pens, plenty of envelopes - I brought everything I would need. I quickly was known as the boot guy because I didn't wear flip flops or tennis shoes, I always wore boots, either steel-toed Red Wings or a tan pair of military-issued Bellevilles. The Bellevilles came from a treatment center in Ohio, they had been given to Judd. and I confiscated them the first time I saw them.

I met a lot of people in treatment and really got along with everyone for the most part. I will say I've never met so many millionaires that needed to bum a smoke - though, it's really not a big surprise, we are all for the most part liars and thieves when we show up for treatment, so it's not unexpected to hear lies and see people steeling from others. It turned out to be a good exercise in telling people no when they asked for a smoke, I would give out a few in the morning and then quit; I was certainly no millionaire, and I wasn't planning on supplying smokes for everyone else.

I stayed in the main facility for about twenty-one days then moved into the IOP phase of the treatment and was moved to a gated apartment community smack dab in the middle of crackville. I guess the objective was if you could stay sober there, you could do it anywhere! I did stay sober my whole fifty-four days of treatment. I wasn't altogether honest my whole stay. I didn't like that the facility took all of your money and debit cards as soon as you arrived and they went to the store for you at first, and later when you were allowed out on your own, they would give you some of your money if you asked in advance. I wasn't very happy about not having access to my own money, so I called my bank and canceled my debit card and ordered a new one, and when it showed up in the mail, I had Judd buy me a carton of smokes and hide my debit card in a pack in the middle of the carton and then glue the carton back shut. When my second carton of smokes came, I had a new debit card and access to my money if I needed it. I never really did need it, but I was much more comfortable not having to ask for my own money.

While I was there, several people ran and used, only to come back and start over again. Two young girls in their early twenties ran together, and only one of them came back; the other was found a couple days later dead on the side of the road from an overdose. The woman that ran the apartment complex had a wall with pictures of everyone that had died who had been a resident, and there were an incredible number of pictures on the wall. It really brought it home that I was fighting a life-or-death disease, and there was evidence all around me of people losing the fight!

While I was at The Watershed, I got a temporary sponsor and worked some steps. We did a speed exercise where I worked all of the steps but not thoroughly. This was the first time that I had done anything past step five. It was somewhat enlightening being that the goal of a twelve-step program is to actually work all twelve steps (Who would have thought?). My temporary sponsor's idea was to get a quick introduction to all of the steps and that they then would be followed by a complete working of the steps with a sponsor after going home. Again, about this idea of further work to be done, I had heard the saying "Faith without works is dead" but had very little concept of what it really meant!

During this time, Marilyn moved back in from Ohio. She and Judd were able to take care of all the bills at home and keep me supplied with a little money and cigarettes. I was going to treatment classes during the days and going to outside meetings in the evenings. I was for the most part busy most of the time that I was there and like every time before I took treatment seriously, I put forth a genuine effort to better myself. We got to go to the beach at West Palm Beach several times, and on Sunday mornings there was a 6:30 sunrise meeting on the beach. I really enjoyed the sunrise beach meeting; I've always felt an awareness of a creator at the beach, probably because I was raised in a cornfield. I wrote another letter, it was my goodbye to alcohol assignment. I titled it "Goodbye to A Lie." Here is what I wrote:

Goodbye to A Lie

I have completed five previous treatment programs, four of which required a Goodbye to Drugs and Alcohol Letter. Which I have written with all the words of sincerity, but I find myself back again, so I am going to adapt this letter to the real issue at hand. I left all five treatments successfully completed. After each one I went home to start my life over, living clean and sober.

My first attempt in 1986 yielded me four years clean and sober, at the end of which I thought myself cured and I picked up!

My second attempt in 2000, six months, and frustrated with life I used again.

My third attempt in 2002, nine months and I blamed jealousy of my wife's drinking for this relapse.

My fourth attempt in 2008, twenty-three months, eighteen of which I spent in intense study of my past behavior in a penal institution. This relapse I blame on a Blue Oysters Cult and Rush concert. I just knew it would be more fun with a drink, and I would be able to control it this time. Of course, I couldn't!

My fifth attempt October 2012, less than a year ago, broken and on the way to treatment after a spiritual revelation, a true awakening of the awareness that I am the problem not the drugs or the alcohol. I hit this treatment with a passion to learn to live life on life's terms. Ready to be completely and totally honest with myself and the center. I was sure that I was ready to accept my defeat at the hands of this disease. For this relapse there is nothing but the lie that I can find to blame. I just drank, days away from six months sober. Completely content I thought, with the success of my sobriety.

In my mind I know that if I drink, I can't stop. I know that if I continue, I will surely die. I've known this for a very long time, maybe from as far back as my first treatment.

I can clearly see the effects drinking and drugging have cost me, a wife of fifteen years, three beautiful children; my two daughters that I no longer get to hold every day, our relationship is on the phone. My son, nine months clean from heroine, raised in my image, with my disease which I taught him. Countless jobs, a house, vehicles, relationships with other family and friends. And the list goes on and on. I see the damage and in my waking mind I know it to be true.

Somewhere in my heart and soul where the rest of me is, the part that only God and I know, the part of me that hides, the part of me that at the worst times becomes dominant. I hold onto the idea that one day I will be able to drink like a gentleman, "not a new idea."

My disease has changed and adapted over the years to keep its hold on me. I have changed in my living mind; I fight to suppress the wrong I do. In my living mind I accept defeat, I am beaten.

I live with a lie, in my heart and soul the part of me that is hidden, the part where good and evil live together, the part that is hard to find. I believe that once God realizes his mistake of making me with this disease I will be fixed. I am able to lie to myself and I am able to hide this lie, even from myself. I can't be broken, it's a mistake, someone else must be to blame, even God!

I am ready to surrender and the only way for that to happen is for me to face this lie. I was made to be what I am; God doesn't make mistakes. I am no more or less important than a single grain of sand on a beautiful beach. Each one necessary, each one waiting to perform its destiny. Be it to blow in the wind or to be swept to another place by the tide. Each one waiting faithfully to fulfill its clandestine duty.

I must look inward to my hidden soul to say Goodbye to A Lie. I am not Hashem! I must face the spoiled child inside my soul. I don't get what I want, only what I work for. I must face the fear of what lurks inside my soul. For I think this is where I hide.

> Forgive me Lord for
> Thinking you made a mistake
> Forgive me
> For lying to myself for all
> These years
> Give me strength to face my lie
> To know the truth
> In my soul
> I am not a mistake
> May I face my soul
> Each new day
> And tell the truth
> I am what I am
> An alcoholic that
> Will never drink like a gentleman

The day finally came to go home, and I said my goodbyes to new friends made at The Watershed, a few of which I'm still in contact with. I made the flight home without drinking and went to a meeting as soon as I got home, something that greatly increases your chances of staying sober! When I got home, I had to look at the fact that I wasn't working any steps with my sponsor, so I decided to ask someone else to sponsor me. I asked Franklin, the first person I had met in AA in the state of Alabama, to be my sponsor. It turned out that Franklin was a retired treatment center counselor, which worked out really well considering my obvious love of treatment!

I worked the first three steps with Franklin over the next several months, but I was in no real hurry. Hell, I had the rest of my life, didn't I? Things were better at home; Marilyn and I didn't seem to have much to argue about, and I went to work on time and worked all the overtime I was asked to work; life was getting better. I no longer paid bills late, and I was able to quit living on cash advances. The world seemed to be changing for the better.

However, I didn't work nearly as diligently on the twelve steps as my sponsor would have liked. I was working a partial program at best and at about five-and-a-half months sober, I hurt my back at work. I had pulled a muscle and was in some very serious discomfort, so I went to the doctor. I was prescribed some painkillers and muscle relaxers and given a steroid shot. I was kind of concerned about what others in recovery would think about me taking painkillers. I felt like the best thing to do would be to keep it to myself, so I didn't tell Franklin or any of my friends that I went to meetings with. I will say that it was one of the first times that I ever took a prescription painkiller exactly as prescribed by the doctor, and I felt that I was doing the right thing by keeping it a secret. Uh oh, a secret, I think I've already said we are only as sick as our secrets! That was another valuable lesson because when it came down to it, I started to experience cravings for a drink and I was already keeping one secret, what would one more really hurt!

I was right at six months sober when I started drinking again, and I was pretty sure that I wasn't ever going to get past six months of sobriety. I was about as defeated as I have ever been. The only real change in my behavior was that I was terrified to drive after I was drunk. I already had four D.U.I.s, all of which I was charged first offense for. My license was revoked until 2025, so I was pretty sure if I got another one that I would be doing five years in an unairconditioned Alabama prison, and as amazing as that sounds, I had the wherewithal to realize that I didn't want to experience this consequence. So, after I would get drunk, I started calling Marilyn to come and get me. Even when I was blacked out and didn't know what I was doing, I still would call Marilyn to come and get me. Sometimes bartenders or bouncers would call Marilyn for me. So, looking back at this I was clearly making my problems someone else's problem because Marilyn also didn't want to see me locked up for five years either.

I woke up on more than one occasion after a black out with a loaded gun in the bed with me. I started waking up with a disassembled loaded gun in the bed with me. Looking back, I realize that I took the gun apart so I wouldn't shoot myself. I was totally miserable, I didn't want to do this anymore, but I couldn't stop, I was fairly convinced that death was going to be my only way out. I was using every particle of my existing willpower to only drink on my days off! I knew that if I drank on the days that I had work, I wouldn't go I would just keep drinking. I was completely miserable on the days I worked I wanted a drink, and I counted the minutes until I had a day off and was finally able to start drinking. In essence I was completely miserable when I drank, and I was completely miserable when I didn't! Again, death was looking more and more like a realistic solution.

This went on for several months until it finally consumed me. I had the weekend off, and Marilyn had picked me up at a bar on Friday night, my car was still in the bar parking lot. I had come home with Marilyn after buying beer and whiskey for the house. I woke up Saturday and started drinking, I drank into the afternoon until the beer and the whiskey ran out then I ordered a pizza for Marilyn and me. On the way to pick up the pizza, I had Marilyn stop at a gas station that conveniently had a liquor store beside of it. I went in and got another bottle of whiskey. When we got to the pizza place, I asked Marilyn to go in to get the pizza; I was literally too ashamed of myself to go in and face the teenager behind the counter. As I sat in the car realizing that I was too ashamed to buy a pizza from a stranger, I decided that I had to do something about this. When Marilyn got back in the car with the pizza, I was on the phone with The Watershed telling them that I had relapsed and that I needed to come back to treatment.

Looking back, it's kind of ironic. I had been homeless, I had been to prison, I had been ostracized from my family, I had lost numerous jobs, I had four D.U.I.s, I had lost my license until 2025, I had lost a wife and being with my children, and through all these things I continued to drink and do drugs. I found my defeat at the hands of a pizza and not being able to face a stranger behind the counter. I told you all that I was fucked up!

On Thursday August 14, 2014, I went back to treatment for what I hope was the last time. I celebrate my sobriety date on August 13. I moved it up one day because I went to treatment for the first time on May 13, 1986, and I stayed clean the longest in my life after that treatment, so I thought the thirteen would be luckier, and I have always been honest about moving it one day. So, moving my sobriety date came later, I got ahead of myself again! Let's go to treatment for the last time. I showed up to treatment in regular fashion, pretty well drunk! After the necessary couple of days recuperating, I was finally able to eat, I set right into recovery.

21

THE BITTER END

July 2, 2018

I find myself unable to continue my story tonight. I am distracted by the haunted memories of friends and acquaintances lost to this Disease of Addiction and Alcoholism, of which unfortunately there have been many. Last night, a friend who I went to school with found The Bitter End; she committed suicide, leaving behind two grown children, a mother, a sister, and a brother. I find myself reminded of the several times that I stood on the precipice of The Bitter End. I am saddened at our loss; my friend was well liked and a much-loved person. I cannot claim to know rather she was one of us "an alcoholic or addict," as that right is solely for everyone to decide for themselves. I can, however, say that she definitely portrayed some of our behaviors. She will be greatly missed.

I have been reminded of countless others who I have known who have lost their lives going to The Bitter End. This is captioned in a reading titled "More About Alcoholism"; in essence, it says that the great obsession of every abnormal drinker is to finally drink like a normal person, and unfortunately there are those who are willing to follow this To the Bitter Ends Insanity and Death.

There are many people who have lost their lives to addiction, and I am tonight reminded of a few of them that I knew personally. I am also reminded of lives taken by people who are in the throes of addiction and alcoholism also of which there are many.

My first memory of an alcohol-related death comes from elementary school. The brother of a neighbor girl, who I might have had a crush on, was in an accident; he was drunk, and the driver of the car he hit was killed. My neighbors left town and moved away. I was much too young at the time to understand; all I knew was a girl I liked was gone, and I never saw her again.

I didn't know then, but I later found out that my mother's sister and children were killed in a drunk driving accident. My mother's sister was the one drinking, so this disease was taking people out of my life before I was ever born. I find it ironic that I would become such friends with Death itself. I lived a great many years in the grips of this Disease, more than willing to die or kill as my friend Death would have it. I was also willing for years to ignore the fact that Death was my friend, and the closer to Death I got while drinking and using, the better it felt!

We lost a good friend in high school to a drinking and driving accident. I also had a friend whose dad lost his life in a motorcycle accident driving impaired. There were also a few suicides of friends growing up. Again, I can't point a definite finger at alcoholism and addiction for these, but there is no question that a maladjusted mind was involved, and I'm well aware that I share a maladjusted mind as well therefore I can't rule it out either.

A very good friend of mine went to jail for nine months, and on the day he was released, he had some coke that he put away when he went to jail. The day he got out he used like before he had left, and it killed him! Another very good friend went to the bar with another friend, and they got into a fight over a girl. One friend hit the other, he fell and hit his head he was in a coma for a while before he died!

In recovery, I have met many people who later lost their lives to this disease, some by their own hands and others by accidental overdose. As mentioned earlier, one of the treatment centers I was in a couple young girls left to go use and only one came back the other went To The Bitter End. It is a very devastating disease, and it has virtually touched in some way everyone. Every household knows someone who has went to The Bitter End. I must admit that the memories bring up a feeling of profound sadness for myself and everyone who has been touched by this disease. I don't understand my creator's plan! I don't understand how I could have stood with Death himself, and yet here I am. I don't understand why I was allowed to live and others are not. I also don't understand how I can feel this way and be ok today. Four years ago, this would have led to a bender and another chance at The Bitter End. I find myself looking at peace in what I face today, I no longer have to understand. I have found acceptance and I have been given a way to learn to live life on life's terms. I can experience pain and anger today; I can feel grief for the loss of a friend, and I can feel sympathy for the pain of her family. I can feel a plethora of emotions and feelings today and not be overwhelmed and have the need to medicate myself so as not to feel them at all. Essentially, I have been given life and a way to live it. I have been given a method that has and is teaching me how to handle myself and life. I have been given an understanding, as have many others, of how to live with this Disease and my maladjusted mind.

I find myself with the feelings of the loss of a friend in a very humble and human place. I don't understand why I do understand. As I feel pain and sadness, I also feel grateful that I don't have to live that way anymore. I feel gratitude for all I have learned and all I have been through, and I realize that everything that has happened, that is happening, and that will happen is part of what makes me who I am! I feel an overwhelming gratitude that I can express love for myself and my fellows today. I know what I have done to get here, and I also know what saved my life from drinking and drugging, as a fellow human in the mix of life I have an overwhelming desire to scream from the mountain tops that there is a solution and if I can learn to live with the disease of alcoholism anyone can!

But alas I live in reality today, and I can remember all the people in recovery that were and still are willing to help me just as someone helped them. So, I suppress my desire to scream from the mountain tops, and I brace myself for the wait and opportunity to show someone what has been shown to me. If I could rub a lamp and make a wish it would be that no one must live with the desire to die in the throes of addiction and alcoholism. It is a torturous hell, and when you are there, it seems totally hopeless of ever escaping. There is however a way out! I don't understand, why I understand, but I sure as Hell am glad that I do! I promise you I know the truth today and I also know how to live with it. As do millions of others, there is a way out. So, to my friend and all of the alcoholics and drug addicts who died the night of July 1, 2018 R.I.P. Know that you were loved and will be missed! May you be in Heaven thirty minutes before the devil knows you're there!

On March 1, 2019, I was told that another one of my very good friends from home has gone to The Bitter End, losing the battle with alcoholism and addiction. My first reaction is gratitude that I have been able to find another way to live. My second reaction is a prayer for all who are struggling, there really is another way to live. My third reaction is a prayer for all who have lost the ultimate battle with addiction may your souls find peace in the afterlife, because I know the terror and hell that you endured while you were here.

RIP my friend, we all loved you! R.I.P. Tigger!

22

ON WE GO

Well, it's been a while since I've written any, as time goes it's been about a year since I've started. I am about three months away from celebrating five years of continuous sobriety, I'd like to say that I haven't been writing because I've been busy, or maybe consumed with the ending of *The Game of Thrones*, but being as I'm trying to write an honest book, I can't say either of those. The truth is I've been afraid that my story isn't good enough to be in a book. I've also been afraid to face some of the things that are going to be written about as I get closer to present time. Even though I am working a twelve-step program and by the grace of God I am not faced with the desire to drink or use today, I am still sometimes driven by fear. There are some things that I don't really want to say or think about but here we are. So, as I face my fears, I also keep a commitment that I made to myself, I wanted to write a book so that's what we are going to do!

As best as I can recall, I'm in treatment again, and I am being rather serious about it. I have found myself in a place where I cannot live with or without alcohol or drugs. There's a ringing in my ears that sounds a lot like Franklin telling me that I've never worked the First Step. I am attending all my groups, I am going to outside meetings "of the twelve-step variety," I am trying to be supportive to other patients who act like they are interested in recovery.

At about fourteen days into what has turned out to be my last trip to rehab, I was trying to get a temporary sponsor. I was going to use a guy that I had been in treatment with a year before who wasn't really working a program; I don't really remember what happened, but for some reason the whole plan sort of fell through. Today I can say that was likely God doing for me what I couldn't do for myself. I was sitting in group one day, and I got the funniest feeling that I could be teaching this group. It's not like the seventh time I've been in treatment or anything (Mom still swears it was eight.), but I think one of them was in detox for only a few days! Let's not split hairs here, I get the funniest feeling that maybe I should just go home and start working the steps with Franklin, go to meetings, and see what happens. It's not like I came up with this idea on my own – it's what was suggested to me every time I've been to rehab! What if I actually did it though? At which time I wrote my last goodbye to alcohol letter, which I titled "Another Letter." It seemed appropriate at the time; of course, I might have just been being a smart ass. Here is what I wrote:

Another Letter

In 1986 at fifteen years old I wrote a heart felt Goodbye to weed letter. I stayed clean four years.

In 2000 I wrote a beaten and broken Goodbye to cocaine letter. I stayed clean for eight months.

In 2002 I wrote what I was sure was my last Goodbye to drugs letter. I stayed sober six months.

In 2012 I wrote Goodbye to alcohol with a new determination and a renewed spirit. I only stayed sober six months, had to celebrate a promotion!

In 2013 I wrote Goodbye to A Lie, the lie being that someday I'll be able to drink like a gentleman.

I believe that everything in creation has a purpose. I am no more or less important than a single grain of sand. On a beautiful beach. A grain of sand may wait an eternity to fill its full purpose, it could end up a pearl, it may be swept to the four corners of the world, it could forever be caught in the current swept back and forth from beach to beach, for whatever is in store it waits and obeys.

I don't have the faith of a grain of sand, I force my will above my Creator's. I go where I want, I sit waiting impatient, I run into trouble like it's meant to be. I lack the faith of a grain of sand.

Yet here I sit full of life, allowed to write Another Letter, with a new goal to have the courage to try again, to have the courage to admit when I'm wrong, to be able to say Goodbye to the idea that my way will ever work.

I took my letter to group and read it, getting the normal responses of "Well done!"

I have this idea inside my mind that I need to go home and start working the program with Franklin. I'm pretty sure that this idea isn't going to be met well by my counselor or the treatment center staff. So, I decide to keep this idea to myself for a few days. I say a little prayer about the whole thing asking for guidance on what I should do! In the meantime, I continue to go to groups and outside meetings, I continue to focus on the fact that I think maybe Franklin had been right all along. You see, Franklin and I had a conversation and essentially Franklin told me that I had never worked an honest first step. Now I have to admit that my first reaction to this statement was to get a little defensive and I snapped back that I'm pretty sure I've worked about seven first steps. Franklin's calm reply was that if I had done an honest one, I wouldn't have had to drink again. I thought now look here old fella just because you have forty years sober doesn't mean you know what I have and haven't done. Now this conversation keeps bouncing around in all the empty space between my ears and the part that keeps standing out to me is forty years sober, obviously this guy knows something! For about three days I keep playing this conversation over and over while I'm trying to decide what I'm going to do.

Eventually I went to my counselor and said, "I think I want to go home. It's time for me to work an honest program, and I believe I'm ready." You would think that my counselor would support my idea to work an honest program, especially being that is the goal of every treatment center I have ever been in. However, I was told that if I left treatment I would go home and continue using and eventually die! Now, I had to admit to myself that this in fact was a possibility. If I didn't follow through with working an honest program, I would definitely go back to using. But I was very confident that I was in fact ready and willing to do whatever it took to work an honest program with Franklin as my sponsor. So, against medical advice, at twenty-one days into treatment I left The Watershed, got on an airplane, and headed for home.

I stayed sober on the trip and went to a meeting and met with Franklin the day I got home! Remember, I said earlier that greatly increases your chances of staying sober. I went back to work at the steel mill, I started working the twelve steps with Franklin, I also became an active member of my family. That sounds kind of funny, but it was the truth. I had only been pretending to be part of a family for a very long time, actually being present and a participating member of a family was something that I was going to have to really work at. Now when I say a member of my family, I mean my house with Marilyn and Judd and also my relationship with Alice and Ophelia. I wasn't including my mom and sister in Ohio; I was still very angry over losing my inheritance from dad, and I was fairly sure I wouldn't be getting over it anytime soon!

So I worked an honest first step with Franklin. We admitted that we were powerless over alcohol and that our lives had become unmanageable. I knew to the hidden place in my soul, down to the little hairs on my toes, that I am an alcoholic, that I have the disease of alcoholism, and that if I put alcohol in my body in any form, I would trigger the allergy that would start the cravings and obsession of the mind. I fully conceded to my inner-most self that I am an alcoholic. Took long enough, didn't it? As for the unmanageable part, I believe the previous work in this book speaks for itself. I continued to work steps with Franklin, and they were fairly easy until I got to the fifth.

I don't want to go into much detail on the second and third step (step two came to believe that a power greater than ourselves could restore us to sanity, step three made a decision to turn our will and our lives over to the care of God as we understood him), not because they are not vastly important because they are. I just don't think I can talk about the second and third step without showing opinions and prejudice. Many of us have been taught from birth the concept of God, we can confuse this concept with religion, however, fitting God into a box or a book for that matter, might just be a little presumptuous of us all. If you can smash the idea that you must believe what others believe, if you can find your very own concept of a higher power, then the journey becomes a blessing. I found my concept and together with Franklin I said the third step prayer and turned my will and life over to my higher power. It sounds easy to do...well my friends, for me it was not. While writing this book and attending meetings I continued to hear a repeated theme that numerous people started their day saying the third step prayer. I shared in a meeting that I thought that people were obviously speaking in a metaphor because no one gets up in the morning and says a prayer. Well, that's what I thought. Turns out that people really do, and I have started to try to practice this in my life as well. I must admit that I fall short of doing this every day when I wake up, I am learning to do it more and as I continue to practice, I find that life continues to improve. I really am slow sometimes but again it's the journey that is a blessing.

Now we move on to the fourth and fifth step, (four made a searching and fearless moral inventory of ourselves, five admitting to God, to ourselves, and to another human being the exact nature of our wrong). Here I ran into a common failing – I wrote my fourth step, but I glossed over a great many things. I was still full of pride and shame, and I didn't want to admit to myself or another human being the exact nature of my wrongs. So, as I came to share my fifth step with Franklin, he saw right through me and said I don't think so! I got more than a little angry over the whole thing, I thought this is my story what do mean you don't think so! Franklin told me he didn't believe I had written an honest fourth step, so he didn't accept my fifth step as being done. I left Franklin feeling a little pissed off, and I sulked for a week or so before I admitted to myself that he was right.

I searched through my treatment files and found what I had written two years ago in Bradford. I read through it, and I had been very thorough because I was writing for myself; I never intended to share this with anyone. So here I felt I cheated a little. I called Franklin and asked if we could get together for another fifth step, and so we did. This time as Franklin read through the more than thirteen pages front and back on yellow legal tablet paper, he kept shaking his head yes, at the end he told me, "Now that was a thorough fifth step." I later confessed to Franklin that I felt like I cheated a little; he asked me if I had written what was on my fifth step. I said I had a few years ago; he then asked if I wrote it how could I have cheated on it. Apparently, I couldn't have cheated because I had in fact written every word of it. After my fifth step was completed, Franklin sent me home to contemplate what I had written. I was to call him after an hour or two of meditating about my fifth step. When I called, he said we are now ready for step six and seven, (six, we're entirely ready to have God remove all of these defects of character and seven, humbly asked him to remove our shortcomings). Now working the first seven steps really encompasses the first year of my sobriety. I must admit, that by this time the desire to drink and or use drugs had been virtually removed. "I, still under extreme anger, drive past a A.B.C. store, and it may look like there is a light behind it so that it stands out in my vision, however I recoil from the idea of a drink or drug as if from a hot flame!" Not my words – it's in the Big Book, yet it is as true as anything I have ever known.

A lot of life happened that first year of sobriety, and working the steps is what allowed it to happen! I asked Marilyn to marry me, and she said yes. We planned to go to Ohio and pick up Alice and Ophelia to go on a camping trip to Arkansas to visit a state park that has an active diamond mine. I went to work, not missing one day, not going in late or leaving early. I tried to help Judd with recovery, but he wasn't very interested, so I tried to be a good dad. I made an honest effort not to hurt others, and it seemed to be making a difference. Just before Marilyn and

I left for our summer trip with the girls, Franklin and I did some more step work (eight, make a list of all the people I had harmed and became willing to make amends to them all). In preparation for nine (made direct amends to such people wherever possible, except when to do so would injure them or others), so when we got to Ohio to pick up the girls, I was able to see my mother and to make amends to her. Mom was the first real amends that I made, and I was very nervous to do so. There were things I had done that I could never undo, and even when I made my amends, I couldn't yet comprehend what all I had really done to her, but I would, it was coming, I would soon understand exactly what I put her through, but we will save that for later.

Earlier in the book, I gave my dad credit for everything good that I know about love and working. Dad was my best friend. Well, here I get to make a little retraction to that statement because I knew that my mom was the most important person in my life. She had made me, she had loved me before anyone else, she had taught me as much about love and life as dad. Moms never get the credit they really deserve. From the moment I made my amends to my mom, our friendship has continued to grow until I realized that she was as much a best friend to me as my dad had ever been. Thank you for being my mom, I love you.

Now we had a really good vacation with the girls. We dug for diamonds in Arkansas, and we stayed on a lake in a cabin for several days fishing and hanging out. We acted like a family, and I started feeling like a real dad. I don't remember catching any fish, but I do remember making s'mores over a campfire, digging in the mud together for diamonds, and Alice scaring the living shit out of Ophelia hiding in the woods beside a trail after dark.

We came back to Alabama and went on day trips to the beach in Florida – I still wasn't going to the beach in Alabama

– and had a great summer. When the time for the girls to go home came, mom had offered to meet us in Nashville to take the girls back to Ohio. We stayed in Nashville over the Fourth of July and watched the fireworks there. It was an amazing trip, and we all had fun. While in Nashville, I got to buy some new boots. I actually have my very first pair of cowboy boots on a shelf in the house, because mom saved them! Only one other thing that happened that first year of sobriety that was kind of a big deal. Marilyn was going to a friend's birthday party in Florida, and I was working nights. So, I asked her to pick me up a scratch-off ticket. I gave her the money, and Monday morning when I got home, I scratched my ticket. It was a $5,000 winner! As it turns out, I stumbled across a 2000 Pontiac Trans Am WS6. The dealership wanted $10,500 for the car. I scraped together everything I had and traded in my Ford Thunderbird and bought the Trans Am, which I still have. It doesn't seem like much, but all of my money always went on drugs and alcohol, so this was the first real thing I bought that I wanted. Had I not been sober, it wouldn't have happened! Well actually it was the second big thing I bought. Several years earlier, I bought a 2012 Honda TRX450ER; it was really a repeat of getting Mort's four-wheeler, as I bought the Honda with the hope that if I had something fun to do, I wouldn't drink as much. I ended up only riding when I was drinking, and that wasn't a very good mix. So, I guess the car was the first thing I had bought sober that I wanted. I had to mention the four-wheeler because it's going to make another appearance soon.

Work was going incredibly well. I continued to not miss any days, and I was always on time, usually fifteen minutes early. Judd was also doing very well at work. He had joined a hunting camp with a coworker and was spending a lot of time at the camp. I spoke to our coworker and told him I was concerned that Judd might be drinking. Our coworker assured me I had nothing to worry about Judd was much too young to be an alcoholic or a drug addict. At this time, I informed our coworker that he didn't have a clue what he was talking about. I proceeded to explain that if Judd was using or drinking, the day would come that he would lose everything – his job, place to live and anything else he might have accumulated. Our coworker didn't believe me, and he again told me I was making too much of a big deal about it. I said we will see! Now this gets a little sketchy because I'm telling my story, however, what I'm about to start going through with Judd is relevant.

The truth is Judd had already been battling addiction for years. Remember, I picked him up in Ohio from a locked down court ordered treatment facility. Promises were made of going to meetings and working a program. Two years earlier when I moved Judd down from Ohio, he did go to meetings with me. Judd even asked someone to be his sponsor, however, I don't think they ever did any step work. Now this isn't really an abnormal thing, and it's one I've been guilty of myself more than once. Coming to meetings and seeing the program, even though a thousand people might call you out or suggest that you actually do steps, the perception of a good alcoholic is often that reading a step is the same as working a step. Another very similar perception is that going to meetings is working a program of recovery. This, however, is not a reality but a lie that we willingly tell ourselves so that we can continue to be sick. Recognizing this lie is part of the rigorous honesty that must be achieved to be able to recover. And here is the real bitch of the problem: no one – and I do mean *no one* – can make someone else have this honesty. Now let's be clear on something right here, the honesty that I'm talking about isn't honesty to your priest, or taxman, or your wife, parents, children, or your dog for that matter. The honesty that is required to be able to work a program of recovery is honesty to yourself, and I'd have to say as humans we are able to believe a lot of really stupid shit! It is possible that some can't acquire this type of honesty without Devine intervention. Case in point was when I asked God why this kept happening to me! Now having said all that, let me say that I tried with all my might to get Judd to accept this honesty. Even though I knew I couldn't, I still tried. Because the bottom line is, I was afraid that Judd would die an alcoholic and drug addicted death.

23

LIFE ON LIFE'S TERMS

During my second year of sobriety, a lot of stuff happened. I was still working on my recovery, I worked on the remaining three steps (ten, continue to take personal inventory and when we were wrong promptly admitting it; eleven, sought through prayer and meditation to improve our conscious contact with God as we understood him, praying only for the knowledge of his will for us and the power to carry it out; and twelve, having had a spiritual awakening as a result of these steps, we tried to carry this message to alcoholics, and to practice these principles in all our affairs). Well, I certainly tried to carry this message to Judd. I will honestly admit that my life had changed exponentially, the desire to use or drink had been totally removed. We will bring this up again later because it's important for you, me and everybody in-between to know that I, in no way, believe I am cured of alcoholism. In my heart and soul, I know if I stop working a program, the desire to drink will return.

As to the events of my second year of sobriety, I mostly worked and attended meetings. I guess the biggest thing that happened that year was, Marilyn and I were married on February 20, 2016. We had a small wedding outside in the gazebo at the Mobile art museum. Judd was my best man. Franklin and his wife Eva, one of Mary's coworkers, and Judd's girlfriend Rita, who was already six months pregnant with our grandson Matt, were there. We had a very nice service and went back to our trailer for the reception. As to the rest of the events of that year, Judd had a small medical issue at work and required a minor surgery. Shortly after his recovery, he broke his foot while showing off on my four-wheeler. Now, I couldn't hardly be mad that he was showing off, as it was for the very pretty, young Southern bell Rita, so I understood. However, with the broken foot came another doctor and more pain medication. The April before my third year sober, Rita was giving birth to my first grandchild Matt. Judd and Rita were living with Rita's grandparents. That year's summer vacation was a week's stay at Destin West a resort on Okaloosa Island. I rented a three-bedroom condo on the first floor beside the swimming pool right off the beach. We invited mom, and she drove down and brought Alice and Ophelia with her. We had an incredible week at the beach; Judd, Rita, and little Matt came over for a few days too! Now I say we had a great time; however, Marilyn had started a new job in Pensacola the Monday after we were married so she didn't have any vacation time, and she worked the whole week we were on vacation. She was able to work several half days, so she did get to hangout on the beach some! We had a great summer, and it was incredible to be able to be present and enjoy being with my family while not needing a drink. Life was good.

In all fairness to my honesty and my recovery, I must admit that I was spending more money than I was making. I had been given several lines of credit because of my credit score and my income. Now this credit card business was all new to me, until three years before, I didn't even have a credit score. There would be a couple more vacations and another car before I was able to reign myself in. Then Marilyn beat it into my head that what I was doing wasn't any too bright. By the time I stopped spending more than I was making, I was nearly $40,000 deep in credit card debt! To my complete displeasure, a friend of mine in recovery pointed out that financial amends was in fact a large part of the ninth step – if I spent it, I have to pay it back. Son of a bitch! I will just say here that I am incredibly lucky to have a wife with more self-control and wisdom than I possess myself. We can look at another common failing in the alcoholic and the drug addict –

from my perspective, I spent so many years in a drug and alcohol induced fog that I didn't mature in many ways. I can still act and behave like a fifteen-year-old. There are many simple life's lessons that I missed or simply don't remember. Ok let's get back to spending money I don't have! There is one more vacation that I'm going to take that I really shouldn't have but I'm glad I did, we aren't quite there yet there's more to the story to add.

After summer vacation in 2016, Marilyn and I started looking for a house to buy. We both wanted to move across Mobile Bay so that Marilyn would be closer to Pensacola for work. Now I will remind you that I have been living in the same trailer, renting from Harry for five years, and I'm only four miles from the steel mill. So, I didn't really want to move across the Bay, but Marilyn helped me again to see it would be for the best. We started house hunting and found one that we liked on six acres in a little town called Stapleton. We put in a bid for the house and were turned down. Marilyn and I kept looking, but we weren't having much luck. About five or six months after we had put a bid on the house, the real estate agent called and said the sale had fell through and the house was about to be put back on the market. We were asked if we wanted to bid again and told that the price had come down! So, we put in a new bid, it was accepted, and we bought the house. Now again this is normal grown-up activities but let's remember using my name and *grownup* in the same sentence might be a mistake. Let's also remember that I had been homeless due to my alcoholism, so buying a house was a really big deal! As it turned out, when all was said and done the house payment with insurance and hurricane insurance was a little less than I was paying Harry for rent. In October 2016, we moved into our house. I spent a few weeks painting and getting the inside ready, and when we moved in, we had a very comfortable home.

Shortly after we moved in, Rita called me and asked me to come over to their house. Judd and Rita had rented a house in Saraland about three months before we moved into ours. I had been suspicious that things weren't going very well for Judd and Rita, but I didn't see them every day so wasn't sure. Judd had asked me for some money several times, and I had given him some; subconsciously, I was aware that it felt very similar to when I would ask my dad for money. I had a funny feeling that things weren't ok. I went over to Judd's, and what I found was even worse than I wanted to believe. Judd had been up for too many days using meth; he was in full-blown drug delusions. Essentially what he saw and what he thought was going on wasn't real. This person I was talking to was not my son, and at that moment he didn't even look like my son. I very carefully talked him down, as best as I could, as he kept explaining to me what he saw, and what he thought was happening. Now here I experienced true terror and fear; I could see my son dead from using – hell, he looked to be about three quarters of the way there. I calmly explained to Judd that he was experiencing serious drug delusions and that he should be hospitalized immediately. Uh oh, that was a mistake. I spent the next forty-five minutes chasing him around the house and yard trying to calm him down.

It started to sink in just how my parents must have felt for years and years dealing with me and my shenanigans.

After a fair amount of chasing, I finally got Judd to calm down. I explained that we had to do something, that I couldn't just leave him like this. I talked him into going to The Watershed, really what happened, was I finally got pissed enough that I told him he was either going to treatment or jail because I was fixing to call the police and ambulance. Judd agreed to go to treatment, we called The Watershed and work the next day he flew down for rehab. I will say right here and now that what I should have done was call the police, but I didn't want Judd to get into trouble. Guess what folks? Consequences equal surrender. I was wrong for trying to get Judd to treatment he needed to make that decision on his own! The shit-show that is coming will back up that statement. I was aware that Rita was using also, so I was trying to convince her to go to treatment too. If I'm going to be wrong once what could twice hurt? In my mind, I had to do something, so I moved Rita and baby Matt in with Marilyn and me. Now that doesn't sound too bad except I neglected to ask Marilyn if it was ok. I'm already headed for the hot seat so let's really light a fire – I also called and asked Mom if she could come down and stay with us. I thought I was going to be able to talk Rita into going to treatment. Now I'll say that my lovely wife Marilyn was thrilled to be in our own house; she was, however, less than thrilled that I appeared to be doing my best to fill all the bedrooms less than a month after we moved in. I argued to get my way when she expressed that she thought I was wrong for what I was doing. Remember, earlier I mentioned progress not perfection. Well, I can't even use that to get out of this one. I was wrong, and I was trying to save someone else, I was trying to fix someone else, I was turning my new house into a halfway house and my wife wasn't happy about it. Believe it or not, Franklin even tried to tell me that I was going about things the wrong way that it was Marilyn's house too and she had a right to be part of the decisions that I was making. Let's remember that I'm closer to a fifteen-year-old than a forty-eight-year-old. So, in short, I was wrong. I was told by my wife and sponsor that I wasn't being fair, but I did it anyway. Now let's remember that I did stay sober through all of this, and I have been able to learn a great deal, still doesn't excuse the fact that I acted like an ass. So now that we have firmly agreed that I'm an ass, let's continue.

Mom showed up just after Thanksgiving, and yes, the house was pretty well full. Judd is in treatment, Rita is staying with us, I'm almost always at work, so guess who gets to cook for more people and clean up? Well, you guessed it, Marilyn. She did, and for the most part we all got along. I'm going to meetings and working a lot of overtime, and somehow, I found a car that I really wanted to buy – a 2008 Pontiac G6 GXP, the car only has 121,000 miles on it, and they are only asking $1,800; it is a great deal. Well, it turns out the transmission is completely shot, it's going to take $5000 to replace it, so the figures add up in my head, and I buy the car, have it sent to a transmission shop, and order a rebuilt transmission from Jasper. I can't remember if I asked Marilyn if this was ok, and I'm kind of guessing by the way it turns out that I was probably still being an ass. When I got the car back, which I fully intended to be driving, I gave it to Marilyn instead, and I took her work car to drive as my work car. Now my ulterior motive was to get out of my Trans Am, I didn't want to keep putting miles on it I wanted to make it my extra vehicle. Geez, I seem to have been doing a lot of me, me, me, at the time.

Well, there's one more big one. Franklin told me that he was going on a cruise in April and that I should come.

Well hell yeah! I called Carnival and booked a suite for Marilyn and me, and we were going on a cruise. Ok, that just about finish up my astronomical credit card debt. However, the very last day that I was ever going to drive my Trans Am to work, I woke up a little late. It was one of the only days in February that was below freezing, and I was flying down a country road at about 85 miles an hour. I passed a pickup truck and was just topping over a hill and there was a box in the middle of the road – a large box with a lid on it probably someone's recycling box at the end of their driveway. There was no way to swerve to miss the box without wiping out, so I mashed the gas and drove on through. The box was frozen, and it shattered like glass. I didn't even stop; I drove on to work. I also should remind you that I don't have a driver's license; it had been revoked until 2025. So, I drive on to work, I get out and look at my car. The hoods destroyed, the front bumper cover is destroyed, the driver's side headlight is destroyed. Nice! So, to round out and really finish my credit card debt, there's about $3000 worth of car parts ordered. I found a body shop right down the road from the house, and I hired a guy to fix my car and do a complete repaint I mean why not. Little did I know it was going to be eighteen months before I'd get the Trans Am back! So, I jumped out of time again, this all happened in February, we have to go back to December for Judd coming home from treatment.

24

RESCUE

I had been sending Judd cigarettes in treatment, and we had been talking almost every day. Judd was going to meetings and working with a temporary sponsor. I had high expectations that Judd was going to be all right. I felt that way because I was alright, I was working a program, and I knew that if it could work for me it could work for anyone. The key to the program working is solely based on the willingness of the individual to work it, though. As we were getting closer to Christmas, Judd started talking about being home for the holidays. I wasn't sure that was a good idea, but I had to admit that Judd was talking and acting like he was doing well in treatment. He told me he was going to continue going to meetings and working the program. He told me he's got this! Now I gave a warning earlier that anyone who says that in recovery is almost always in trouble. The very reason is that the ability to stay sober comes from a power greater than ourselves; had we been able to do it on our own, why the hell are we in treatment, or jail, or homeless, and the list can go on and on. By that point, we had proven that we don't have this. Now accepting this, is another matter entirely!

So, I missed the warnings that Judd was throwing at me. I wanted to believe that Judd was in fact going to work a program like I was, again if I could do it anyone could! It will become clear that with Judd, I miss the warnings and signals, it's because I love him my fear of losing him clouds my judgment. Long story short, I called the treatment center and talked them into releasing Judd the day before Christmas Eve 2016. When Judd got home, I suggested that he and Rita go to a meeting. Remember, it greatly increases your chances of staying sober. I had to work night shift that night so I went to work hoping that Judd and Rita would go. Marilyn had driven to Ohio to spend Christmas with her family and the day after Christmas she was going to bring Alice and Ophelia down for a week to visit. I went to work looking forward to having all my kids in the house just after Christmas. It was just going to be mom, Judd and Rita and little Matt and me in the house for Christmas. Judd Rita and little Matt went to spend the night at Rita's grandma's.

About midnight, I get a call from Rita's grandma, Sue. She was upset and explains that Judd and Rita are both drunk and are fighting. Sue begs me to come over and see if I can help get them under control. I'm pretty much pissed; Judd just got home from treatment, and the same night he is drunk! Obviously, they didn't go to a meeting like I suggested. So, what do I do? I leave work and head over to Sue's house. What I should have done was call the police – remember, consequences equal surrender. I love Judd so much that I want to fix him, I want to convince him that recovery is the answer, I want him to realize that there is a solution for what ails him. I'd have better luck staying dry while pissing up a rope! I make it to Sue's, and I can see myself twenty years earlier drunk, pissed off and fighting the world. I confront Judd, I try to calmly "I'm pretty well pissed at this point" tell him you have one chance either get your ass in the passenger seat of my car or I'm calling the police! I must have been convincing because Judd stopped arguing and got in the car. I apologized to Sue for the kid's shenanigans, and I took Judd home. Now, why was I apologizing? I didn't do anything wrong, except come and try to save Judd from more trouble. When I got home, I told Judd to keep quiet and go to bed. The next morning, I had to tell mom what had happened, she wasn't happy about it either. Judd apologized to Rita and her family and went back to Sue's for Christmas.

The day after Christmas, Marilyn and the girls showed up, and we celebrated Christmas with a house full. We had a great week with the girls, and for the most part we all had fun just being together. After Alice and Ophelia flew home, things settled back down to normal. Judd went back to work. On our days off, Judd and Rita would go to a morning meeting with me. I had extremely high hopes that the relapse had proven to Judd and Rita that there was indeed a problem. For the next couple of months, things seem to be going all right, so mom decided early in February to go back to Ohio. Judd and Rita were leaving on their own and going to meetings while I was working. Then one night Marilyn pulls me aside and says that she thinks Judd and Rita are using. I let Marilyn know that the kids are attending meetings on their own, though I had nothing other than Judd's word to substantiate that statement. I further informed Marilyn that I thought she was just angry because the kids were living with us. "Man give them a chance already!" I said. Yep! You guessed it, I'm completely wrong. Marilyn was right, they were using, and I didn't want to believe it. The elephant in the room! And to top it all off, I acted again like an ass to Marilyn to defend what I believed.

Over the next couple of weeks, Marilyn continued to express suspicion that something was wrong with the way Judd and Rita were acting. I was being told that they were attending meetings and looking for a place to rent. I finally started to realize that maybe they were lying to me when Judd forgot his wallet on the way to work and Marilyn had to run it to him so he wouldn't be late. When Judd finally made it to work to relieve me, he went into the bathroom and stayed there for a very long time. Now our job requires a pass down at shift change, so the next operator knows what's going on. So, I waited. When Judd finally came out of the bathroom; I could tell he had been using. Rather than have a confrontation at work, I delivered the pass down, clocked out, and went home. Now here again, I'm completely in the wrong – we run heavy machinery and you really need a clear head to be safe. I was sure by what I had just witnessed that Judd didn't have a clear head. The next day, I went to night shift to work overtime, and Judd had the weekend off. Over the weekend, Judd's and Rita's behavior became even more erratic. The elephant in the room is sort of hard not to notice when it starts shitting on the carpet.

When I got off work Monday morning and came home, took a shower and tried to go to bed. The tension in the house was so strong you could almost see it; I definitely felt it. Around nine and still unable to sleep, I got up. I went to Judd and Rita's bedroom door, knocked, and said "I think you two need to come out here so we can talk." I walked away and fifteen minutes later I was still waiting so I went back to their door and knocked again.

Judd says, "What do you want?"

I can tell Judd doesn't even sound like himself. I open the door and walk into the room. Judd is laying on the bed with tears openly running down his cheeks, and Rita is sitting on the bed holding Matt.

I ask, "Where are the drugs?"

Judd says, "There aren't any."

I ask again, "Where are the drugs?"

Judd leaps off the bed and grabs my throat and is choking me as hard as he can! Rita is screaming, "No Judd, Judd stop!" I can hear Judd saying something, but I can't understand it. I can feel the black circle closing in I'm about to pass out when Judd let's go and walks away. I'm completely filled with terror; I instantly realize that the monster inside my sons' body is obviously in control.

I walk backwards out of their room and head into mine and close the door. I don't know what to do! I'm as full of fear and genuine terror, as I have ever been! My son just attacked me, and he is obviously slap out of his mind on drugs. I realize that there are guns in my room, and I instantly fear being shot or having to shoot Judd, so I immediately hide the guns hoping I'm making the right decision.

I leave my room and head back for Judd and Rita's room. Judd is ranting and raving that they are leaving, and he tells Rita to pack a bag. Again, I backpedal out of their room and go outside. I can't let them leave with Matt; Judd isn't even close to acting rational. I call mom and tell her what just happened and I ask her what to do. Mom says, "Call the police, right now." I know inside that is the right thing to do, but I don't want to, I don't want Judd and Rita to get into trouble. Well, you might ask, "How stupid are you?" but there are many people placed in the same situation every day. The love you feel for a child, parent, spouse or sibling easily can cloud our judgment. If a stranger were in my house and choked me, I wouldn't think twice about calling the police, and there's a fair chance that I would put a bullet in them before I made the call. The absolute worst thing you can do for a drug addict and alcoholic, though, is to keep bailing them out of trouble. Remember, consequences equal surrender. I knew what I needed to do, but I still didn't want to do it.

I went back into the house and to Judd and Rita's room. I told Judd, "Leave Matt here with me, and I'll let you leave." That didn't go over very well. Judd started cussing me and saying Matt is his son and he will go with them. Well, that was when I knew I couldn't let him leave with the baby, so I went back outside and called the police. At this point, I should make a humble apology to the rest of the world that I was about to turn my fully drug insane son loose on if he had been willing to leave my grandson. I am sorry.

As it turned out, the police made it to the house before they were able to leave. Judd and Rita were both arrested and charged with child endangerment. While the police were waiting for children's services to show up, I tried to talk to Judd. He screamed that he hated me and a few other things, but I walked away. I was completely sure that he didn't have a clue as to what he was doing or saying. Once children's services showed up the police left. Marilyn came home from work because I called her and asked her to. We were interviewed and asked if we would like to keep Matt, we said yes, we would. We were told to take him to a clinic for a drug test. We did and the results were shocking, he tested positive for three different narcotics. When I told them that I knew Judd and Rita wouldn't give drugs to a baby, they explained they didn't have to, if they hold the baby when on drugs, it will transfer from sweat to the baby's skin.

I called mom and asked her if she could come back to Alabama. Mom had only been home for two weeks; she repacked the car and headed south. I also called my sister Terry; she sounded shocked to be hearing from me! The truth was that after the incident with Judd and experiencing the fear of what he might do, I realized how my family had to have felt about me and my so-called shenanigans. I had for a long time believed that Terry acted the way she did about me because she must be greedy or something. After Judd attacked me, it became clear to me that Terry was only trying to protect Mom from me and my violent behavior. So, I called and said, "I owe you an apology, I had misunderstood, I thought you were after something. I didn't realize that you were just trying to protect the family from me. I'm sorry for misjudging you, and for whatever it's worth you were right." Terry graciously accepted my apology.

Marilyn and I both worked full-time and being responsible for a baby was going to take some getting used to! I was incredibly thankful that I was sober and working a program, able to be responsible enough to take care of Matt. A few days after this all went down, Sue bailed Rita out of jail. About four days after it all happened, Judd called and apologized and asked if I would bail him out. Judd told me he had been having delusions from the drugs for several days after he was arrested. By day four, he was starting to come back to our planet! Rita also called and asked if we would bail out Judd. My reply was that I thought Judd was right where he should be, I wasn't going to bail him out, and I would appreciate it if you don't bail him out either. Several days later, Rita talked her Paw Paw into bailing Judd out.

I had been specific in asking Rita's family not to bail him out and thought I could ask the judge to court order Judd and Rita to treatment. I later found out that Paw Paw thought Judd was too good of a worker to be left in jail. As for work, Judd was considered a no-call no-show even though I had told our company that he was in jail. The third day Judd had missed work, my boss came to me and told me that if I bailed Judd out so he could come back to work, he could save his job. I told the boss that I didn't think bailing Judd out was the right thing to do. So, they terminated his employment. Not bailing Judd out was almost as hard as calling the police. I didn't want Judd to lose his job, as it was a really good job. I took a lot of shit from my coworkers for not bailing him out. However, the coworker who Judd had joined the hunting camp with came to me and apologized. He said everything I said would happen if Judd was using or drinking did! I told him that we were really both drug addicts and alcoholics, and I was positive about what would happen, it was inevitable! I still took a lot of shit from my other coworkers – after all, what kind of dad let's his kid get fired, especially when all I had to do was bail him out; surely, he has learned his lesson. No one knew that I had years earlier went and got Judd out of a court-ordered treatment to bring him south to work at the steel mill. They also had no idea that Judd had already been to multiple treatment programs for drug addiction. Sometimes the worst thing you can give an addict or alcoholic is a paycheck. I myself have experienced the allusive drinking paycheck! There were many times that I was trying "or so I thought" to stay sober. But when I would get my paycheck, it wanted a drink so bad, I really had no choice but to have one too. Damn paycheck! All kidding aside, payday is a real struggle for alcoholics in early recovery. A paycheck can trigger lots of memories and desires of using! If you are struggling with the paycheck dilemma, you likely can find the solution in the first step.

Now Judd and Rita know they are facing a good amount of trouble, a decision is made to go to treatment. Seems logical to me, even familiar. Some suggestions are given that they might consider going to separate treatment centers, however they decided to go to a treatment center in California that claims to be for couples. Now I might have been born at night, but it wasn't last night! How can you possibly find any recovery if you go to treatment with your wife? You will inevitably spend your time focusing on your partner. Recovery is a process that requires focusing on oneself not someone else. I believed that this treatment was doomed before it even started. I wasn't far off the mark either, but it was far worse than I could have ever imagined.

25

ARE YOU SHITTING ME?

The treatment center in California was actually run by two using addicts. They were using the treatment center to supply their income for their addiction. On a personal note, that is either brilliant or completely evil, depending on which side of the recovery line you happen to be standing on. I know some, though not all of Judd's and Rita's California adventures, but they are not mine to tell. Maybe if Judd and Rita get on the right side of recovery, I can talk them into a book of their own. I sometimes think my daughter's perspective on life with alcoholic parents might also be an interesting read. My thoughts. Anyhow back to my story.

The next several months went by with me working lots of overtime, going to meetings on my days off, and playing with my grandson. It was really amazing to have a baby in the house and actually be sober to remember all of the incredible things that babies learn. Rolling over, crawling, learning to talk, learning to walk. Shamefully, I was using while my children went through the same development. So, getting to experience something that I had really missed was a blessing that I hadn't expected! I would take Matt to my morning meeting on my days off, my home group was very welcoming to Matt attending meetings with me, no one complained about having a baby in the meeting. Matt and I were both welcomed and loved, and we quickly became regulars in attendance. Now the cruise with Franklin was getting closer, and I wasn't sure what to do. When I had bought the tickets, we didn't have a baby in the house with us. Mom offered to stay home with Matt while we went on the cruise. That was an option, but I didn't think it was fair for Marilyn and me to go and leave mom home to watch her great grandson. We talked about canceling our tickets, then I had an idea! I called the cruise line and asked if I could change my suite to a double bed and have a crib added! And that, my friends, is how I handled that, I took Mom and Matt on the cruise to Mexico with us. Told you I was a thinker! I might have forgot to ask Marilyn what she thought before I bought another ticket. Told you I was an ass!

When April 12, 2017 came, we got to go on a trip. Just before his first birthday Matt got to tour the Mayan ruins in Mexico. Again, Matt was a hit on the cruise ship; evidently there aren't a lot of babies going on Mexican cruises! Seemed perfectly reasonable to me. We did all have an incredible time together, and it turned out to be another blessing that I wasn't expecting. Uh-oh, flashback time! Now to be perfectly honest, this wasn't my first cruise to Mexico. Years earlier, my ex-wife had won an all-expense paid cruise to Mexico from the portrait studios where she worked. It was a five-night cruise it included air fare to South Florida all meals and nonalcoholic drinks. The ship was to leave early afternoon and stop for a few hours in Key West then move on to Cozumel Mexico. My memory of the trip is a little foggy; I remember a bad plane ride, starting to drink the second I was on the ship, and spending the thousand dollars in spending money on alcohol. I know – not that great of a flashback is it? Oh well, what's important is that I seem to be getting a do over, a chance to experience a trip I've already been on, one I can share with my family and one that I will remember forever. Man am I telling you, this recovery thing sure can be amazing!

So, our current trip to Mexico with mom and little Matt was a blast. We toured some Mayan ruins, swam in the Gulf, and I picked up another pair of cowboy boots, a nice pair of seven panel Caiman. After we got back from Mexico, Franklin told me that he bought a pair of boots too but that his feet had swollen and he didn't think he was going to be able to wear them, so I bought them too, I was sure I would be able to wear them just fine. Told you I like boots!

We were preparing for Matt's first birthday party, and Judd and Rita asked us if we could wait until May 1st to have the birthday party, as they then would be home from treatment. I had been talking to Judd the whole time they were in California, and by the pictures they were posting on Facebook, it looked more like vacation than treatment. I was trying my best not to judge; I might have, could have, tried a little harder. We waited for the first weekend in May to have Matt's first birthday party. The party went well. Judd, Rita, and Sue came we had cake and ice cream; Matt opened presents. But the overall feeling was awkward, there was a tension, an uncomfortableness being around each other. I had already attained an attorney because I expected there to be upcoming difficulties concerning Matt's custody. Boy, did I call that one!

About the middle of May, mom decided to go home. We had enrolled Matt into a daycare, and we were becoming fairly adjusted to having a baby in the house. Marilyn planned on flying to Ohio to get her mom – nicknamed "Butch" – and flying back. Don't ask me how her mom got the nickname Butch, she is very small. Anyhow, Butch stayed for a few weeks, and when Marilyn drove her home, she took Matt with her and dropped him off at Abigale's for a visit with his other grandparents. When Marilyn came back, she brought Alice and Ophelia back for summer vacation. Our vacation was a calm one, we went to the pool, the beach, we grilled steaks, and burgers. We also had bonfires and made s'mores. Overall, the visit was a very pleasant.

There was, however, a very unfortunate thing that happened while the girls were on vacation with us. About the third week they were here, I got a call from children's services. They informed me that Judd and Rita were in the process of signing their parental rights over to Sue; once they had done that, I would have to give Matt to Sue! As you can imagine, I wasn't very happy; as a matter of fact, I was pretty well pissed! I called my attorney, and he informed me that I really didn't have a choice all we could do is comply and fight for custody in court. I put children's services off for as long as I could, but the day finally came when I had to give Matt to Sue. I later found out that Judd had went to children's services and accused Marilyn and I of being abusive; he also accused me of being a drunk and told children services everything I had done to him as a child. Someone from children's services called me and told me, "Your son really hates you." Now I'm of two minds about this whole thing. First of all, Judd's lying and manipulation to get whatever he wanted was on the whole a complete work of art. It was masterfully executed, and children's services bought it hook, line and sinker! However, on a personal level I was quite devastated, Judd knew I was sober and had been for several years. He also knew that there was absolutely zero abuse toward Matt. My feelings were hurt, I was angry that Judd had lied and there was absolutely nothing I could do about it. Oh, but there was. I talked about it in meetings, I shared how I felt, I was given support and advice on how to accept what had happened. I eventually did accept it after some struggles. The real blessing was that through it I didn't pick up a drink or a drug. Wow, this program thing is really working in my life! Ain't that something!

Just before the girls were going to fly home, we went to see The Blue Angels fly at Pensacola Beach, it was on July 8th. We all got up early and we were on the beach setting up as the sun was rising. We set up our canopy and decided to go find some breakfast. We had to wait for about forty-five minutes for the restaurant to open, there was already a line forming so we decided to wait. Just as the restaurant opened a little storm broke lose. Marilyn asked, do you think the canopy will be ok? Sure, it will be fine. I wonder if I'll ever listen to my beautiful wife... We ate breakfast and enjoyed being together. After breakfast, we headed back to the beach to find our canopy completely destroyed, our towels soaked, our bags of snacks all wet and covered with sand. Ophelia's coat was all wet and the pockets were full of sand! Wait a minute, Ophelia's coat? It's fucking ninety degrees! We are on the beach and my Yankee kids are dragging coats with them! So, we set to cleaning up our mess, and I'm pretty well pissed now, why didn't someone suggest that we check on the canopy? Oh wait, they did, didn't they? Son of a bitch, deep breath, it's going to be ok. It didn't feel like it was going to be ok at the time. Now it's quite possible that I was still struggling with the whole Matt thing, and I was likely more than a little unstable. I yelled at Ophelia for having her coat on the beach, but I was really angry that I hadn't listened to Marilyn when she told me probably more than once that I should check the canopy. Now it's barely past 9 a.m., and The Blue Angles don't fly until closer to 1 p.m. So, we have five or six more hours on the beach in direct sun; if I don't do something, we are all going to be blistering from the sun. Traffic is a nightmare, we got here so early to try to beat the worst of it. The Blue Angles bring in a crowd of somewhere north of 50,000 spectators. I'm sure if I try to drive, I'll never get another parking spot, so I take off walking for the surf shops to buy umbrellas so we can have some shade. Two hours later and an apology for yelling at Ophelia, we have umbrellas for shade. We watch the show and have a great day on the beach. Now on a side note I did learn something that day – now when we go to the beach with our canopy, we take four five-gallon buckets and a foxhole shovel to fill the buckets with sand and anchor the canopy at all four corners. Isn't learning fun! So, the girls flew home when the time came (their first time flying alone); it was an emotional goodbye at the airport. Life got back to normal for the most part, though we didn't get to see Matt for several months, and we prepared ourselves for the upcoming custody battle. Now in all honesty, I must have spent many hours contemplating how it would turn out, holding court in my head. They were not the most pleasant few months.

Finally, the day for court came and we showed up with a witness that we thought would surely help our cause. However, Judd and Rita didn't show up for court, and that essentially took our witness out of play. When it was said and done, the judge decided to give custody of Matt to Sue because I didn't have a driver's license and he felt like my employment was at risk. We were granted one weekend a month of visitation, though. It took a couple days and several meetings for me to accept that it had worked out the way it was supposed to. Again, I was angry at myself for the wreckage of my past, for something that I couldn't change.

We started getting our visitation with Matt and did our best to be present to the situation and we love every moment that we get to spend with him. We later found that Judd and Rita didn't show up in court because they were out using again. They were eventually kicked out of Sue's over their shenanigans and after a few weeks in the woods sought another treatment facility. We didn't learn about what had been going on until they had come back from another treatment and started talking to us again. I would love to say that they started working a program and everything was better, but that's not how this plays out.

Let's talk a little about how I related to what was happening with Judd and Rita, and how I had been to my parents and family. When I knew that Judd and Rita were using, I lived in a constant state of fear. I was always waiting for the phone call that told me they had been found dead. You might think this a little extreme, but I'll assure you, it isn't, especially today with all the cases of death connected with Fentanyl overdose. Uh oh, I feel a little flash back coming on.

When I was using in my hometown, before I went to prison, before Abigale and I divorced, a using friend that I would buy meth from came by one day and told me there wasn't any meth available, but he had something else. He gave me a brown school paper lunch sack full of Fentanyl patches. Now, it struck me a little funny that he didn't want them for himself; he told me that he thought you could chew the patches to get high. Sounds legit. I'm not sure why, but I threw those patches away without ever using one. Now that was very unlike me; I would use anything that would get you high. Very likely it was God keeping me alive because I can find no rational reason why I didn't try using the patches.

So back to living in constant fear that Judd and Rita were going to overdose and die. I was more than aware that it was a very realistic possibility; hell, I had woken up from a coma in the hospital, and they told me that I had died. So it was very much a reality to me, suffering the fear myself. I realized that I had been putting my whole family through the exact same fear and anxiety that each time the phone rang it could be the call that tells you your loved one is gone! Well, isn't that a happy fucking coincidence! For all of you that already know, it's not ok at all! It can become debilitating, it's a horrible way to live. So, I had the crushing reality that I was feeling the same things that my loved ones felt every day! I have described the fear of impending death, let's move on to the lesser fears, such as being robbed, being attacked, having your car stolen, having your house burned down while you are in it "a personal favorite if you remember" or worse, having to take the life of your loved one in self-defense! I'm quite sure the list can go on and on, now how the hell can we learn to live with all these fears? Well, we can, and we do. They always become a nagging presence on the edge of our conscience. I will say that if you are experiencing these fears, they are probably justified and protecting yourself should be number one, not protecting the ones that are using. That unfortunately is a little harder than it sounds because I still don't want to cause Judd or Rita anymore trouble and I am continuously writing that consequences equals surrender! Ok, so some prudent steps can and should be taken locking doors and windows, hiding keys and jewelry, hiding guns and ammunition, locking up tools and outbuildings. Adding an alarm system probably isn't a bad idea either. My whole point is we are only victims if we allow it, we have a life to get on with and that's what we do!

26

NO MIDDLE OF THE ROAD SOLUTION

After Judd and Rita come home from another treatment center, we begin to re-establish communication. Sometimes on our weekend with Matt they would come over to visit. Judd and Rita also appeared to be going to some twelve-step meetings, though they preferred going to church instead. I suggested several times that I thought they might get a little more out of going to meetings and working a program of recovery. They did appear to be making an attempt of working steps, but as we know there really isn't a middle of the road solution.

There is a passage in the Big Book that we read in recovery that talks about there not being a middle of the road solution. After some thought and reflection, I am very aware that I attempted this numerous times in my life, another way to look at this is there is no middle of the steps solution. I've done the 1 2 3 shuffle; this is when I worked the first three steps and started to experience some relief and eventually felt like I was doing something to change and since I was doing it, I could probably control my drinking and using. Now many people are going to have to experience this for themselves; I hardly think I'm the only one with a hard head that can hear without listening!

I have also done the 1 2 3 4 5; this is almost the middle of the steps and is what I did my first trip into recovery. I can say that my life did change, and I was able to maintain sobriety for four years. I was still using my will more than reaching out for my higher power's will, and eventually my will was to use. I share a lot in meetings, that I learned everything I need for recovery in my first treatment. It's akin to "Everything You Need to Know You Learned in Kindergarten." Then why, you might ask, did it take so long to get a solid foot into recovery? Well, that is a good question and some of the answers lie in living on my will, and some lie in not working a full program. There are twelve steps for a reason, and if you are willing to use them your life will change. I keep slinging this word, willing, and there are a great many different levels of willingness. For instance, I'm willing to get the wife off my back, or how about I'm willing to get the judge off my back, and the ever elusive I'm willing to get the monkey off my back. With all these, once the weight on my back starts to lighten there comes a phenomenal ability to forget why. This is also a direct result of not working a full program, as the goal when you reach the end of the twelve steps is to think about others more than yourself. I should point out here that I will never be perfect and that I am still able to be selfish and I sometimes slip back into thinking about myself first; thank God the program was designed by a group of people that took all of this into account, and I am allowed to claim progress not perfection!

There is a great deal to learn about yourself when working a twelve-step program, and there are no time constraints to reaching step twelve. What counts is starting the journey. We are promised that we will be amazed before we are halfway through. In the past, however, I have started to be amazed and took credit for the changes happening in my life and have picked up a drink or a drug with the belief that I had changed. Sometimes failure is a part of the journey, and I must admit to a lot of failures to reach this point, and it is only in hindsight that I see that many of my failures came with warnings, and a great many people who had gone through the same thing. Because I'm selfish, stubborn, and full of self-will, I didn't heed the warnings, and I didn't listen to others who saw eminent disaster ahead.

Over the next year, things seemed to be getting better. Judd and Rita were going to have another baby, and we continued to work on being a family. There was, however, the ominous presence of waiting for the shoe to drop! On April 13, 2018 (Friday the 13th) Emma was born, my first granddaughter. she is a beautiful little bundle of joy! Judd is working with Rita's family business and doing some remodeling jobs on the side. They seem to be doing better. We celebrated Matt's second birthday a few weeks after his little sister arrived. We had a cookout and grilled steaks and had cake and ice cream, a regular family birthday party. While we were eating Judd told me he had been thinking about calling my boss to see if he could get his job back. I told him it couldn't hurt to ask. We also talked about his sisters coming for summer break. Alice had a boyfriend "Lance" who had offered to drive her and Ophelia to Alabama. I wasn't sure I liked the idea at all, remember that's essentially how their mother and I got together. After talking about it I figured it would be better to go with it than have Alice decide not to come. It was going to be a much shorter vacation; Lance's parents were going to come down for a week in Destin and Alice and Lance were going to go and stay with them. Also, Abigale and her husband Robert, the kids' stepdad were going to come down for a week and stay in Destin. Judd and Rita were making plans to go and stay with them as well as Ophelia. Of course, we were invited to come over and spend time on the beach, all of us together. We had a big summer planned, and we were all, for the most part, excited.

Just before the girls were to come down for vacation, my Boss pulled me aside and told me that Judd had been calling him and asking for his old job back. He wanted to know how Judd was doing. I told him that he had a new baby girl and that as far as I can tell he seemed to be doing well. Now remember, I didn't really see that much of Judd, but when I did, he appeared to be sober. My boss told me he wanted to rehire him, and that to do it he was going to have to get permission from several rungs up the ladder. I called Judd and told him that he may be able to get his job back. He was thrilled and said that would make everything better! I completely missed it! Red flag!

As it turned out, he was rehired right before Abigale and the girls came down for vacation. We had another great summer vacation together and I got along well with Lance. Being present and a part of a family was incredible; I no longer felt ashamed about all of the years I had missed, and I had zero doubt that working a program of recovery was restoring my life! We spent time at the beaches in Destin, we had dinner with Lance's family, we took a trip to the French Quarter in New Orleans, we bought cigars in the Quarter, and we spent an evening at home on the porch smoking them. I even got Judd, on one of his days off, to help clear a couple of the pecan trees on the property. It was an incredibly good summer; we all had a great time. It was kind of sad when the time for everybody to go home came, but we all knew we would get to do it again next year!

Judd was back to work for about six months when he started showing signs that things might not be ok. Leaving work early, showing up late were little things, but they started adding up. I asked him if everything was all right, if maybe he thought working a twelve-step program might help? He assured me that everything was fine, that he's got this! Another red flag, maybe double red flags! But I again missed it, as I wanted to believe him. About a month later, Judd told me that he and Rita had decided to go back to The Watershed for treatment.

27

THE DREAM

As you might imagine, I was a little stressed at this time, and I had a rather peculiar dream. Experiencing using dreams is not uncommon in recovery. We have spent a good portion of our lives under the influence of drugs and alcohol. In early recovery, I experienced many of these types of dreams, often waking with feeling of guilt and shame, upon waking not sure if I had in fact used! Now as I learned to share these dreams and the resulting feelings that they produced, I learned that I didn't have to hide them in shame. We all experience these dreams, and when we learn that by sharing our fear, guilt, and even our shame we experience freedom from the oppressive feelings that we ourselves are producing, essentially to share the weight of our fears, lessens the fears themselves! The same is true for all our hated emotions, guilt, shame, embarrassment, when we share. we experience the gift of others identifying and sharing their own experience, and we find that we are not alone, that we are not the only one experiencing said emotions. The real gift is when we learn to laugh at our feelings with others, we begin to learn how to live with ourselves without having to hide behind drugs and alcohol. What we are experiencing is freedom from ourselves and it's a kind of magic for someone like me! Ok, I've slipped off the dream that I intend to share. but I guess that's ok too.

About six months earlier, I was in a meeting where there was a lot of sharing going on about praying the Third Step Prayer in the morning before you start your day. Now six months ago, I was three months from my four-year sobriety birthday. As I listened to all of the comments about how starting the day with The Third Step Prayer had really manifested a real change in people's lives, as the golden thread came around the room and it was my turn to share or pass, I remember saying that I thought everyone must be speaking in a metaphor because when I wake up I piss, brush my teeth, get dressed, and go to work; there isn't any time for anything else. However, I did share that I often remembered to say a prayer before I fell asleep, which seemed entirely reasonable to me. I was not met with ridicule or even any strong suggestions that I might change my thinking. I heard many people talk about putting cigarettes under there bed in the morning, so they had to get on their knees to get them and while they were there, they said a prayer. Well, I smoke but not until I'm at work, so that's out. I heard others talk about putting post-it notes on their mirrors in the bathroom to remind themselves to say a prayer, and it often was referred to as the Third Step Prayer. Now I had done the third step, and my sponsor and I said the Third Step Prayer, but honestly I had to look it up after the meeting.

God, I offer myself to thee, to build with me and do with me as thou wilt. Relieve me of the bondage of self, that I may better do thy will. Take away my difficulties, that victory over them, may bear witness to those I would help of thy power, thy love, and thy way of life, may I do thy will always!

Well seems like a pretty good prayer, I thought, but saying it first thing in the morning, well I don't know about that! So, over the next several weeks I kept hearing about this repeatedly, eventually I thought maybe I could try this too. Well getting up at 4 a.m., I was usually at work before I was even awake, but I continued to think about what I had heard, that everyone who claimed to do this in the morning experienced a better day, so I decided to give it a try. Now I'll say that my efforts at first were very minimal, I did however take a screenshot of The Third Step Prayer so that I could look at it when I wanted, and at first it was usually on the days that I went to my morning meeting at 7:30 a.m. that I would look at the prayer and say it. Some mornings I would remember and actually start my day with the prayer. Now let me be very specific here because I still wake up on days and forget to pray. Remember, we claim spiritual progress not perfection (thank God), but I have also experienced the same difference in my days when I do wake up and pray.

Before I get to the dream, I'd just like to say that the relevance of the Third Step Prayer to me really hinges on the "relieve me of the bondage of self"; it was myself that had to get out of the way to start to experience recovery, my selfishness, my wants and desires, my willingness to live in a lie. So, I greatly appreciate the need to be delivered from myself.

Ok, ok the dream. I am on a houseboat. When I look out the window, I see a resort and a long boardwalk that leads to the resort and then open water as far as I can see. The houseboat is docked to the boardwalk. Marilyn and I are in the houseboat together, and she is getting ready to leave for work. We are arguing, about what, I can't remember, but it is a heated argument, and we are screaming at each other. Marilyn says something to me that really pisses me off to the point that I shut down; I remember feeling angry and hurt over what she has just said. Though I don't remember what it is, I sit in a chair, grab a magazine, and start flipping through the pages. Each page is a different alcohol – Jack Daniel's, Black Label Jim Beam, Patron, Paul Masson, Root Bear Vodka, Absinthe, Makers Mark, Goldschlager, Jägermeister, Blanton's, and Crown Royal. As I'm flipping through the pages, Marilyn is still yelling at me. I'm getting angrier and angrier, keep flipping pages, and seeing more alcohols. As Marilyn is about to leave, she looks back and says, "If you want to drink, we can drink," and she walks out the door to go to work. As soon as she leaves, the back door opens, and the houseboat begins to flood. At which point I wake myself from the dream. It's 3 a.m., and as I'm coming to, I realize I'm already saying The Third Step Prayer. I am instantly relieved of the fear, shame, and guilt from the dream, it was only a dream.

That morning at my meeting, I shared the recollection of the dream. The next day in my morning meeting, I find myself sharing it again, and it isn't until this time that I realized the real significance – it wasn't the dream but how I woke up, it was how I was saying The Third Step Prayer in my subconscious I was using a tool against my fears and my feelings. In just six months of trying to say a prayer in the morning – something I often fail to do but continue to try – I have and am learning a defense against myself. Deeper yet is this is how I've learned everything I know about recovery; I've learned it from others who learned it before me, and I find that the golden thread isn't just going around during the meeting it's moving through time, as I'm being taught what others were taught before me, who were taught by others before them, who were taught by others before them. It leads back to recovery, it's a gift that I've been given that I can only keep by giving it away, and The Golden Thread connects us all, all the way back to Bill W who with help from some truly amazing people started this Golden Thread of recovery, and it works today as well as it worked for them in the beginning. I've asked before how recovery really works, and the most common reply is "It works really well!" All I can say is that for a drunk that was lost, hopeless, unemployable, homicidal, and suicidal, recovery has taught me and is still teaching me a way to live with myself without drinking or using drugs. I continue to experience the feelings of freedom and joy. I am currently living in such a way that I never dreamed possible, and I realize through this dream that I get to be a part of The Golden Thread of recovery so long as I am willing to learn and share what I have learned with others. I have heard it said many times, why don't you just try this and see what happens and at any time you like we can always refund your misery. For me today, all I have to do is take a drink and I can have all the misery and pain back, and that, my friends, isn't something that even crosses my mind.

28

EMINENT DISASTER

Ok, where were we? Oh, Judd and Rita have decided to go back to treatment. So, they fly back to The Watershed in West Palm Beach. As you might imagine, work was less than pleased; Judd had only been back a little over six months. On their third day in treatment Judd called me and told me that he had been fired. I called our boss, and he told me he couldn't talk about it. Not sure what to do – and truthfully, I shouldn't do anything – I didn't want Judd to lose his job. So, I asked a lawyer I knew if it was legal for the company to fire someone for going to treatment. His immediate response was no, that Judd was protected under the Americans with Disabilities Act. So, armed with this information and slightly pissed off that the company fired Judd, I called our local office and once more asked why Judd had been fired. Again, management told me they couldn't talk about it. I said "That's fine, but I can talk about it." I informed them that I thought they were in fact breaking the law, that under the Americans with Disabilities Act, Judd's job was protected. I then told management that I was only trying to head off the inevitable lawsuit, and maybe I should just call the corporate office and ask them what they thought. Two hours later, Judd was fully reinstated to his position! Now I really shouldn't have stuck my neck out so far, as I had risked my own job calling management and basically threatening them with a lawsuit. Here I was again, covering up for Judd; I just couldn't stop myself. Truthfully, the underlying fear that he might die from his addiction pushed me into doing a lot of things that I shouldn't, as we are about to see I was only prolonging the inevitable.

Marilyn and I were getting along great, except when Judd and Rita were brought up. She kept telling me that I was doing things I shouldn't be doing, like sending cigarettes every couple of weeks, often two cartons at a time. We came to find out that they were basically homeless again when they decided to go back to treatment. I wanted to believe that they were going to actually work a program of recovery, so it didn't really matter why they went. I kept doing more because I thought it might work. The truth is I was so afraid of them dying in a gutter that I didn't want to tell myself the truth. Judd and Rita were in treatment for about sixty days, they had relapsed there while being AWOL several times, so it wasn't going well. I believed it was going to get better.

I allowed them to come home, and I gave them three weeks for Judd to earn a paycheck so they could move out. Just before they came home, my old landlord Harry stopped by and said he had a place for rent. Wow, that was easy, now they have a place to live right beside work. I did everything I could to make it better...except what I should have done which was nothing. I knew in my heart that I couldn't make Judd and Rita stay sober, but I was sure going to try! Marilyn was less than happy that I was allowing Judd and Rita to stay for three weeks. That probably stemmed from the fact that I again decided that it was ok, I neglected to ask my beautiful wife what she thought. Well, that's because I knew what she thought! Marilyn was very disappointed with Judd and Rita; she really didn't believe they were going to stay sober. Marilyn told me that if I was going to let them stay, I needed to call mom and ask her to come down, as she didn't want Judd and Rita left in the house alone. I said, "Come on, that's going a little far isn't it?"

During all of this, we were making plans for our summer vacation. Alice was graduating high school, and we were invited to be there. Well, that's not actually accurate; we were told our presence was required. I was very proud of Alice and thrilled to be wanted in attendance to witness her big day. So, we were making plans to go north at the end of May. The plan was coming together, we would go to Ohio for a week for graduation. Afterward, Alice, Ophelia and Lance would follow us back to Alabama for a couple of weeks. Our time together over the summer was growing shorter, as the kids all had jobs; they all worked at the same restaurant in Ohio. So, we were very lucky they were coming at all. Whenever Marilyn and I started arguing about Judd and Rita, I would deflect and start talking about our plans for vacation.

When Judd and Rita come home from treatment, they stay for three weeks, during which we went to meetings while Judd went back to work at the steel mill. We had Matt and Emma over for a weekend. We spent some time putting new carpet into Harry's trailer. As far as I could see, everything was working out. The whole time, though, Marilyn was very suspicious of anything Judd or Rita did. We had several more arguments, and I was pretty sure she just needed to give it a rest. I may have even started to develop a little resentment over the whole thing.

The day came, and Judd and Rita moved out. The next week I passed Judd, as I was leaving work; he was coming in a little late. He waved, as we passed, and my Spidey sense started going off! Two days later, we were supposed to work a night shift together; we were already going to be a man down. The shift really requires three operators, and we were going to have to get through it with just the two of us. Judd called and told me he was going to be a few minutes late. I wasn't very happy but ok. Judd ended up being about forty-five minutes late. My Spidey sense was really going off now. I called Judd and asked him if he was ok, to which he replied "sure." A few minutes later, I called him back and told him that I thought he was lying to me and that he wasn't ok at all! Judd drove down to our break trailer and got out of his Taylor; I drove down and got out of mine. I asked Judd what he was doing. He told me he was leaving that he couldn't work with me! I said, "Judd, if you leave you will be fired." He replied that I couldn't fire him. Now I'm pretty well pissed at this point; I tell him that he obviously has forgotten who I am, and that if he leaves, he is fired! Judd walks out and doesn't look back. I have no choice but to call my boss and tell him that I need some help. I can't possibly cover three positions for a twelve-hour shift. He asks me what happened to Judd, and I told him. Judd was terminated on the spot.

I later found out that Judd and Rita had relapsed the day they moved out, and Judd had been awake for the better part of a week when he walked off the job. My boss asked me if I was ok, and I told him I was extremely pissed off over the whole thing. I, however, didn't have the heart to tell him I wasn't sure what pissed me off more, Judd leaving or my wife being right again! I immediately went back to the overwhelming dread of waiting for the phone call that told me my son was dead.

Marilyn and I almost canceled our trip to Ohio, but we had promised Alice that we would be there for her graduation. We asked all our neighbors to keep a close eye on the house and then went to Ohio. We had a very nice time in Ohio spending it with both of our families. The two weeks that we spent in Alabama with Alice, Ophelia and Lance were also very nice. We did our regular trips to the beach, a trip to the French Quarter, and a trip to the naval museum in Pensacola to watch The Blue Angels practice. We had another great vacation.

About two weeks after the girls went home, I got a call from Harry. A detective was there looking for Judd and wanted to know if I knew where they might be. I told them I didn't have any idea. That's not exactly true – I told them if they started searching crack houses, they might get lucky. That night, Marilyn and I saw Judd on security footage in an armed robbery of a gas station! Now my fear for Judd's and Rita's life really kicked into high gear. I really believed that they would be found dead either from overdose or by their own hands. Two days later, Judd was arrested and charged with armed robbery. I'd like to tell you that Judd had changed his life by working a twelve-step program. That's not, however, how this book is going to come to an end. Remember consequences equals surrender. Judd has another opportunity to work a twelve-step program and change his life, but that my friends will be up to him.

I, on the other hand, have been continually blessed with progress in recovery. Just a few months ago, my driver's license was reinstated, and that wasn't supposed to happen until 2025. I continue to be amazed at the life I have been given. I guess since we are coming to a finish, I'll let you in on a little secret – as I'm writing this, it's September 24, 2019, 2:28 a.m. I'm at work. I've written the entirety of this book while I've been operating a ninety-ton Taylor in the slab yard of the steel mill! I have one more night of work, and I will be taking another vacation. Marilyn and I are flying up to Ohio. Ophelia has been asking me for the last two years to take her to a Luke Bryan concert. On Saturday, Luke Bryan will be performing in Pleasantville on a farm, just twelve miles from the farm I grew up on. We are all going together as a family, and I am very much looking forward to this trip. I have another secret; Lance is going to propose to Alice at the concert. Ophelia told me earlier tonight. Oh, if you haven't guessed, we are terrible at keeping secrets!

I once heard my dad say that if he wrote a book, it would change the world. I thought, "Damn, that would be some book!" Well, with love in my heart and the life ahead of me, I realize that if just one person struggling with alcoholism or addiction reads this book and thinks maybe there really is hope, if that one person joins a twelve-step fellowship and decides to work the steps, then this book could in fact change the world. I wanted to write a book, and that is exactly what I did. Fucking Amazing! I hope it hasn't been too boring, for me it feels good to have completed a goal.

So how do I end my book? With another story, of course.

29

A VISIT FROM AN ANGEL

This is an old story, and I don't remember where I first read it, but after doing some research, I found there are many variations. The author is unknown. So, I'm going to tell this story in my words with a little twist to serve my higher powers purpose.

A young alcoholic in recovery was struggling with the concept of a higher power when he was visited by an angel!

The young alcoholic exclaims, "Why have you come? You frighten me."

To which the angel replies, "I have been sent to you, being that you are struggling with the concept of a higher power. You still wish to only believe in yourself. So, I have been sent to offer you a gift."

Being an alcoholic, even though frightened he asks, "What kind of a gift!?"

"I am here to offer you a chance to see heaven and hell! If you are so inclined to accept this gift, I can take you there now, and I will return you to this place and time when we are finished."

Finding himself very intrigued, the young alcoholic nods once in acceptance and asks where we will go first.

"First, we will go to hell, but be tranquil, we will not be forced to stay long. To travel there, you must hold my hand."

The young alcoholic gets up and crosses the room, when he takes the angel's hand. He feels an electric charge, and his fears are lessened. He feels more alive than he has in years.

The angel asks, "Are you ready?" and with another single nod they are off flying weightless though time.

They come to a door, and they go in. The room is not large, and in the middle is a table laid with a great feast, every kind of food a person could want. The food smells fresh and warm and the young alcoholic's mouth begins to water.

But around the table the people are screaming in pain. They gnash their teeth and lash out at each other in anger and hate.

The young alcoholic notices that the people around the table are very thin and sickly. He also sees that their arms are chained to the table and that their hands have been changed. Their left hand is a fork over three feet long, their right hand is a spoon the same length. And try as they might no matter what they do they cannot get food to their mouths. They are covered with old and new wounds from where they have attacked each other in their misery and pain.

The angel asks, "Have you seen hell?"

With a single nod, they turn and walk out the door.

They come to another door, and they step through. This room is exactly the same, the same table, the same feast, the same chains, the same spoon and fork for hands. Yet the room is completely different. The people around the table are all well-fed and healthy, they are laughing and talking together. The young alcoholic sees someone spoon up a bite and reach across the table to feed another. Bewildered by what he sees, the young alcoholic looks to the angel.

The angel asks, "Have you seen heaven?"

With a single nod of his head , they are traveling back, and our young alcoholic finds himself standing in his room with his hand in the angel's.

He says, "I don't understand – heaven and hell were exactly the same."

"No, my young friend. In fact, they were quite different. You see, in Hell they are only able to think about themselves, and that leaves them hungry and in pain for all of eternity. They are consumed with hate and anger, and they are stuck in their misery.

"In Heaven however, they all think about someone else and in doing so they get to spend their eternity with love and compassion, full and warm, with the joy of knowing they are helping others."

The young alcoholic releases the angel's hand and asks, "Why have I been given this gift?"

To which the angel replies, "We only wished to help you in your recovery." He smiles warmly. "And we love you." With that, the angel vanishes.

Our young alcoholic falls to his knees to pray in earnest, "Thank you God for allowing me to see the truth. Thank You God for making me who and what I am and Thank You God for putting recovery in my life, that I might learn to help others."

My dad and his first combine

My family, the Vances

Me reading my essay,
"What the American Flag Means to Me"

Grandpa Vance

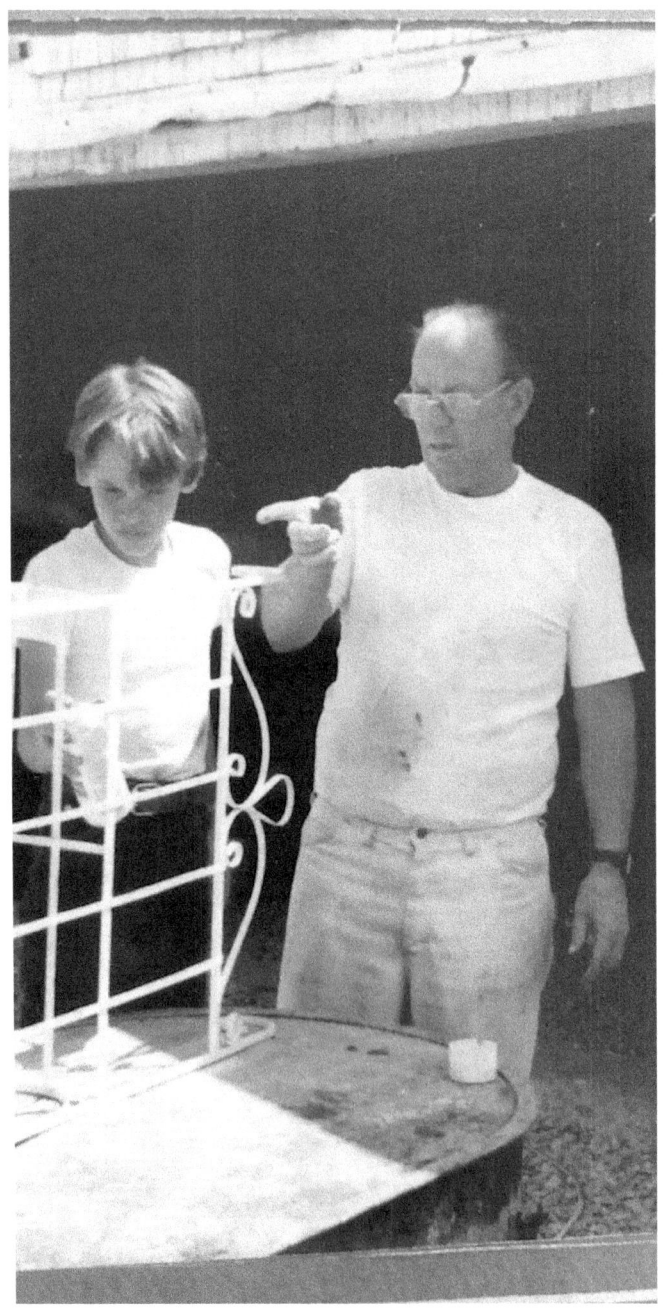

Grandpa O'Malley

My first motorcycle

My first deer

My first move to Alabama

Me on my four-wheeler

My 1970 Oldsmobile Cutlass Supreme

Aerial view of the farm

My prison tattoos

My first pair of cowboy boots

www.ingramcontent.com/pod-product-compliance
Lightning Source LLC
Chambersburg PA
CBHW060900120626
46553CB00001B/147